Changing Shape

Changing Shape

The Faith Lives of Millennials

Dr Ruth H. Perrin

scm press

© Ruth Perrin 2020

Published in 2020 by SCM Press
Editorial office
3rd Floor, Invicta House,
108–114 Golden Lane,
London EC1Y 0TG, UK
www.scmpress.co.uk

SCM Press is an imprint of Hymns Ancient & Modern Ltd
(a registered charity)

Hymns Ancient & Modern® is a registered trademark of
Hymns Ancient & Modern Ltd
13A Hellesdon Park Road, Norwich,
Norfolk NR6 5DR, UK

British Library Cataloguing in Publication data

A catalogue record for this book is available
from the British Library

978-0-334-05831-1

Typeset by Regent Typesetting
Printed and bound by
CPI Group (UK) Ltd

Contents

I would like to express my immense gratitude to all those who so generously shared their stories and made this work possible. In addition, for their support and encouragement, I would like to thank Drs Robert Song, Sarah Dunlop, Andy Byers, Mathew Guest, Pete Ward and Joss Bryan, as well as Chris Juby, and David Shervington at SCM Press.

The project was made possible by support from the William Leech Research fund and St John's College, Dublin.

It is dedicated to Hollingworth Perrins.

Introduction:

Millennial Faith in Britain

Allow me to begin with an understatement: we are living in interesting times.

Most of us are somewhat bewildered by the events unfurling around us in twenty-first-century Britain. As I write, the 'Will it or won't it happen?' Brexit clock is ticking. By the time you read this we will have more idea what that even means (or perhaps not!), but it is merely one among myriad ongoing changes. For historians and social scientists, it is fascinating to watch the developments (most news bulletins contain material for multiple doctoral theses!), but living through the current social, political and economic changes is creating an atmosphere of uncertainty and anxiety; we are aware that none of us can predict what the future is going to look like.

This is true also for the British Church. Five hundred years on from the Reformation and subsequent creation of the Church of England, it is unclear what the future of Christianity in Britain will be. Those of us concerned by that need to be like the ancient leaders 'of Issachar, those who had understanding of the times, to know what Israel ought to do' (1 Chron. 12.32). This book is my humble attempt to help us understand and answer one of the most pressing questions being asked in the wider British Church: Where did the young people go?

Memory-less Millennials and the Anomaly of the Active Affirmer

Despite the vestiges of cultural Christianity that persist in the UK, few doubt that Britain is a 'post-Christian' nation. Some argue that what has passed is the remnant of Victorian moralism, others that Britain's religious commitment has always been erratic. Either way, for the first time, secularism has become the dominant reported worldview. In the 2013 national census, 51% of the population described themselves as having no religion, including 70% of adults under 30. A 2014 Win/Gallup survey found the UK to be one of the most irreligious countries in the world; church membership stood at 10% of the population with attendance at 5%.[1] This pattern is particularly acute among younger generations. In 2018 just 0.5% of 18–24 year olds were reported as attending Anglican congregations and the London Churches Census identified 5.4% of 20–29 year olds attending church (the lowest of any demographic group).[2] Given that London has a considerably higher Emerging Adult population and church attendance than the wider UK, it is not unreasonable to estimate that merely 2–3% of those under 30 regularly attend church.

So what has happened to young adult faith?

For one thing, although Millennials are often referred to as the 'missing generation' within churches, the absence of young people is not a new phenomenon: it has been creeping up on the Church for decades. Peter Brierley shows clearly how that decline manifests with a particular downturn among those now in their forties and fifties (known as Generation X).[3] According to Linda Woodhead, 'The massive cultural shift from Christian to non-religious Britain has come about largely because of children ceasing to follow the religious commitments of their parents.' This has occurred over decades, generation by generation until today 'Children brought up in Christian homes have a 45% chance of ending up as "Nones", whereas those brought up "no religion" have a 95% probability of retaining that identification.'[4] A slightly different pattern emerges among young Catholics, who make up 10% of those self-describing as religious today.[5] Mathew Guest argues that although 'Roman Catholicism is the denomination least successful at retaining its younger members as regular church attendees once they are at university, most see this not as a decline or abdication, but as a realistic moderation of perspective. They do not cease to be Catholic. Their values might evolve, but their attachment to the religious tradition of their childhood is often an enduring bond.'[6] However, in 2006 Sara Savage et al. described most British teens as 'memory-less' when it came to even the basic tenets of Christianity.[7] The generational chain that had passed on religious knowledge had been broken, and broader institutions no longer reinforced that worldview. Today, those teens have grown up into the young adult Nones.[8] This decline is the result of a century-long trend exacerbated by social changes since the 1960s. Millennials are not particularly irreligious (opposed to religion), they are just the most recent of multiple generations of religious decline. Having been raised in a neo-liberal, pluralistic society, most are not hostile to religious faith. Half have no contact at all with religion, and many more simply have no interest. Woodhead describes them as 'Maybe's, Don't Knows and Doubters rather than Dawkins-esque atheists'.[9]

This makes depressing reading for those who care about Christian faith in Britain, particularly for those from traditional denominations who are bearing the brunt of that decline. However, as Grace Davie noted, religion in Britain is a persistent paradox; despite the predictions of secularization theory, it simply isn't going away. Certainly, popular attitudes have shifted away from religious obligation towards religious consumption (people now opt in rather than opt out of belief), but she also argues that the secularization of Europe is globally anomalous, and Peter Brierley observes that patterns of immigration have significantly influenced both Christianity and other religions in Britain.[10] In some (typically urban) parts of the country, large churches full of the young are thriving.[11] Evidently, there continue to be British young adults who buck the statistical trend, and the evidence is that those who *have* opted-in to Christian belief (or continued to follow the religion of their upbringing) are typically devout. Faith is central to their identity. Davie again summarizes, 'Fewer people are now religious but those who are take their religious lives more seriously.' During research into Christian faith in universities, Guest et al. labelled this group 'Active Affirmers'.[12] This book is about their faith journeys.

Rationale for this Research

Countless books (blogs, vlogs and articles) exist on Millennials; apparently almost everyone has an opinion on them. Frequently people take delight in telling me their horror stories of unreliable, entitled, self-absorbed behaviour from young people. But that is not my experience. My interest in Millennial Active Affirmers is rooted in 20 years of Christian ministry. In that time, I have been privileged to work with hundreds in both church and para-church settings and have observed their ongoing faith journeys with interest. Some have continued into adulthood with their Christian faith and religious identity firmly intact and are pillars of their church congregations. Inspired by their beliefs, others have made radical choices and sacrifices or have found ways to sustain a religious identity through very dark times. On the other hand, there are those whose faith has faltered or waned, and those who have intentionally renounced what was once so important to them. In truth, when they were 20 years old, I could not have guessed the direction their faith would take.

Of course, there is nothing new in enthusiastic young devotees modifying their beliefs, but at a time when church attendance is at an all-time low and faith groups are increasingly aware of their minority status, it is urgent that we understand the experiences, beliefs and faith journeys of young Active Affirmers.

It is also worth noting briefly that both academic and Church attention is already shifting away from Millennials and towards the younger Generation Z, currently in their teens and early twenties. I am fascinated by Gen Z – they tend towards being independent, feisty and often curious about religious faith (knowing almost nothing about it). Nonetheless, my ministry and research interests are with how Millennials have and are emerging into adulthood – something that may well shed light on those following behind them too.

I anticipate that some readers of this book may be motivated by academic or research interests. Minorities are always fascinating and although there has been considerable investigation into the religious beliefs of Millennials in the West (including some in Britain), there has been limited exploration of the process of their faith development. In the United States, Christian Smith undertook a large-scale, long-term project into faith change from teens into very young adulthood, but I am unaware of any studies of Millennial faith development in the UK.[13] I hope that this will function as a springboard for subsequent research.

I also suspect that many of those picking this up are pastorally motivated; concerned about the faith of their own or younger generations and the state of the British Church more widely. I sit in the intersection of these groups – a qualitative researcher whose questions are rooted in ministerial praxis. Being an 'insider-researcher' has the advantage of being able to recruit, understand and identify with research participants. However, that familiarity also creates the potential to miss important trends or to lack objectivity. Obviously, I have endeavoured to be objective, but having invested most of my adult life in the Millennial generation, their faith matters to me. I found myself deeply moved and disturbed by what I was told numerous times during the research that underpins this book.

That research project was qualitative in nature. Understanding statistics and overall trends is helpful in painting a broad picture of the state of Millennial faith, but also has limits. Religious belief is personal, complex and multifaceted; no two faith journeys are the same. My aim in writing this, then, is not to be predictive, nor are these findings universal, claiming to describe the experiences of all Active Affirmers. Qualitative research is not about percentages and predictions. It asks the 'Why?' questions, listens carefully and endeavours to make sense of individual journeys. Nevertheless, the patterns that are identified might be helpful in indicating wider trends and answering those central questions about why Christian faith flourishes or declines during early adulthood.

The data on which this book is based was gathered from a sample of Millennials in North East England during 2016/17. However, 80% had spent at least part of their twenties living elsewhere, and feedback from speaking engagements across the country has convinced me that these findings illustrate experiences many British Emerging Adults identify with. I have lost count of the number who have told me, 'You just described my life!' I hope therefore that this book will be helpful for the wider Church and those interested in identity and faith formation among the young more widely.

The Research Project

Measuring faith is a challenging thing and people adopt different tools to do so. In order to understand how and why their faith had changed I decided to conduct interviews. Forty-seven individuals aged 29–37 who had been Active Affirmers in their early twenties took part. Most were recruited with the help of church leaders or by snowball sampling and personal contacts. Unfortunately, I was unable to recruit any young Catholics but 23 Protestant congregations from varying traditions were represented, plus 16 individuals who described themselves as ex-Christian or were de-churched.[14]

In terms of demographic make-up, participants were 46% male, 54% female. Six international individuals were included as representative of the diversity within the British Church. Three were Nigerian, one American and two Eastern European. Participants represented a broad relational spectrum (although none told me they were LGBTQi+ and all were cis gendered). Half were married with children and a quarter single, but there were also married non-parents, divorcees and those in long-term or cohabiting relationships. Although 45 of the 47 had a degree or postgraduate qualification, their socio-economic background was more diverse than that might indicate. Several were the first in their family to attend university and had lived at home, working in order to fund their studies at local universities. Others had gained degrees later in their twenties after starting a family or beginning a career.

After providing background information on their religious upbringing, participants gave a retrospective account of their twenties, with minimal prompting so I could hear what was important to them rather than make assumptions.[15]

Clearly there are methodological limitations to retrospective interviews: how far people can accurately remember what they believed a decade or more ago; how far they understand their faith now, and the transitions it has undergone. Similarly, what they chose to include or exclude in the account they give, or how far they misremember, exaggerate, or reinterpret events to present themselves in a positive light. Ultimately, I was surprised and humbled by how open and candid most were in sharing highly personal information – including reflections on their mistakes and regrets. Some commented that taking part had felt like a form of therapy or allowed them to see patterns they had never previously identified in their faith journey. Many became emotional while reflecting. Despite the methodological limitations, careful listening and analysis of an individual's account is a valuable way to begin to understand their faith journey, and doing so for nearly 50 Emerging Adults provided a large amount of fascinating and rich data. All participants, congregations and locations have been anonymized and given pseudonyms.

I am enormously grateful to all those who took part.

The Structure of this Book

In the light of my interests and background this book is structured somewhat unusually. Each chapter contains a mixture of scholarly theory and reflections on British Millennial life supported by research findings. However, they also contain ministerial reflections and questions to facilitate reflection and discussion. My hope is that members of different generations in diverse contexts might read and consider the findings together. At this point in its history the British Church needs to engage in mutual listening and learning and I hope that this book might stimulate that.

The book is in three parts.

Part 1: Setting the Scene – Being an Emerging Adult paints a picture of life for Christian Millennials and introduces some key theories. Chapter 1 considers those Active Affirmers who buck the secularizing trend and some of the cultural patterns that have shaped their religious faith. Based on the accounts of the participants, Chapters 2—4 explore both the privileges and pressures of Active Affirmer life. Chapter 2 considers their experiences of coming to adulthood in a decade of austerity, their economic realities and health; Chapter 3 describes the relational realities around friends and family; and Chapter 4 looks at romance and parenthood.

Part 2: Changing Shape – How Emerging Adult Faith Develops focuses more closely on faith development. Chapter 5 examines how far Millennials do and don't match earlier faith development theories and considers some key factors in conversion and faith formation. Chapter 6 considers the journey to apostasy that some experience. Chapter 7 looks at the experiences of those who retain a Christian faith while rejecting church, and Chapter 8 examines the journeys and patterns of those who continue to be churchgoing Active Affirmers in their thirties.

The concluding Chapter 9 considers not only how the British Church might respond to Emerging Adulthood, but also what it might learn from younger generations in promoting authentic Christian faith in the twenty-first century. It includes participant responses to the question 'What would you like me to tell church leaders on your behalf?'

Notes

1 'Christianity in the UK', *Faith Survey*, https://faithsurvey.co.uk/uk-christianity.html (accessed 06.09.19).

2 '"Not As Difficult As You Think": Mission with Young Adults', *Church Army*, www.churcharmy.org/youngadultsresearch (accessed 06.09.19).

3 Peter Brierley, *UK Church Statistics No. 3: 2018 Edition* (London: Brierley Consultancy, 2018).

4 Linda Woodhead, 'The Rise of "No Religion" in Britain: The Emergence of a New Cultural Majority', *Journal of the British Academy*, 2016 (4), 245–61.

5 Stephen Bullivant, *Europe's Young Adults and Religion: Report 2018* (St Mary's University, London, 2018). Available from www.stmarys.ac.uk/research/centres/benedict-xvi/docs/2018-mar-europe-young-people-report-eng.pdf (accessed 06.09.19).

6 Mathew Guest, 'University Challenge', *The Tablet* (28.09.13), 10–11.

7 Sara Savage et al., *Making Sense of Generation Y* (London: Church House Publishing, 2006).

8 10% identify as Catholic, 11% Protestant/other Christian, 6% Muslim and 3% other religion. Bullivant, *Europe's Young Adults and Religion*.

9 Woodhead, 'The Rise of "No Religion" in Britain', pp. 245–61.

10 Grace Davie, *Religion in Britain: A Persistent Paradox* (London: John Wiley & Sons, 2014).

11 Peter Brierley, *Pulling out of the Nose Dive* (London: Christian Research, 2006).

12 Mathew Guest et al., *Christianity and the University Experience: Understanding Student Faith* (London: Bloomsbury Academic, 2013).

13 Christian Smith, *Souls in Transition: The Religious and Spiritual Lives of Emerging Adults* (Oxford: Oxford University Press, 2009).

14 25% Anglican, 21% Charismatic New Church, 15% Baptist, 8% Fresh Expression, 6% Black Majority Pentecostal, 4% Methodist.

15 Participants completed an online questionnaire providing background information about their religious upbringing and faith aged 20.

Then, in interviews ranging from 45 minutes to two-and-a-half hours, they gave a retrospective account of their twenties, marking key events on a visual aid. They were invited to share as much or little as they felt was significant with minimal prompting – just a few concluding questions. I wanted to understand what *they* thought was significant, not impose my own assumptions. The interviews were recorded, transcribed and analysed using NVIVO software. Obviously, they and any congregations or locations referenced have been anonymized.

PART I

Setting the Scene:
Being an Emerging Adult

I

Bucking the Trend:
Emerging Adults Who Resist the
Secularization Narrative

As already established, there are those among the Millennial generation who have bucked the national secularizing trend and either continue to follow their family's faith or have converted to Christianity. The challenges and benefits of being part of that religious minority will be explored more fully in due course, but (particularly for those from older generations) it is helpful to understand what influences Millennial values more widely and consider how that shapes the ways in which they express Christian faith. Before doing so, though, two key terms need explaining: 'Millennial' and 'Emerging Adulthood'.

Who Are the Millennials?

The term 'Millennial' is widely (and often wrongly) used in popular culture. Naming generations began with the work of Karl Mannheim in 1928. Popularized in 1950s America, it describes 'A unique type of social location based on the dynamic interplay between being born in a particular year with the socio-political events that occur throughout the life course of the birth cohort, particularly when the cohort comes of age.'[1] It can be summarized as 'Groups of people who travel together through time and share a unique perspective that shapes their cultural understanding and civic roles.'[2] In other words, people born at the same time, experiencing similar events in their formative years are likely to understand and respond to the world in a similar way.

This theory has proved popular as a way of distinguishing between groups born within a certain time span. Broadly accepted descriptions are:

'Baby Boomers' (the large cohort born from the end of the Second World War to 1960).

'Generation X' (named in Douglas Copeland's 1991 novel, born between 1961 and 1980).

'Generation Y' or 'Millennials' (following Generation X, born from 1981 until near the millennium – around 1995).

'Generation Z' (those born from 1995, now approaching early adulthood and becoming known as the 'I-Gen' (Internet Generation).

Criticisms of Generation Theory are legitimate. To anticipate that all individuals born within a 20-year window will have the same experiences and responses is unrealistic; particularly given the increasing speed of cultural changes in the West. Cultural shifts are more gradual and continuous than specific cut-off dates permit for. (Indeed, 'Xennial' has been coined for those at the Gen X/Millennial crossover.) It is obvious that myriad social, personal, economic and cultural factors influence perspective and behaviour. Added to this, 'Millennial' is often used as a ubiquitous term for anyone young. I am regularly asked to address ministerial concerns around Millennial students and young people. Current undergraduates are barely Millennial and young people are most definitely not! However, despite these (and other) limitations, Generation Theory can be helpful shorthand for understanding those shaped by broad cultural trends that cause cross-generational tensions. Conflicts between Baby Boomers and Millennials are well documented by the press on both sides of the Atlantic. Voting patterns in the British European Referendum (the Brexit vote), the subsequent British general election and 2016 American Presidential campaign well illustrate these. The prospects of those coming to adulthood in a decade of financial austerity, projected to be the first to have a lower quality of life than their parents, contrasts with elders who benefitted from post-war social and structural transformation. Where Millennials are stereotyped and castigated as the entitled 'Generation Snowflake', heading off on another gap year to take endless selfies, so Boomers are presented as (and resented for) going on retirement cruises, having benefitted from free education, cheap housing and financial security.

Clearly these images (whatever their level of accuracy) represent privileged groups and, in truth, most scholarly research undertaken into Millennials focuses on middle-class, educated groups. In the North East we recognize that there are large numbers of young adults for whom the idea of a gap year is an impossibility and that much of what is described in this and other research hardly reflects their experience. There is much to do in order to understand the lives and faith of non-privileged young adults. Nonetheless, recognizing the limitations but acknowledging widespread academic and popular use, I will use the term 'Millennial' to describe those born between the early 1980s and mid-1990s – including my research participants.

What Is Emerging Adulthood?

A second important definition is that of 'Emerging Adult'. This theory will be unpacked more fully in Chapter 2 but was proposed by the American developmental psychologist Jeffrey Jensen Arnett in 2000.[3] He argued that there is no longer a predictable path to adulthood. Cultural and socio-economic changes mean that rather than completing normative tasks of adulthood (like finishing education and beginning a long-term career, or marrying, buying a home and starting a family), it takes younger generations much longer to self-identify and live as adults. Previously one might have a period of experimentation and self-discovery between adolescence and young adulthood (usually around 17–22), but individuals were expected to be adult members of the community by their early twenties. Arnett argues that this is no longer the case; rather than following an established map towards adulthood, younger generations have both the freedom and pressure of needing to create a 'self-biography' from myriad options – particularly with regards to relationships and employment.[4] This has resulted in an extended period of identity and worldview formation (including faith formation). Emerging into a stable adulthood can take Millennials most of their twenties. In short, 30 is the new 21!

Of course, there are limitations to this model too. Critics argue that it represents only the experiences of Western privileged elites and is not normative for many of the world's young adults; something Arnett himself acknowledges. Older Millennials (now approaching 40) do not necessarily recognize this as the pattern of their own development and it is worth noting that those who are religious are still most likely to marry young and follow historic hetero-normative patterns.[5] Yet Emerging Adulthood does describe the process many young British Active Affirmers follow (given that they are often educated and middle class). It is a helpful framework for understanding the processes and patterns in both their identity and faith formation and helps explain some of the tensions and frustrations experienced between generations.

Millennial Active Affirmers – Snowflakes or Altruists?

The sport of criticizing younger generations has a long history. As far back as ancient Greece there are records of elders despairing over and denigrating their juniors. However, Millennials are perhaps the most analysed and written-about generation to date. Descriptions of them include emotive judgements: 'self-indulgent narcissists', 'Generation Me' and 'the dumbest generation ever'.[6] Jean Twenge, famous for some of these labels, attributes many Millennial problems to the advent of the smartphone. Others put the blame on 'helicopter parents' who have hovered over their children providing continual attention, affirmation and poor boundaries. Christian Smith paints the picture of a highly individualistic, sexually promiscuous, socially, politically and ethically disengaged generation whose consumerism, drug and alcohol misuse are the result of endemic boredom.[7] Others are more sympathetic. 'Generation breakdown' reflects the levels of poor mental health many suffer.[8] 'Mosaics' describes the eclectic, consumerist nature of Millennial identity construction.[9] Others are more positive, describing them as 'Altruistic Individualists', concerned that their life should be fulfilling and make a difference rather than prioritizing finance or status.[10] Advances in travel and technology have certainly increased Millennial global connectedness, raising concerns and awareness about environmental, ethical and social issues. Yet they are least likely to be involved in volunteerism, religious or political organizations. In short, Millennials are a paradox: often strongly idealist but not always equally activist. However, Millennial Active Affirmers *do* tend to be activists. We will explore the choices of the participants in this study more fully in due course, but it is accurate to say that most had been, or remained, highly involved in religious volunteerism or community service in some form. A majority worked in the public or charity sector and were deeply concerned about the well-being of the disadvantaged and marginalized. Of course, there are regional factors in this pattern, but activism is also a historic part of evangelical Christianity to which most had links.[11] Although further research is needed, it is possible that Millennial Active Affirmers are more socially engaged than their peers by virtue of their religious faith.

Understanding Millennial Values

Emerging Adulthood – shaped by a happy-midi narrative?

Many of the tensions between current generations are underpinned by changing social values and a misunderstanding of what motivates each other. Of course, we must be cautious of any sweeping generalizations about vast swathes of the population, but there is evidence of some underpinning values that many Millennials identify with which are helpful to understand.

I often ask groups of Baby Boomers what they think the most 'memed' verse on the Internet is. They typically assume John 3.16: 'For God so loved the world that he gave his only Son, that whoever believes in him shall not perish but have eternal life.' The answer, however, according to research by CODEC, is Jeremiah 29.11: '"I know the plans I have for you", declares the LORD, "plans to prosper you, and not to harm you, plans to give you hope and a future."'[12] I have to confess that one of my favourite games is to get groups of Emerging Adults to read the whole of Jeremiah 29 and consider whether this verse is appropriate to lift out of context. However, understanding its attraction clarifies Emerging Adult thinking more generally. Accusations of self-absorption, prosperity theology and entitlement may have some validity, but this verse is deeply comforting to those who are uncertain about the world, uncertain about their identity, and uncertain about the future. As will become evident, uncertainty is what underpins the whole season of Emerging Adulthood. It should hardly be surprising that young Christians are looking to God for security and hope, and this verse summarizes it in a way they can understand.

Writing in the United States, Christian Smith famously coined the phrase Moralistic Therapeutic Deism (MTD) to describe the quasi-Christian worldview of many American Millennials. He considered that they understood God as being a 'Divine butler and cosmic therapist' whose job was to make them happy and stop them 'being jerks'.[13] Although some of these traits are evident among British Emerging Adults, the dominance of secularism in the UK means their worldview is framed differently. Savage et al. coined the phrase 'happy-midi narrative' to describe what they had found underpinning the values of those aged 16–25 in 2006.[14] Rather than holding strongly principled views, aspiring to change the world, achieve great success or accrue wealth, most young Millennials simply wanted a happy life. Some of this was formed by a sense of powerlessness; that there was little they could do to change all-encompassing political and economic systems. Instead, they were responsible for controlling their own lives as best they could in order to achieve happiness. Thus, if part of their life was not meeting that requirement it was their responsibility to change it. However, this was not entirely self-centred; it extended to their friends and family (hence 'midi' narrative). As they have grown older in turbulent times (and have been further researched), Millennials are now well documented as holding several core values that both contribute to and are underpinned by this happy-midi framework. Three of the most significant are authenticity, tolerance and collaborative participation.

Authenticity

Charles Lindholm writing in 2008 noted that: 'Authenticity has become taken for granted as an absolute value in contemporary life.' He attributed this to the alienation and estrangement of living among strangers; the inevitable outworking of Western urban industrialization.[15] Having grown up in such contexts, Millennials often claim to be authenticity seekers, aspiring to a life that has meaning and integrity. That can come in many shapes and forms, but they admire those who embody sincerity. One of the core problems many report with all forms of authority, including the Church, is hypocrisy. This is not only as highlighted in abuse scandals but also the failure of believers to action the values they purport to hold; particularly with regards to relationships, finances and the poor. James Bielo calls authenticity the 'organizing trope' for 'Emerging Evangelicals' – young Americans who have rejected what they perceive as commodified, impersonal, evangelical mega-churches. Instead they have opted for small-scale expressions of faith, centred on relationality forms of worship drawn from historic Christian spirituality.[16] How this pattern manifests in the UK will be explored more fully later, but the valuing of authenticity means that Millennials are less likely to be nominally religious than older generations. Although there is evidence of a proportion of British students continuing to define themselves as Christian for historic, natal or cultural reasons (including significant numbers of young Catholics), the valuing of authenticity is well illustrated by the dramatic numbers of Millennials purporting to be 'Nones'.[17]

This desire for authenticity outworks in other ways. Regardless (or perhaps because of) the advent of social-media-fuelled superficiality, many Millennials report a strong desire for community. This usually manifests in a high valuing of friends and family. Despite the number coming from divorced homes (or again, perhaps because of it), family is important to Millennials. This includes biological family and constructed 'family' of close friends.[18] Of course, technology has facilitated the ability to remain in almost continuous contact. Social media in multiple forms – Skype, FaceTime, WhatsApp and collaborative online gaming (among many others) – mean that contact with friends and family has never been easier, yet, ironically, there is also a reported epidemic of loneliness. A highly mobile lifestyle, technologically mediated social interaction, unstable and short-term romantic relationships combined with an idealization yet delay of marriage, mean that many crave meaningful social contact.[19] Debates continue as to whether online communities (including religious ones) constitute genuine relationship but, as will be explored more fully, authentic relationships are one of the key factors in faith development among Millennials.

A third way this authenticity outworks among middle-class Millennials in particular, is in the valuing of creativity and uniqueness. The Barna group refer to them as 'Mosaics', piecing together a bricolage of beliefs, values, fashions and interests from multiple sources to create 'unique' identities.[20] The oft-mocked bearded Hipster is one such stereotype. Ironically, piercings and symbolic tattoos have become almost ubiquitous expressions of Millennial individuality. The Internet and related technologies mean that blogging, vlogging, music production, self-publication and crafting are normal ways for Millennials to express their creativity to a global audience. Unique experience is also highly valued and is where many spend their disposable income. Travel (as opposed to tourism), diverse forms of live entertainment and eating out are documented online by the all-pervasive selfie. This craving of authenticity of course exists within a highly consumerist culture of mass production. And although some Emerging Adults eschew such systems and pursue alternative lifestyles, for many pragmatism outweighs such principles. Amazon, Uber and the latest technological gadgets are part of their unique lifestyle. Nevertheless, Millennials claim to value the unique and creative as the outworking of authenticity.

Tolerance

A second (related) core Millennial value is that of tolerance. This is shaped by the multi-cultural nature of British society and access to the Internet, which have resulted in unparalleled exposure to a plethora of beliefs, worldviews and practices. As Peter Berger observed, in culturally diverse contexts it becomes harder and harder for any given worldview or religion to claim absolute authority; inevitably they become a matter of personal preference.[21] Indeed, 90% of the British population (both religious and non-religious) affirm ethical liberalism, 'The conviction that each and every individual has the right, if not the duty, to make choices about how he or she should live her or his own life.'[22] Millennials, raised in a liberal, pluralistic context, expect to be allowed to be 'true to themselves' and to 'follow their heart' and are supportive of others doing the same. The radical change of attitudes towards gender, sex and family since the 1960s, including the social and legal acceptance of LGBTQi+ rights, has led to widespread lifestyle changes. Over a similar time frame the rise of feminism and the Social Sciences have validated human experience as a (and sometimes *the*) legitimate source of authority – increasingly giving voice to those ignored within historic power structures. It can be argued that these are the inevitable outworkings of the Enlightenment and Protestant Reformation, but individualism, the authority of experience, and the right to self-determination are understood as self-evidently moral by most British Millennials.

This is where orthodox religions become problematic. Those that, based on theist or collectivist worldviews, hold traditional or conservative perspectives on gender, sex and marriage are perceived as discriminatory and oppressive, denying the right of individuals to be true to themselves. Ancient understandings of freedom as the mastery of bodily desires have been replaced by freedom as the right to self-expression. Consequently, many who retain affiliation to traditional and conservative churches are selective on which teachings they embrace and are likely to be more liberal than their religious leaders.[23] This is also a point of tension between generations. Those whose value systems categorize lifestyle, behaviour and religious doctrine in absolute terms find themselves in tension with contemporary tolerance. Likewise, those who value duty, commitment and stability are often frustrated and bewildered by Millennial insistence on self-actualization, and (as will become evident) this can affect Active Affirmer willingness to remain within conservative religious communities.

For those who experienced the theological conflicts of the past decades (usually over charismatic gifts, women's leadership, sovereignty and penal substitution), the advent of the 'Agreement Generation' (as they are sometimes called) is refreshing.[24] Millennial tolerance means they tend to look for points of affinity rather than differences both within and beyond the Church. Of course, this can also have detrimental effects on the formation of religious identity with individuals unclear about doctrine or praxis and avoidant of potentially divisive subjects. Older generations are also wont to accuse Millennial Active Affirmers of religious consumerism; selectively picking and choosing beliefs and practices to suit their personal needs. There is some truth in this, as many do access a plethora of spiritual resources, drawing on diverse Christian (and other) traditions, often in an unreflective manner. Clearly there are philosophical and theological problems with this, but it is the result of growing up in a consumerist culture that prioritizes choice, convenience and pragmatism. Millennials are not the first generation to be denominationally ambivalent. For decades many British Christians have selected their congregation based on worship style, convenience and personal preference. Millennial religious consumerism is inherited but also amplified by cultural shifts, highly mobile lifestyles and technological developments. They can (and do) listen to teaching and worship from across the globe and have unprecedented access to spiritual ideas and resources. Their challenge is not a lack of information but how to discern and make sense of it in order to develop a coherent system of belief that will help them negotiate the demands of adult life.

Holding tolerance and authenticity as core values also means that Emerging Adults often prize experience over objectivity. Living at the intersection of rationalism (in the form of scientific and technological knowledge) and relativism, they are often most concerned with whether something will help with the challenges they face. Of course, there are those for whom objectivity, logic and pursuit of philosophical truth are foundational to their belief system, or those who profoundly identify with the religious traditions within which they were raised. However, in a society that increasingly disregards external authority and values personal experience, this is how many Emerging Adults measure the veracity of religious belief. If religious tradition is true in your experience and helpful to your life, then it is legitimate for you to believe and practise it. It cannot, however, be imposed on others as objective truth.

This explains in part the growth of charismatic and Pentecostal churches – experiential, therapeutic and personally empowering forms of Christianity.[25] The rise of interest in ancient and highly liturgical traditions (as illustrated by increased attendance at Anglican cathedrals) may also be an expression of the same phenomenon. The Reformation may have rationalized Christianity, removing the numinous and often presenting faith as a series of propositions, but it would seem that many Emerging Adults are drawn to experiences of

God rather than assent to correct doctrine. [26] To the horror of their traditionalist or rationalist elders, many Emerging Adults are likely to ask, 'Does it work?' rather than 'Is it true?'

Collaborative participation

A final value pertinent to this discussion is the desire of Millennials to take part. Raised with pupil-centred learning and used to adult attention, Millennials anticipate being listened to. They have been consistently encouraged to tweet, like, vote, comment and become involved in discussion on all levels. Consequently, they are unwilling merely to observe or comply, they want to join in and voice their ideas. Critics argue that this rarely constitutes a willingness to take genuine responsibility or commit but is 'empty slacktivism' – little more than clicking an online petition or tweeting their reaction.[27] However, over the past few years there has been an increase in Emerging Adults engaging in forms of social and political protest. Although some argue it is the younger Generation Z instigating these movements, Millennials have been involved in gun control and Black Lives Matter protests in the United States, and the #MeToo movement and the Extinction Rebellion protests in the UK. Students overturning politically safe seats in the 2017 British general election and rise of the Corbynista are examples of the increasing politicization of Emerging Adults. Similarly, the Internet and legal changes since the 1990s have made it much easier to initiate and promote start-up businesses, not-for-profit organizations and charities. Without trying too hard I can think of a dozen Millennial Active Affirmers of my acquaintance who have done just that.

It is also well documented that employers (Boomer directors and Gen X managers) can find Millennial employees frustrating. Their anticipation of having a voice appears precocious, and their desire for meaningful relationships with their elders can irritate those who view employment in transactional terms. For those who expect deference from juniors, Millennials seem presumptuous and entitled. This is not necessarily the case (though of course it can be!); often they just want to be valued and included. However, reluctance to unquestioningly comply, unwillingness to commit long term or work excessive hours are, in part, what has contributed to the narrative of a Snowflake Generation. Given their happy-midi narrative, if Millennials are professionally unhappy, they consider it their responsibility to find employment that *does* make them happy.

As with religious denomination, Millennials are not typically loyal when it comes to institutions (although they often are to people). They anticipate short-term contracts and change as the norm. Where former generations might have expected a job for life, starting on the bottom rung and working their way up, Millennials are conscious their job could evaporate at any point. It is wise, then, for them to keep their options open and pursue opportunities to develop transferable skills. This is not a trend exclusive to Millennials, for brand loyalty is rare for most modern generations; something supermarkets, utility and service providers are fully aware of. Consumer choice has significantly contributed to the reshaping of the British high street just as it has the Church. Millennials are just following this model in the workplace. Since job satisfaction is more important than finance, should a job be unfulfilling, relationships unpleasant or the demands detrimental to their happiness, they are likely to look for alternatives. Conversely, if they feel valued, included and have positive relationships, Millennials will typically make creative and significant contributions to the teams they belong to.

So Where Are Millennial Active Affirmers?

Some readers will probably recognize these traits in the Millennial Active Affirmers they know. Others will be realizing that these are values of the privileged among that generation. I imagine more may be wondering where Emerging Adult Christians – the Active Affirmers – are hiding.

Geographical variation

In addition to their small numbers, Millennial Active Affirmers are not equally distributed in terms of either geography or denomination.[28] They are most likely to be found in university cities (since almost a half undertake tertiary education)[29] or urban centres that offer graduate employment opportunities.[30] Unsurprisingly, then, churches with the highest proportion of Emerging Adults are in those locations. Clearly this can make the lack of Millennial Active Affirmers acute in small towns and rural locations. As we will explore, for both teenagers and Emerging Adults, peer groups are highly important for identity and faith formation. Without peers in their smaller congregations, and in the face of their minority status as Christians in all other spheres of their life, many Emerging Adults either withdraw from church, access alternative spiritual resources or commute to larger congregations in local towns and cities. These act as what Nick Shepherd calls 'plausibility shelters' – providing reassurance that there are other young Christians out there, and it is legitimate to hold the beliefs they do.[31] I was given several reports of Emerging Adults from rural areas driving long distances to attend (or take the youth groups they lead to) large, lively contemporary worship services in urban locations. Such congregations have a centrifugal effect, drawing in younger believers and leaving smaller, more traditional congregations without any. Similarly, as they become parents, Millennial Active Affirmers are concerned about the faith of their children and are likely to look for churches with a lively children's ministry – being willing to commute to do so.

It is hard to know with any accuracy how many Millennials retain an active faith but have withdrawn from church. Steve Aisthorpe discovered large numbers of de-churched Christians in Scotland, many of whom could not find the style of church they wanted to attend. However, he provided no age-related figures.[32] Data exists from the United States, but the context is so different that they cannot be considered comparable. It seems likely that some of the 50% who grew up in Christian families may have retained some measure of faith even if they are unwilling to engage with church. Indeed, a quarter of this research sample fit that description, but without further research it is only possible to speculate how many de-churched Millennial Christians exist in the UK.

Denominational patterns

In terms of denomination, Brierley suggests that British churches demonstrating growth and Emerging Adult attendance are typically charismatic, evangelical and Pentecostal. For example: New church networks such as New Frontiers, Pentecostal denominations like Hillsongs and Black Majority and Orthodox congregations (bolstered by immigration) have seen growth, where traditional denominations have dramatically declined. Many of these growing denominations have church-planting strategies, often focusing on young adults and situated in the city centres and suburbs where they live. The Centre for Church Growth reported 125 ethnically and generationally diverse charismatic and Pentecostal churches planted in urban areas of North East England since 1980. Although mostly small, their combined Sunday attendance was conservatively estimated at 12,000.[33] Several Anglican dioceses and networks are following suit, investing large sums in planting 'Resourcing churches' that aim to revitalize local congregations and attract Emerging Adults. Holy Trinity Brompton currently reports 52 congregations linked to its Church Revitalisation Trust. Similarly, in 2018 the Church Army reported on the successes of smaller Anglican church plants and 'Fresh Expressions' of church in reaching Millennials. Their findings parallel some of mine, but in short: accessibility, relevance, relationship and inclusivity were core factors in attracting and retaining unchurched Millennials.[34]

As already mentioned, among younger generations loyalty to Protestant denominations is negligible. Those who are unchurched have no understanding of the differences between forms of Christianity at all. Similarly, only 8% of respondents in a 2015 Evangelical Alliance survey considered denomination an important factor in selecting a church and 94% of the participants in this study had attended multiple denominations.[35] For Millennials, their minority status, paucity of theological (and often biblical) education, combined with an emphasis on tolerance mean that they are less likely to be denominationally tribal. Consequently, although they might initially look for a congregation of a certain denomination, Emerging Adult Active Affirmers are more likely to choose a church based on style, convenience and peer group, or pragmatic factors like childcare provision. Typically, they are looking for experiential worship and engaging, pragmatic biblical teaching, a spiritual home that will provide community, and ideally a place where they might be able to contribute in some way. Even those who choose to attend large or mega-churches report that community, not anonymity, is a priority, and most have mechanisms for creating a sense of relational intimacy via mid-week small groups. A final note on denomination is to acknowledge that attendance at Cathedrals has increased by 10% over the decade to 2017.[36] Most of this growth is in mid-week service attendance. There is no data to indicate how many of these participants are Emerging Adults, but it seems likely (given the experiences of participants in this study) that some are drawn to highly liturgical spirituality and the anonymity of the context, particularly in times of crisis.

Diversity of spiritual resources

A final introductory comment on denomination and spirituality (which will be explored more fully in Chapter 5) is that Millennial eclecticism means that most Active Affirmers will supplement whatever teaching they receive in their church with other spiritual resources. Short courses run by evangelical and charismatic churches such as Alpha or Christianity Explored are widely undertaken.[37] Mega-gatherings become

annual pilgrimages for many. These include teaching conferences and arts festivals lasting from a weekend to a full week's
holiday. Several newer festivals such as David's Tent and Big
Church Day Out focus predominantly on music, while some
denominations and larger churches have their own 'in house'
conferences – for example, Catalyst (New Frontiers), Focus
(HTB), and International Gathering of Champions (KICC).
Mega-gatherings range across the theological spectrum from
the conservative evangelical Keswick Convention and Word
Alive, through more charismatic events such as Spring Harvest,
New Wine or Soul Survivor and the progressive Greenbelt
festival. The majority of Millennials I have interviewed in two
academic studies cited such events as highly significant in their
spiritual journeys as resources to supplement their weekly
church attendance.

In addition to attending such events, Millennial Active
Affirmers commonly access global spiritual resources. Popular
American and Australian preachers, writers and worship leaders
have significant followings among British Active Affirmers.
Books, blogs and websites are common sources of spiritual
information, and accessing online worship, podcasts and live
streaming from large, lively churches is widespread. For a
mobile generation, listening online can be part of a discern-
ment process for deciding whether a congregation is one they
might want to join before physically visiting. Churches that
are technologically adroit are therefore more likely to attract
such seekers. There is also evidence of non-believers watching services remotely before deciding to attend, in part because
many un-churched Millennials simply do not know what goes
on behind the door of a church.[38] One individual told me her
friend had asked if she needed a membership card – like the
gym – to attend church with her.

Given their propensity to regularly relocate, Active Affirmers
carry this diversity of Christian spirituality with them. On
occasion their trans-denominationalism will cause problems
(particularly when they run into ecclesiological boundaries of
which they were unaware). Others will make active decisions

to change tradition, or move to smaller, more family-orientated churches at some point, but few are entirely loyal to the doctrinal values of their congregation or church leader. For those from older generations or deeply committed to a particular tradition this can be surprising, even disconcerting, but it is nonetheless true. In every research project I have undertaken, the vast majority of Millennial participants have a denominationally diverse history and access materials from a wide (sometimes conflicting) range of sources.

Active Affirmer Social Activism

One other trend in Millennial Christianity worth briefly commenting on is a move towards social activism. This is shaped by global influences, such as the trickle-down of liberation theologies into the British Church, radical international Pentecostal ministries such as those of Jackie Pullinger, and the New Monasticism movement. The advent of the gap year has also meant that many Active Affirmers have spent extended periods undertaking short-term mission, church and charity-based activities. Exposure to realities of the developing world at such a significant age can be profoundly influential on both their faith and aspirations. Closer to home, by 2014 the Message Trust's Eden Project had sent hundreds of young volunteers to live and minister in teams on some of the poorest British housing estates. In addition, Millennial Active Affirmers have grown towards adulthood in a decade of financial austerity with increasing awareness of the poverty in their local communities and their own relative privilege. As the Welfare State struggles to cope, many churches have stepped into those gaps: Christians Against Poverty, the Trussell Trust, support of refugees, asylum seekers and the victims of human trafficking all tap into Millennial Altruism. In addition to the participants in this research I am aware of dozens of Active Affirmers involved in prison ministry, homelessness charities, child welfare and youth work, 'pay as you feel' and community cafes, education, social work, training and rehabilitation of prisoners, addicts and other vulnerable groups. Churches that demonstrate compassion and relationality by engaging with the poor and vulnerable look like the kind of communities altruistic, authenticity-seeking Millennials might want to be part of.

The Anomaly of London

Finally, in a study on Millennial faith the interesting anomaly of London's church attendance figures cannot be ignored. Some estimates are that half of Emerging Adults attending church in the UK do so in London. Of course, the city attracts huge numbers of British and international Millennials. Those aged 25–34 are double the national average, and its BAME population (who are more likely to be religious) is four times higher than the wider UK. It also has 11 mega-churches (defined as 2,000+ worshippers per week). Most of these are Black Majority churches, bolstered by young migrants (KICC had 5,500 attendees before its relocation and Jesus House has 3,000). However, Hillsong London and two evangelical Anglican churches fit this description. Holy Trinity Brompton (HTB) has 4,500+ attending its various congregations and 2,300 attend All Souls Langham Place.[39] These churches have a strong emphasis on proselytization and hospitality, and significant financial resources to devote to them. Clearly, in a city such as London many Emerging Adults find themselves socially isolated and the sense of community created in these churches is attractive. In *Aliens and Strangers*, Anna Strhan quotes a young woman explaining that church had 'made London bearable'.[40] However, not all London's churches are huge. There are considerable numbers of congregations meeting the needs of different ethnic and migrant groups, and poorer areas have seen the greatest church planting and growth, in part prompted by 'ecclesial involvement in humanitarian activism'. These and other factors are explored in *The Desecularisation of the City*. What remains unclear is whether this pattern of

Emerging Adult church attendance will eventually spread beyond London, given the trend of Millennial relocation out of the city as they age.[41]

Questions for Discussion

As promised in the introduction, each chapter of this book has some questions for discussion – ideally across the generations. They will be most effective if all parties have read the chapter but could be used even if that's not the case. In terms of this chapter, it might be helpful to discuss:

- How far does Emerging Adult Theory match the experiences of those Millennials you know and/or in your area? If not, then what *are* their experiences, challenges and needs?
- What is your response to the popularity of Jeremiah 29.11 among young Active Affirmers?
- Which congregations in your area function as 'Plausibility shelters' for young Christians? Why does that appear to be the case? (And how might you support them – given that they are trying to care for large numbers experiencing a demanding life stage?)
- If you agree that authenticity, tolerance and participation are important to Millennials, then where are the opportunities and challenges for your faith community?
- What spiritual resources are people within your context accessing? What is the impact of that on their faith?
- How far do you identify tendencies towards: a happy-midi narrative; reluctance to commit; or altruism in the Millennials you know?

Notes

1 Julie A. McMullin et al., 'Generational Affinities and discourses of difference', *British Journal of Sociology*, Vol. 58.2 (2007), 297–316.

2 James T. Sears and J. Dan Marshall, 'Generational Influences on Contemporary Curriculum Thought', *Journal of Curriculum Studies*, 32.2 (2000), 199–214.

3 Jeffrey Jensen Arnett, 'Emerging Adulthood: A Theory of Development from the Late Teens through the Twenties', *American Psychologist*, Vol. 55.5 (2000), 469–80.

4 Ulrich Beck and Elisabeth Beck-Gernsheim, *Individualization: Institutionalized Individualism and its Social and Political Consequences* (London: Sage, 2012).

5 Brian Willoughby and Spencer L. James, *The Marriage Paradox: Why Emerging Adults Love Marriage yet Push it Aside* (Oxford: Oxford University Press, 2017).

6 Jean M. Twenge, *Generation Me: Why Today's Young Americans are more Confident, Assertive, Entitled – and more Miserable than ever before* (New York: Free Press, 2006); Mark Bauerlain, *The Dumbest Generation: How the Digital Age Stupefies Young Americans and Jeopardizes our Future: Don't trust anyone under 30* (New York: Tercher, 2008).

7 Christian Smith, *Lost in Transition: The Dark Side of Emerging Adulthood* (Oxford: Oxford University Press, 2011).

8 Beck and Beck-Gernsheim, *Individualization*.

9 David Kinnaman, *You Lost Me* (Grand Rapids, MI: Baker, 2011).

10 Jeffrey Jensen Arnett, 'The Dangers of Generational Myth Making: A Rejoinder to Twenge', *Emerging Adulthood*, Vol. 1.1 (2013); Robert Wuthnow, *After the Baby Boomers: How Twenty and Thirty Somethings are Shaping the Future of American Religion* (Princeton, NJ: Princeton University Press, 2007).

11 The Evangelical Alliance report a similar pattern of philanthropy in their survey (October 2015). Activism is also one of the core values according to Bebbington's famous quadrilateral definition of Evangelicalism. The others being: conversionism, biblicism and crucicentrism. David Bebbington, *Evangelicalism in Modern Britain: A History from the 1730s to the 1980s* (London: Unwin Hyman, 1989).

12 David G. Ford, Joshua L. Mann and Peter M. Philips, *The Bible and Digital Millennials* (London: Routledge, 2019).

13 Christian Smith and Melinda Lundquist Denton, *Soul Searching: The Religious and Spiritual Lives of American Teenagers* (Oxford: Oxford University Press, 2005).

14 Sara Savage et al., *Understanding Generation Y* (London: Church House, 2016).

15 Charles Lindholm, *Culture and Authenticity* (London: Blackwell, 2008).

16 James S. Bielo, *Emerging Evangelicals: Faith, Modernity and the Desire for Authenticity* (New York: New York University Press, 2011).

17 Mathew Guest et al., *Christianity and the University Experience: Understanding Student Faith* (London: Bloomsbury Academic, 2013); there is also evidence from the Benedict XVI Centre for Religion and Society that young Catholics are more likely to self-identify as religious than young Protestants even if they rarely attend Mass. Stephen Bullivant, *Europe's Young Adults and Religion: Report 2018* (St Mary's University, London, 2018).

18 Bella DePaulo, *How We Live Now: Redefining Home and Family in the 21st Century* (New York: Atria, 2015).

19 Willoughby and James, *The Marriage Paradox*, explores this in detail.

20 George Barna, *Real Teens: A Contemporary Snapshot of Youth Culture* (Ventura, CA: Regal, 2001).

21 Peter L. Berger and Thomas Luckmann, *The Social Construction of Reality* (London: Penguin, 1975).

22 Linda Woodhead, 'The Rise of "No Religion" in Britain: The Emergence of a New Cultural Majority', *Journal of the British Academy*, 2016 (4), 245–62.

23 Smith found that 30% of American Millennials matched this pattern. *Souls in Transition: The Religious and Spiritual Lives of Emerging Adults* (Oxford: Oxford University Press, 2009).

24 Rob Warner documents these in *Reinventing English Evangelicalism 1996–2001: A Theological and Sociological Study* (Milton Keynes: Paternoster, 2007).

25 Grace Davie, *Religion in Britain: A Persistent Paradox* (Chichester: Wiley & Sons, 2014), 8.

26 Peter L. Berger, *The Sacred Canopy: Elements of a Sociological Theology of Religion* (New York: Random House, 1967).

27 Tyler Wigg Stevenson, *The World is not Ours to Save* (Leicester: Inter-Varsity Press, 2013).

28 None of my participants were Catholic (though a few had converted to Protestantism from a Catholic upbringing), so this work only reflects on Protestant forms of British Christianity.

29 www.ucas.com August 2018 (accessed 06.09.19).

30 www.centreforcities.org (accessed 06.09.19).

31 Nick Shepherd, *Faith Generation: Retaining Young People and Growing the Church* (London: SPCK, 2016).

32 Steve Aisthorpe, *The Invisible Church: Learning from the Experiences of Churchless Christians* (Edinburgh: Saint Andrew Press, 2016).

33 David Goodhew, *New Churches in the North East* (Durham: Centre for Church Growth, 2016).

34 '"Not As Difficult As You Think": Mission with Young Adults', *The Church Army*, www.churcharmy.org/youngadultsresearch (accessed 06.09.19).

35 Greg Smith (ed.), *21st Century Evangelicals* (Watford: Instant Apostle, 2015).

36 Peter Brierley, *UK Church Statistics No. 3: 2018 Edition* (London: Brierley Consultancy, 2018).

37 Developed by Nicky Gumbel, the Rector of Holy Trinity Brompton, the Alpha course has become a global phenomenon. Their website claims that 1.2 million people in the UK, and 23 million people worldwide, have tried this introduction to Christianity. HTB report 1,000 attending their central courses annually. Christianity Explored is an alternative developed at the more conservative evangelical All Souls Langham Place.

38 '"Not As Difficult As You Think"', 9.

39 Andrew Davies et al., *Megachurches and Social engagement in London*, www.birmingham.ac.uk/schools/ptr/departments/theologyand religion/research/projects/megachurches/index.aspx (accessed 06.09.19).

40 Anna Strhan, *Aliens and Strangers: The Struggle for Coherence in the Everyday Lives of Evangelicals* (London: Oxford University Press, 2015).

41 David Goodhew and Anthony-Paul Cooper (eds), *The Desecularisation of the City: London's Churches, 1980 to the Present* (London: Routledge, 2019).

The Privilege and Pressure of Emerging Adulthood: Economics and Health

As I listened to the accounts of their twenties by nearly 50 individuals, I was repeatedly struck not just by the opportunities they had enjoyed, but by how challenging the twenties are to live through. Of course, in many ways that is nothing new – establishing life as an independent adult has always been demanding (I remember the drama of my own twenties!). However, it appears that those pressures are now exacerbated by both technology and relentless and rapid cultural changes. As Zygmunt Bauman noted at the turn of the century:

> Social structures are now malleable to an extent unexperienced by, and unimaginable for, past generations; but like all fluids they do not keep their shape for long. There are, in short, no longer traditional patterns, codes, rules or 'pre-allocated reference groups' that individuals can look to as stable orientation points in their lives and be guided by. Rather, individuals now face an array of conflicting life-choices on their own, meaning that they face them in increasing isolation and with little prospect of assistance from any collective body or system.[1]

For Millennials, this 'liquefaction' of Western society provides an unstable backdrop to an acutely unstable life stage.

In the previous chapter the theory of Emerging Adulthood was introduced briefly. The aim of this, and the following two chapters, is to explain more fully the implications of that for the Millennial Generation, to consider some of the unprecedented opportunities and challenges they face, and to begin to consider how these might shape religious faith. By way of illustration, aspects of British Millennial life will be examined through the accounts of the participants. Clearly such narratives are complex and unique but for the sake of clarity they have been categorized. Broadly speaking they fall into two categories: Economic realities (explored in this chapter), and relational realities. Participant experiences with family and friends are examined in Chapter 3, and romance and parenthood in Chapter 4.

Developing into Adulthood

Not so long ago, people knew what being an adult looked like. It probably looked very similar to the lives of their parents and grandparents. For good or ill there were established patterns to follow from childhood into adolescence and then adulthood. The so-called 'markers' of adulthood were:

- Completing education and becoming financially independent by beginning a (probably lifelong) career.
- Marrying a member of the opposite sex and moving from the parental home into a marital one (which ideally you would have bought).
- In good time, beginning a family.

Once those tasks were accomplished (probably in your early to mid-twenties) you were an adult member of society.[2] Of course, there were exceptions, and the constraints of this heteronormative pattern created a range of problems and abuses, but it was what most people expected their life would look like. The window of identity, worldview and faith formation (as individuals moved from dependency on their parents to independent adulthood) was anticipated to last from the ages of about 17 until 22. Even for the few undertaking tertiary education, being a graduate meant being a grown-up. Today few people follow this predictable trajectory. Put simply, individualization and social changes mean there is no map to follow.

Among the middle classes, extended education and associated debt, the challenges of short-term or erratic employment and the advent of the gap year mean that most Millennials relocate multiple times during their twenties. By choice or necessity, many delay establishing a career by exploring multiple professional options or taking short-term, low-skill jobs. In terms of establishing a stable place of residence, property prices in many parts of the country are prohibitive, rents exorbitant and mortgages unattainable. Emerging adults might rent, lodge, share with friends, cohabit or undertake 'Yo-yo housing' (repeatedly moving in and out of their parents' home).

Changing attitudes towards sex, gender and marriage also mean that establishing a stable relationship and family unit also needs longer and may take myriad forms. Individuals might choose to remain single, date or engage in 'hook-ups' (sexual interactions with no expectation of ongoing relationship). Alternatively, they might establish long-term monogamous heterosexual or homosexual relationships. Cohabitation is the norm (often financially expedient rather than a precursor to marriage), with civil partnerships and/or marriage usually taking place after the age of 30. Although most delay starting a family (the average age this happens is currently 29.5 for women and 33 for men), those patterns are also diverse, including natural and assisted pregnancies, adoption and 'blended' families (namely step/half siblings).[3]

As discussed in the last chapter, Millennials aspire to an authentic identity – to be 'true to themselves' – but they need to do so by continually negotiating and renegotiating most aspects of their lives. Of course, there are familial, social and, for some, religious influences that still shape expectation at some level, but today's Emerging Adults have both the opportunities and demands of creating their own unique path to adulthood; a 'self-biography'.[4] All these options combined with continual change and limitless access to information (and disinformation) via the Internet and social media mean that establishing a stable, adult identity takes considerably longer than it did for generations with fewer choices. This can be liberating, exciting and self-indulgent but also uncertain, stressful and emotionally overwhelming.

Recognizing these trends, Jeffrey Jensen Arnett coined the phrase 'Emerging Adulthood' to describe this extended period of identity formation between adolescence and young adulthood. Initially (writing in 2000) he argued that it had extended to 25. Subsequently many agree that 30 is the age at which many finally feel and begin to function as young adults; often spending most of their twenties in an extended period of identity formation. Arnett argues that Emerging Adulthood is marked by five traits:

1 *Identity explorations*, answering the question 'Who am I?' and trying out various options, especially in love and work.
2 *Instability*, in love, work and place of residence.
3 *Self-focus*, as obligations to others reach a life-span low.
4 *Feeling in-between* or in transition, neither adolescent nor adult.
5 *Possibilities/Optimism*, although pessimistic about society more widely, many are optimistic about their personal future and have an unparalleled opportunity to transform their lives.[5]

Recognizing cultural and socio-economic variation, an additional quality was subsequently added:

6 Developing the *Ability to care for others*.[6]

As mentioned in the introduction, there are vociferous critics of this theory; particularly that it only represents Western privileged elites and that Emerging Adulthood bears little resemblance to the lived experience of many. In the United States, Osgood et al. described a set of six pathways to adulthood, which included three non-EA categories:

- *Fast Starters* – who begin work in their teens and 'settle down' at a younger age.
- *Parents without Careers* – often teen parents with low levels of education.
- *Slow Starters* – known in the UK as NEETS – not in employment, education or training.[7]

These are helpful in describing the reality of many younger Britons who do not have the same luxury of choice. Over half do not attend university, often remain living close to (or with) their families and have children or begin employment much younger.[8] Further research from the United States provides evidence that those young women who transition directly from school to parenthood (without tertiary education or any sort of career) are at higher risk of experiencing psychological distress and a declining physical health.[9] Similarly, those from lower socio-economic groups are often squeezed out of the low-skilled jobs market by underemployed graduates and find themselves in the so called 'gig-economy' or on zero-hours contracts. Unstable employment is particularly acute in former industrial and rural areas or for those who have been in care. Young men from these groups are at greatest risk of unemployment, homelessness and all the associated social problems. Emerging adulthood, then, does not describe the lived experience of many British young adults. To date I am unaware of any research into Active Affirmers who belong to non-elite groups in the UK. It seems likely, given the middle-class nature of much of the British Church, that there are very few.

It is also important to recognize that the 12% of young adults from BAME groups do not necessarily follow the Emerging Adult narrative.[10] The importance of family, culture and religious belief often remain significant and at odds with British liberal secularism, and it is worth noting that this can be particularly acute for young British Muslims, who make up 6% of the young adult population and (like young Christians) experience ethical dissonance from their secular peers.[11] The accounts of the African participants in this study highlighted some of those cultural differences. As international postgraduate students they bore some marks of Emerging Adulthood, but their experiences, priorities and values were different from those of the British participants. They all expressed concern about Western lifestyles and their familial and marital arrangements were markedly different. However, despite the limitations, Emerging Adulthood does describe the experience of many young Britons. Much of their twenties can be spent trying to negotiate instability and establish an adult identity – including a coherent religious faith.

Privilege or Pressure?

In truth, Millennials face both challenges and privileges, many of which are shaped by developments in technology. I enjoy shocking those I know with stories of the single-dial telephone, attached to the wall in our hallway during my teens in the 1980s, and of having to walk half a mile to a phone box for a private conversation. There are of course those who are spoilt and entitled or have unrealistic expectations, but one generation's luxury is another's necessity. The technology that changed my grandmother's life was a twin-tub washing machine. My father did his PhD using a computer the size of a room on which he was allocated an hour a fortnight. I consider both my washing machine and laptop vital to modern life. Criticizing Emerging Adults for embracing available opportunities and technology while doing the same oneself is disingenuous (it's not just Millennials who are dependent on their phones!).

It is true that for the privileged the opportunities to travel, own sophisticated technology, indulge in an experiential life-style and purchase luxury items are unprecedented. Sold the dream of the happy-midi narrative by society, the media and even their parents ('You can be anything you want to be darling!'), Millennials have high expectations of what life should be like. How far this is the naive optimism of youth and how far it is specific to their generation is debateable. It could be argued that older generations have similar expectations of an affluent, comfortable – even indulgent – middle or old age! However, most Millennials do not live a life of unadulterated indulgence. One of the consequences of all the instability – be it the result of choice or not – is that life feels very uncertain. Many come from divorced backgrounds, others are geographically distant from support networks or relocate so regularly that establishing one is difficult. Despite (or perhaps because of) technological advances, loneliness and poor mental health are significant problems among the young. Jean Twenge famously argues that the collapse of young adult mental health in the United States can be attributed directly to the launch of the Apple iPhone in 2006![12]

Similarly, Millennials have come to adulthood in the aftermath of the 2008 economic crash and a decade of austerity. Many are burdened with student debt and the knowledge that buying their own home is a virtual impossibility. The global consequences of the 9/11 attacks, subsequent 'war on terror', the migrant crisis and now the Brexit vote have also shaped their view of the world. Although better able to cope with some cultural shifts than their elders, Emerging Adults are highly connected and aware of global problems. The world appears a fundamentally unsafe and unjust place and few have a coherent political, philosophical or religious framework within which to make sense of such events. Being a 'None' means humanity is probably on its own, and climate change, global inequality and the current political environment do not indicate that older generations can be trusted to resolve the problems. All those in authority are suspect; politicians, corporations, journalists, banks and religious organizations have all proved themselves to be untrustworthy in recent years. Indeed, research by the World Health Organization suggests that for Generation Z, perceived existential threat is a key factor in making British teens among the least happy in the Western World.[13] One commentator christened them 'Generation K' (after Katniss Everdeen, heroine of the Hunger Games trilogy), explaining, 'They feel the world they inhabit is one of perpetual struggle

– dystopian, unequal and harsh.'[14] Despite their freedom and privileges, for many Emerging Adults all this technologically mediated uncertainty and pressure, be it existential, cultural or personal, is a toxic cocktail resulting in high levels of anxiety and depression – an epidemic of poor mental health.

Of course, each generation has its pressures. Generation X grew up in the shadow of the Cold War, the AIDS epidemic, miners' strikes and Thatcherism. The 2018 armistice centenary has reminded us of the harrowing experiences that now-deceased generations endured in two World Wars. But to compare a 20-year-old from 1916 in military uniform with a contemporary student (as people are wont to do on social media) is unfair on many levels. The world has changed beyond recognition and being an Emerging Adult is different; with unprecedented choices, privileges and expectations on one hand, and yet relentless uncertainties on the other. A self-biography is a mixed blessing!

Real Life for Active Affirmer Emerging Adults

Before explicitly exploring the faith journeys of those I interviewed in Chapters 5 to 8, it is important to understand the life experiences of Millennial Active Affirmers. Christian faith is not merely a set of doctrinal principles adherents objectively assent to. It is influenced, challenged and inspired by lived reality. As circumstances change, individuals need to consider and renegotiate their beliefs if they are to remain coherent and relevant. Surrounded by a wider culture of secular pluralism, many Emerging Adults appear not to have a single conversion experience that sets their religious belief in place permanently, or a relatively short period of religious exploration (17–22 as Fowler and others anticipated).[15] Rather, faith development functions more like a spiral where throughout Emerging Adulthood they continually re-evaluate whether Christianity is coherent and relevant, gradually forming a religious identity.[16] Understanding the joys and challenges that inform these processes is vital in order to make sense of them. We will consider these in two broad categories: economic realities and relational ones.

Economic Realities of Emerging Adulthood

A key task of Emerging Adulthood is to complete education, begin employment and take financial responsibility for oneself. Arnett found that this is one of the key ways in which Millennials self-identify as adult. Of course, the wider economic environment has a significant impact. Although those from more affluent backgrounds (as many Active Affirmers are) have been somewhat buffered by the so-called 'Bank of Mum and Dad', British Millennials have emerged into adulthood in a context shaped by the 2008 global economic crisis, during a decade of high property prices and austerity cuts.

In some parts of the country (like the North East, where this research was undertaken), various aspects of this are acute (finding employment) while others work to their advantage (low property prices). In others the financial challenges are the other way around. However, three economic themes were repeatedly raised by participants as they told the story of their twenties – all of which had an impact on their faith and religious identity: education and debt, experiences of employment and accommodation instability.

Extended education and debt

A key factor in the experience of Millennial Active Affirmers is the expansion of higher education instigated by a New Labour government in the 1990s. The policy aimed to encourage 50% of young people into tertiary education and, in order to finance this, replaced local government grants with student loans. Inevitably, greater numbers of graduates flooded the employment market. Thus, in order to distinguish themselves, increasing numbers undertook postgraduate studies, accruing the associated debt. Among this sample only two did not have a degree and half had postgraduate or professional qualifications. The subsequent increase of student fees to £9,000 per annum in 2012 means that at the time of writing the average student graduates with a debt of £32,000 – something unprecedented in British education. The fact that the government anticipates only 30% will repay their loan in full (once reaching the £25,000 earning threshold) indicates the number who are unlikely to earn high salaries despite their qualifications.[17]

Although these participants had completed undergraduate education before the 2012 fees increase, eight had chosen to study at local universities, living with their parents. This is common among students from lower-income households (particularly in the North East) but is a pattern that is increasing nationally as young people try to minimize the cost of education. For some this stability had been positive and they had found new faith communities in order to explore their beliefs. However, as will become evident, lack of exposure to alternative theological traditions can have long-term consequences for faith development. For example, the narrowness of her world and faith was something Claire had become frustrated with in her mid-twenties, resulting in poor choices she is still resolving.

Twenty-four was my turning point of, *Am I going to follow God, or am I going to run away and do my own thing?* I think that's what I should have done in my teenage years. It frustrates me that I didn't properly get into university life and get it out of my system then. Instead, I did it in my twenties when I had responsibilities.

As financial pragmatism becomes an increasingly important factor in considering higher education, churches need to be aware that the potential for these choices to influence faith development is significant and the emotional weight of debt is considerable for young adults – even if they will never actually be in a position to repay it.

Employment

Unsurprisingly the subject of employment was discussed widely by participants; the joys, challenges and instability of it were highly influential on their faith development, particularly after graduation. Mathew Guest and Kristin Aune correctly argue:

> Life post-graduation requires that a different kind of terri-tory be negotiated, one in which the moral and religious convictions of youth are more directly up against economic and family demands. Given the employment limitations of austerity Britain, we might expect the ideological principles fostered in campus life – whether religious, moral or political – to be especially vulnerable to disillusionment at the present time. Put more simply, the ideals of young adulthood are especially difficult to maintain during periods of economic constraint.[18]

In the current economic climate few Emerging Adults secure permanent jobs on completing education. Those who are middle class often have the social and financial capital to embark on gap years (often unpaid), internships and other forms of work experience, both for personal fulfilment and to increase their employability. The opportunity afforded by an extended period of independence and flexibility means travel and exploration of personal interests may well be financed by service-sector jobs. Much has been written about the irresponsibility of 'Generation Snowflake' but inevitably the expectation of multiple short-term jobs creates minimal loyalty to employers and a concern to gain transferable skills. Their underpinning happy-midi narrative means Emerging Adults are far less likely to remain in jobs that are not stimulating, or to tolerate unpleasant working environments; they consider it their responsibility to look for another. Similarly, their desire to participate and expectation of being listened to can make Emerging Adults appear precocious to older employers who anticipate duty, diligence and compliance in junior staff.

The professional journeys of these participants both illustrate and challenge this narrative. Although there are specific cultural and economic realities for the North East, they are not unique. Newcastle upon Tyne, like other cities with Russell Group Universities, offers wider private and public sector opportunities. The Tees Valley, hit by decades of economic underinvestment, has much in common with other regions built on heavy industry. Northumberland, sparsely populated and dependent on agriculture and tourism, faces the same challenges as other rural communities. Likewise, since 40% had lived in other parts of the UK (or world) during their twenties, their stories offer important reflections that are likely to mirror others across the nation.

Some had graduated immediately after the 2008 financial crisis, which shaped their initial experiences of trying to secure employment. Graduate-level jobs were scarce in the North East and the collapse of the Northern Rock bank made the situation worse. A number spoke about the exodus of their graduate friends to look for work in London, though Frankie also described how many of his less educated friends joined the military – one of the few local employment options. Some had taken short-term jobs in call centres or retail, but for those who experienced extended involuntary instability or unemployment the effect on their self-esteem and faith appeared to be both profound and long term; it made them doubt whether God could be trusted. A decade on, Harry explained:

I came back from [a gap year in Africa] with a confident expectation that God was going to help me. [But] I kept nearly getting jobs and then strange things happening. I got a job and then the agency closed their branch. [Another time] I got a job and they said they would offer me twenty hours a week and it just never materialized, I waited but they never rang. Another I know I got a glowing reference for – but they just didn't want me. I used to think things were God helping me out, now I realize you can't look for circumstances that are [actually] coincidences to help you out. You can't rely on circumstances to drop into place. You can't rely on God to tell you what you should do; you can't rely on God to tell you what career to choose, you need to choose.

Those trained for public- and charity-sector roles had found it easier to secure first jobs but during their twenties nearly half had retrained or changed profession. For some that had been inspired by a sense of vocation or divine direction. For others it had been because employment in the profession they had trained for was erratic, or they had discovered they were unsuited for it. A number described how the stress of work (in combination with other factors) had made them unwell, forcing a lifestyle change. This was particularly acute among teachers who, mirroring widely reported national trends, described the pressure of workload, OFSTED inspections, poor support, bullying and anxiety about the needs of their pupils. Rob explained:

> This sense of calling [I had was to a] fairly rough area, [with] lots of social needs. [I was] impacting lives, not just the children but the families as well. Being part of that community was really amazing, but it took its toll. It started having an impact on my mental health. Originally stress and anxiety that then descended into full-blown depression to the point where I couldn't function.

Several scholars have noted an altruistic tendency among Millennials, and inspired by their faith many Active Affirmers choose to enter caring professions. Guest and Aune found clear evidence of Christian identity shaping the professional aspirations of students. For some it provided a moral critique of neo-liberal values, for others a sense of divine calling and purpose. This included perceiving opportunities for evangelism in the workplace but also for alleviating suffering and exerting ethical influence on the shaping of society.[19] Social activism has a long history within evangelical Christianity and this has seen a recent resurgence, particularly among the middle-class young in response to current levels of poverty. However, the stories of these participants suggest that faith can stimulate both positive and negative consequences. In many cases participants described their faith (and faith community) providing comfort, encouragement and a measure of emotional resilience through the challenges of their professional role. Conversely the level of conscientiousness and compassion their beliefs inspired potentially contributed to poor boundaries and over-work. They were, after all, 'working for Jesus'. Learning to deal with vulnerable, chaotic and sometimes violent clients in overstretched environments, while their own identity and personal lives are unstable, can push Emerging Adults to and beyond breaking point. Even for those who had followed a religious vocational path there were accounts of Christian charities and churches providing little financial recompense or managerial support but expecting much from enthusiastic young employees. It is hardly surprising that this would have a detrimental effect not just on their professional well-being but their faith and attitude towards faith communities.

Although (mirroring regional employment patterns) there were fewer in the research sample, the private sector also placed high demands on junior employees. Scarcity of professional opportunity, poor management, employment insecurity and dealing with redundancy, plus the pressure of excessive travel and long commutes were all described. Of course, these are aspects of employment many recognize, but for Emerging Adults this is the first time they have had to deal with such challenges or develop professional coping mechanisms.

For Active Affirmers this can be compounded by the lifestyle of colleagues, which is often at odds with their own. It is well documented that Christian students form close (sometimes insular) communities to avoid the wider drinking or hooking-up culture in universities.[20] However, in an employment context, exposure to colleagues (including managers) with conflicting values is inevitable and can impact religious belief. Discussion with colleagues was cited as significant in the process of faith loss by three participants, and colleagues were those with whom extramarital affairs were most likely. Some participants described being uncertain how to maintain integrity among senior colleagues whose values conflicted with their own. Miriam said:

> There was a constant pressure as a Christian as well. You are working in a secular environment and you are surrounded by people [and] the way they behave is often so un-Godly. My colleague was quite devious ... liberal with the truth. You are thinking, *How do I navigate my way through without making things worse or kicking things off?* I was known for standing my ground on some things [but] I think I just felt battered from it.

Of course, much of this is the sort of culture shock young people of every generation have experienced on entering the adult world of the workplace. Millennials are not the first generation to have entered the workforce during a period of financial austerity; for some generations unemployment rates have been far higher. But Millennial expectations, their happy-midi narrative and the promise they have been given that they can be anything they want to be, mean that the gap between their hopes and the reality of an economically, politically and socially uncertain environment can be acute.

Clearly, some had thrived, been promoted and found great satisfaction in doing their job well. They often described the way in which they felt they were serving God through it, changing lives or having a positive influence. For some, work was their primary social network – a source of close friendship and support. Opportunities to travel, study, develop skills and self-confidence were all described. Others considered that God had opened doors in the form of ideal or unexpected employment opportunities that had been a source of considerable encouragement, reinforcing their faith. A number talked about the significance, professionally and personally, of older colleagues with faith: the senior doctor who had helped them think through ethical issues; the line manager who became a spiritual mentor; the headteacher who had head-hunted them for a job. The evidence I saw was not that Millennials were flighty snowflakes, flitting from job to job. Those in this sample had worked long and hard. Some had realized after a period that this was not the profession for them and had taken steps to find a meaningful alternative. Most had poured energy and commitment into their jobs and only changed when their mental health had failed, they felt it had become untenable for them to stay, or an opportunity arose for seniority. Others had found rhythms that worked by going part-time, taking less stressful jobs or stopping paid employment to stay at home with their children. Millennial Active Affirmers do appear to have a happy-midi narrative – they want to be happy at work, but they are also often altruists who want their professional lives to make a difference, and in a region like the North East the need is obvious. Almost none of them spoke about finances or status as their motivator (although culturally British people tend not to). Certainly, they were interested in professional development if it allowed them to make a greater difference or do something more interesting, but they typically only mentioned salary when it had been problematic. What most appeared to aspire to were professions that would accomplish personal satisfaction, a healthy lifestyle and an altruistic outcome.

Accommodation and relocation

One of the central sources of volatility during Emerging Adulthood is that of where to live. It is well documented in the press that in many parts of the country, young adults are essentially priced out of the property market. Unless parents can afford to help them acquire a mortgage, many find themselves trapped as part of 'Generation rent'. Among those I interviewed, most had relocated multiple times during their twenties (the average was four times in ten years). Although a number had remained living with local parents while studying, participants described a kaleidoscope of accommodation situations. A number had followed the pattern of 'yo-yo housing' – moving in and out of their parents' homes. Some described family tensions around this but they were usually with siblings rather than parents, with whom most appeared to have amicable relationships. This appears to be a cultural shift, something more akin to southern European models, where Emerging Adults often live with their parents much longer.[21] In these cases the motivation was pragmatic, usually based on finances. Circumstances had changed in some way and so returning home was convenient and (apparently) supported by their parents. However, those now in their thirties living in their parents' home found that difficult. For some, marriage breakdown was the cause, for others it was their mental health or just employment circumstances. Whatever the cause, it appeared that after the age of 30 they viewed living with their parents differently. Harry explained, 'I didn't envisage this – living back at home with my mum and two dogs!' And Felicity, who had moved home aged 29 when her housemate married, said:

Initially I struggled. I'm looking to buy my own house now, but initially that was the hardest time. I'd moved home, started the new job (which was harder than I imagined), and my best friend got married. It was just a combination of the whole change, a mix of all of these things. I think the reality of being in your late twenties and moving back home was a bit difficult.

They seemed to feel that living with parents was acceptable – up to a point. That point came in the late twenties when they should have established a place of their own. Some, like Felicity, were working towards that but others without the prospect of independence were dispirited.

Part of what is unsettling about accommodation for Emerging Adults is that their peers are typically in the same fluctuating lifestyle. Even if they are living in a great house with good friends (and many had), that season was only ever temporary.

It might last a year or two but then someone got a new job and relocated, bought a house or got married. This broke up their pseudo-family and forced them to find new house-mates or relocate. Some had bought a house with a friend, which made change both emotionally and financially demanding. Others described less fortunate house-sharing situations: clashes of personality, lifestyle, or finding themselves in the role of carer for vulnerable housemates. Some recognized that their mental health had made them demanding to live with. In more than one case their housemate had moved out, leaving them in a doubly challenging position. Conversely, Will had a demanding job caring for vulnerable people and a housemate diagnosed with a terminal illness. He explained:

It has been quite hard. [In my job] you are there for every-one else and then you are going home where [my housemate] had to let everything out, and I've been the one that has had to take the brunt of it. Screaming, swearing ... that doesn't bother me, but where is my outlet for that?

He has subsequently had to process his housemate's death.

Those who are not able to rent with friends (for example when relocating to a new region) often find themselves renting a room or lodging. Obviously, that is hit-and-miss; it can be great or dreadful – particularly if they don't know the region they are moving to. Living in an unfamiliar location, with people you don't know, while beginning a new job would be demanding regardless of age, but it is very common for Emerging Adults. One young woman described how her shift pattern meant she barely saw those she had rented a room from and, being new to the city, she had few friends.

Given property prices in the North East, 70% had been able to buy a home at some point in their twenties. A few mentioned parental assistance in that process, but it was not the norm. Several had been able to buy homes in areas they preferred – typically rural, coastal or middle class. Others had bought their first home in more deprived areas or purchased properties that needed considerable renovation. Both had proved challenging. Some described being intimidated by neighbours with mental health problems, evidence of crime and drug use, or simply feeling unsafe in what they had hoped would be their dream home. This too was integrated with their faith, and in some cases hopes of positively influencing the neighbourhood. Pete recounted:

> My wife had got some prophetic feeling ... we went to view a house ... we didn't even go for a second viewing. We were just like, *The Lord is telling us that this is the right house.* It was on a street where two other people from church lived, so it was all community living and maybe we will convert the street, kind of stuff. Then we moved into it and it was just horrendous, it needed loads of stuff doing to it. I remember just thinking, *We've got no floor. We've got bare walls and there's plaster everywhere. Right, you are going to have to learn a lot of new DIY skills!*
>
> The area we were in we had one [neighbour] who clearly had mental health issues. You could hear her swearing at us through the walls. Then we've had drug users in the downstairs flat. There was nowhere for the kids to play out. I regret buying it, we didn't go for a second viewing. If it was a word from the Lord, he was a bit of a knacker to tell us to buy that house!

By contrast some thrived having intentionally chosen to live in such neighbourhoods. They appeared to have greater capacity to cope – often motivated by a sense of God's calling and resultant compassion for their vulnerable neighbours. For example, Rachel explained:

> I felt like God was saying to move to the inner city, so that's what I did with my sister and a friend who I had lived with on and off all these years. We lived there for five years. If I'm really honest, most of my life was about naughty kids and their families. This bit of my life, when I moved to the estate,

was incredible. The kids knew where we lived, they came round for tea twice a week. Their mum knew where I lived, so she would come and knock when her husband beat her up.

A number spoke about how their faith and accommodation situation interacted. Like Pete, others had intentionally bought houses close to their church or members of their congregation, aspiring to create community. One couple, relocating from further south, deliberately rented for some time as they explored what church to join – wanting to buy property near it. Others did drive considerable distances to church and had bought based on lifestyle or financial factors, but again and again a desire for community was what they described.

For some their faith had been profoundly impacted by the provision of somewhere to live in extreme situations. Miriam, whose mental health had been very poor, told me:

My housemate then told me that she was moving out so I either had to take on the whole flat or find somewhere else to live. I remember being away on holiday, only just having started going back to work, so still in quite a bad way. [Ultimately] I moved in here where God provided. It was a real time of provision. I didn't have the contents of a house in terms of furniture. God turned up things. My old landlords gave me these [chairs]. There were lots of things like that, where God just kept providing.

Mandy, pregnant as a teenager, described how what she understood as God's provision of accommodation had led to her conversion.

I had this vision of myself as a single mother in a council flat with grotty window-sills and flaky paint. It was just horrifying and terrifying. I didn't even know how to put the washing machine on. I wasn't self-sufficient at all. I did pray about it, out of absolute desperation. I rang the council and went to their office. The man very casually said, 'Oh, we're building some housing association houses on the new estate. Would you like one of them?' Just like that. No waiting, no anything. So, from then on, what had been a scary prospect became quite an exciting one. I had absolute, complete certainty that that was God and that a response was required from me.

Many of the stories I was told about faith were in the area of provision in difficult circumstances, and for Millennial Active Affirmers, accommodation was one of the most demanding to navigate. Certainly, other generations have experienced volatility in their early twenties when it comes to housing, but it is easy for older, now settled generations to forget how demanding continual change and instability is. For many Emerging Adults, unless they are fortunate to have financial assistance, the prospect of buying and thus establishing a stable home is distant at best. To return to Jeremiah 29.11, Emerging Adults want the assurance that God's plans are to prosper and not to harm them, to give them a hope and a future. What many aspire to is a stable home and community, something their parents and grandparents could often take for granted.

Emerging Adulthood and Health

As will have become evident from these accounts of economic reality during Emerging Adulthood, the theme of health – in particular, mental health – frequently recurred. I had not anticipated how striking this would be, or for how many their health had influenced both their life and faith. Much has been written about the deterioration of mental health among younger generations. The introduction of the smartphone, development of social media, 'helicopter parenting', unrealistic expectations, economic and social instability, and decline in coherent worldview have all been cited as potential causes. The consensus is that the adolescence and student years are particularly acute points for depressive symptoms, anger and low self-esteem. These typically improve as individuals go through Emerging Adulthood, with those who achieve stable identity, relationships and employment doing best.[22] However, for those who do not achieve these tasks, mental health can dip again in the late twenties as individuals feel that they are failing to achieve their aspirations and are being left behind.[23] There was evidence of this within the stories of these Active Affirmers. Most were more emotionally stable in their thirties (some significantly more so) but the extent to which both physical and mental health were central events to their identity formation was striking. In total, half spoke about them; 20% describing physical health challenges and 35% moderate to serious mental health problems (unsurprisingly, there was some overlap).

Physical health

Some participants described acute or emergency scenarios they had experienced. These included traffic incidents, accidental injuries and emergency surgery. A number also described similar events or deaths among close friends and family. Inevitably the shock of such traumas influenced their faith as they tried to make sense of apparently inexplicable suffering. Four explicitly described the phenomenon of post-traumatic faith growth – where their beliefs and religious identity had become stronger as a result of those negative experiences.[24] They had come to understand them as a form of divine rescue, something that had instilled a sense of meaning and increased devotion in their faith. Chloe was certain that God had saved her life for some higher purpose and was consequently endeavouring to evangelize as many people as she could. Wayne described a profound experience of the presence of God in his hospital room. He was certain that divine providence had caused a world-class surgeon to (improbably) take his case. Wider research shows that frequent spiritual experiences increase the likelihood of developing resilient faith even if life circumstances are traumatic. These very dramatic initial experiences seemed to have put that process in motion, creating an underpinning event through which subsequent experiences were interpreted.[25]

For others the miraculous healing they had hoped for had not taken place. Several described the process of trying to make sense of death, often for the first time. Some of these were anticipated, but others had been shocking and traumatic. Individuals from or working among those from chaotic backgrounds typically reported multiple deaths in their narratives, which took a toll on their mental health. However, they also appeared to reinforce their commitment to ministry, intensifying their sense of the urgency of social or evangelistic activity. In terms of processing death, most appeared to have come to a place of acceptance that allowed them to move forward in their faith rather than undermining it. It was noticeable, though, that the support they had received in those times was significant in whether they managed that process or not.

More challenging, it appeared, was making sense of ongoing or chronic health problems. This was particularly acute when they were undiagnosed. For example, it took ten years of repeated medical episodes before Frankie's illness was diagnosed, something that undermined much of his academic and professional life. Andrew struggled with inexplicable chronic chest pains, which made him very anxious, causing him to end a relationship rather than 'inflict my problems' on his girlfriend. Miriam's back pain and chronic fatigue were shaped by her work pattern and ultimately forced her to resign, while Deborah's fertility problems were relentless and painful, causing her to be off work for long periods.

When one's peers are engaged in the opportunities for leisure and social activities that Emerging Adulthood affords, or are moving forward in establishing a life for themselves, to be restricted by chronic illness is not only painful and confusing but also socially isolating. Making sense of why a good God would allow such things, or not heal them, is theologically complex, particularly for those from charismatic and Pentecostal traditions. Andrew described his anger at God for the unfairness of his situation, and Miriam wryly said, 'It was an interesting ride with God!' Those whose faith had survived this process often recognized how their beliefs and religious identity had grown through prayer, the encouragement of others or exploration of alternative theologies of suffering. Andrew ultimately reflected: 'God sustained me through that time.' He had no clear answers to his questions but, with the support of his pastor, had reached a point where he felt able to trust God regardless of his health.

Mental health

For more than a third of those participating, struggles with their mental health had been a significant part of their Emerging Adulthood. These included eating disorders, post-natal depression, insomnia and psycho-sexual problems, but by far the largest number described episodes of anxiety and depression. For some these had been relatively short term and were resolved with the help of medication, counselling and emotional support. Others described acute episodes, using language like 'meltdown', 'burnout' and being 'unable to function'. Three young men spoke of feeling suicidal at points. Chris said, 'I felt empty inside, it was a very dark place', but admitted to hiding his profound unhappiness from everyone and continuing to pretend at home, work and church until he could no longer bear the façade. His reluctance to seek help from either medical or religious sources appeared to be rooted in a sense of shame that he was failing to live up to the roles of 'good son, good Christian, good husband'. Ultimately, he chose no longer to be a husband or Christian, and is still rebuilding his identity and learning to manage his mental health several years later. Robbie also described the shame he had felt at becoming unwell, particularly because his depression was triggered by professional choices that he was certain God had directed him to take. He felt that he was failing God by being unable to cope. It was evident that there continues to be stigma around emotional and mental health, particularly for Millennial men, which their religious identity can sometimes compound rather than help.

Instead of acute episodes, other participants described repeated patterns of low mood, sadness and anxiety that plagued much of their twenties. For several, depression had not only been the characterizing experience of their Emerging Adulthood, but something they continued to battle in their thirties. Theresa, Miriam and Clare all described the repeated ebb and flow of their mental health struggles, and Marcus continued to have episodes of overwhelming anxiety. The phrase many used to describe their relationship with their mental and emotional health was: 'I'm learning to manage it.' Few appeared to be expecting God to heal them; instead they were learning to recognize and anticipate the episodes and adjust their life-style and coping mechanisms accordingly. Their expectation appeared to be that God would sustain them but that medical and psychiatric support was most likely to cure them, or at least allow them to function. Although some expressed a resistance to the idea of taking antidepressants, few expressed theological tensions around accessing a diverse range of spiritual, emotional and medical resources. They appeared to have a pragmatic approach to managing their mental health. Even Diane (whose conversion as a teenager had transformed her life-threatening eating disorder) held that in tension with ongoing anxiety issues. She had concluded:

> I don't believe in sudden changes in life. I think it just takes time, and you don't need to change things quickly. I think in a lot of churches they are pushing the teaching that focuses on changing your life. Something is wrong with your life and you need to be constantly changing it. Do you love God enough? Maybe not. We can pray so that you will love God more. I started to realize that life is a bit more complicated.

In terms of the causes of mental health struggles there were three common factors: existential crises, identity struggles and overwhelming daily pressures. In most cases these interacted with each other. Several spoke about the existential dilemma that underpinned their depression. Of course, creating a coherent worldview is one of the tasks of Emerging Adulthood but for some individuals that had become acute and caused them to pursue religious faith in order to make sense of the world and themselves. The events that led to Penny's conversion began with the deterioration of her mental health:

I started getting real problems with anxiety. The problem was that I was questioning all sorts of deep things like *Why am I here? What is the point of my life?* I hated how I looked. I just didn't like myself. Ironically, I was working as a volunteer for Samaritans. I was talking to suicidal people on the telephone and in the meantime thinking *Why do I even exist?* It got to the point where I would wake up in the morning and have one deep breath and then the rest of the day [my breathing] would be really horrible; I couldn't take deep breaths. I was crying a lot and was basically depressed. My friends were very nice, but I was asking questions that they couldn't answer. I was questioning the very meaning of life. I was searching for my purpose.

Will, too, had reached a point of existential desperation as a student and, like Penny, had begun to explore religious faith. For her that had been a long-term journey whereas for him an experience in church had transformed everything. He said:

I was at a point that I was thinking about suicide to be honest. [I felt] a lot of depression and anxiety and a lot of fear. I wouldn't show it on the outside to anyone, but inwardly that was what was going on. I just went to bed [one] Saturday night and thought, *If I don't ask Jesus into my life tomorrow morning, I don't know what is going to happen.* My parents are strong Christians, and I'd never dismissed God entirely, but it just came to me. I'd tried everything else but the gospel, but Jesus. I woke up that Sunday morning and went to the first church that I could get to. It happened to be an amazing church; full of three hundred people. The pastor was just sharing the gospel. It hit me, that realization that that was what I needed and that was what I had been craving. I felt like I went into church with an invisible rucksack on, and I didn't feel a difference when I accepted Jesus into my life, but when I walked out, it was like that rucksack had been cut off. I've never felt anything like it.

For others, by contrast, doubts about their existing faith were part of that existential trigger. Almost all of those who had become apostate described the interaction of their faith and mental health. The process of their worldview disintegrating combined with social isolation and, in several cases, marital breakdown had made them ill. Several were clearly still struggling at the time of their interview. It was also striking how self-aware many of the participants were. Evidently, for some this was a result of the work they had done with counsellors. They spoke about their upbringing, difficulties in relationships with their parents or their own insecurities. Marcus identified his depression as rooted in his struggle to come to terms with his father's death while he was a teenager, and Pete as rooted in the emotional unavailability of his parents.

For most, though, their mental health had suffered from the sheer pressure of Emerging Adult life. Most commonly cited were the pressures of work, particularly for those in caring professions. Teachers and social workers were most likely to describe how they had simply been overwhelmed by workload, stress and the emotional demand. Their senior colleagues were struggling too, but at the very start of their careers, still developing professional skills and emotional resilience, it had simply been too much. Laura was emphatic that all other aspects of her life had been great, 'Oh it was undoubtedly the pressure of work that made me ill!' Research shows that full-time employment and high job satisfaction militate against depression in Emerging Adults, but when their dream job becomes a nightmare that inevitably undermines their well-being.[26] Disappointment, frustration and anger were all expressed that their desire to help, which they believed to be in line with God's plans, had been thwarted by overwhelming professional pressures such as Ofsted inspections and budget cuts. Many of these participants were clearly highly capable activists, involved in multiple church activities with busy social lives too. They appeared to be running at maximum emotional and physical capacity and all it took was one extra pressure for that to become too much. A health scare, relationship failure, family incident or new baby and they became overwhelmed; unable to 'juggle all the balls' (as one put it).

How their beliefs interacted with these struggles was a key part of their faith journey. Almost all of them described struggling to make sense of where God was in these dark times or why prayer was not resolving pressures or healing them. Some had succeeded in making theological sense of their experiences, particularly as stimuli for personal growth or increasing resilience. Will explained:

> I would say that my biggest passion in life was always people, my biggest fear in life was always people. Social anxieties I've always struggled with it. Not so much now. It is getting better and I'm getting healed from that. But if you had said, this [people-orientated job] is what you will be doing, I'd [have said] said, *Absolutely not!* God turns your weaknesses into strengths. He just blesses you with stuff that you can't handle, and you have to depend on him. I still do that.

Similarly, Harry described the necessity of his faith and using prayer to manage the anxiety his insomnia caused: 'I have to trust God for the process of going to bed.' Several described how retrospectively they could see God's presence with them 'walking in the dark times' and expressed gratitude for friends, family and church members who had done the same. However, it was also common for them to describe how attending church exacerbated their anxiety. Miriam identified social and spiritual aspects that both damaged and helped her mental health:

Going to church was the hardest thing I ever did. Getting through the doors was so hard, and doing it on my own was just so difficult. I think it was that spiritual vulnerability. There's something about even being in a spiritual place where you feel like you are made more vulnerable, and the fear that went with it of not being able to cope. There were times when I was in church that I just had to go for a walk, I just couldn't cope with being in there anymore.

Also, Christians say stupid things that are really not helpful. I'd lost all this weight, and I was barely eating – I probably hadn't even brushed my hair. I remember this lovely lady who was in her late fifties asking, 'How you doing?' 'Not so great.' 'Ah, still? But you are looking fab!' I was thinking, *If I eat any less, I will be taken into hospital.* I was in the worst place I'd ever been, and she was telling me I looked great because I'd lost a whole load of weight! I just remember thinking, *This is so messed up!*

One thing I've noticed through ill health is that a lot of Christians can't handle you saying that you are not fine. They ask the question, 'You alright?' And they want the glib answer. I got very good at saying, 'So-so', or 'Not so great today'. Fobbing them off a bit. These were often people that I perceived as mature Christians who just couldn't handle people not being OK. I just felt like, *If you don't want to know, don't ask the question.* I used to find that quite difficult, but I guess I knew I needed to keep sticking at church. I had a group of friends who tried to encourage that and were really supportive. If needs be [they] went to stuff with me to make it easier going through the door. I didn't find it easy being faced with a room full of people.

Theresa explained how the Reformed theology of her evangelical upbringing became twisted by her mental health:

I definitely had to stop reading the Bible so much. As a good evangelical girl, you had to have a quiet time in the morning. My boyfriend and Christian friends were just saying, 'Please just stop reading the Bible because your brain is not well!' I'd always be skipping to creepy things and interpreting them in crazy ways to back up: 'You are evil; it is all your fault.' I'd grown up in a church culture that maybe was a bit more negative. I didn't have the strength to resist the automatic creepy interpretation that my brain would go to.

Equally, she and others described how the large social setting, theology and emotive worship of their charismatic churches were problematic:

Going to church was pretty awful. If you are a semi-charismatic, long-term illness doesn't fit with that healing culture. The first six or seven months I [thought], *This [depression] isn't going to last.* [But] a year later I was coming to a more peaceful acceptance, [that] this is something that needed to happen. *I need to go through this, and that's sort of OK.* But I remember specifically going for prayer ministry at church and saying to this couple, 'I didn't come for prayer for healing.' Almost quite aggressively. 'I know that I am on the path to healing with my depression with my counselling. I just need prayer to get through this week, because it has been a dark week.' They still prayed for healing. I was like, *Aaah I can't stand being around people because you don't listen!* Big gatherings where everyone was, *Woohoo!* [and] you just feel awful were hard. CU was worse than church, because I also knew everyone, so you feel more conspicuous. At least in church you can [just] sit. There would be drunks or people who had come as a friend of someone, so I felt, *I'm in that group.* That was hard, but it wasn't as hard as feeling super conspicuous.

She became increasingly concerned with the effects of what she saw as 'black and white' teaching and eventually began to attend a rural Anglican congregation. One of several participants who expressed enthusiasm for non-emotive liturgical worship, she said:

It was fine to not feel enthusiastic. If you were committed and believed the right things, or willing to discuss stuff, that was OK. It was nice to be somewhere that was quite dry. Compared to all the old biddies who had been there their whole lives and weren't even sure what they believed, I was back in the 'most committed' section, and that felt nice as well, rather than [being] the one who was awkward and doubting.

It seemed that much of Theresa's identity had been shaped by her mental health struggles. As a student she had become the 'go-to girl for mental health' in her campus group. Many people went to her for advice about how to understand and manage their own emotional well-being. She described running discussion groups for other Active Affirmers on the subject, and had found a sense of meaning and purpose through that. However, unlike Miriam and Theresa, Marcus had not found any form of religious beliefs or expression helpful and subsequently become apostate. He, too, expressed frustration at the lack of honesty about struggle or use of lament in his church:

I would find communal worship difficult because there would be all these people singing stuff and I'd be going, *Do I really believe that? Is this true? Is this my experience? Do I really believe this?* In particular I used to tie myself up in knots about Communion. *Do I really believe this? Am I really in a right relationship with God or with other people to do this?* I [did it] as an act of faith, but it was always that angsty thing, rather than a positive thing.

We also had a fantastic worship band, but they really didn't get the idea of lament. It felt like there was this whole group of people in the church that were really struggling with mental health issues, or their faith, or whatever, and the church as a community wasn't acknowledging that in the way that they worshipped. Once we sang a Tim Hughes song (I can't remember its name) [but] I could see people I knew were struggling to really engage with the song and I was engaged with the song. It was something that I could sing wholeheartedly and was expressing how I was feeling. I said after the service that I found it really helpful and asked if we could do the song another time. It was kind of like, 'Well, we picked it because it tied in with the theme of the service, and I don't think it is necessarily appropriate the rest of the time because we are supposed to be encouraging people toward some kind of positive place.' I found that quite difficult.

None of this will come as a shock to those working in Emerging Adult Christian ministries. Most of us recognize an increase in the number and severity of mental health problems among those we work with. Of course, rates of diagnosis have increased too, but it is important to recognize that even the most devout Active Affirmers can experience such challenges. Religious faith does not insulate individuals from illness or the pressures of this developmental phase. It can help in terms of providing spiritual and emotional resources, social support and a sense of meaning. But equally, religious activity (particularly in the large, enthusiastic settings where Active Affirmers tend to congregate) can exacerbate the sense of feeling anxious, overwhelmed, or a failure. Millennial desire for authenticity means that worship or theological teaching that does not ring true becomes problematic and is likely to push those with physical or mental health problems away from faith communities rather than encourage them in. Indeed, chronic illness, in any form, tends to isolate people from the very support they need. For Emerging Adults, the sense of being alone, in pain and being left behind as their peers move on with what life is 'supposed' to look like, can be deeply distressing. They need all the wisdom, support and inclusion they can get to form a coherent theological framework that will allow their faith not just to survive but to grow.

Questions for Discussion

- What do you identify as the positives and negatives of the need for Emerging Adults to create a 'self-biography'? Do you consider it to be a privilege or pressure?
- How far are the young people in your community 'Emerging Adults' or do they match Osgood's alternative categories more closely? How far does your faith community recognize and respond to that diversity?
- To what extent are debt, insecure employment and fluctuating accommodation pressures you recognize younger generations facing? What forms of practical, emotional or spiritual support does (or might) your faith community offer for those experiencing these pressures?
- What struck you most strongly from the descriptions of Millennial physical and mental health struggles and in particular that interaction with their faith? How are they similar/dissimilar to your own experiences? How might your faith community better accommodate or support those who are struggling with these sorts of issues?

Notes

1 Zygmunt Bauman, *Liquid Modernity* (Cambridge: Blackwell, 2000), 7–8.

2 M. J. Shanahan et al., 'Subjective Age Identity and the Transition to Adulthood: When do Adolescents become Adults?', in R. A. Settersten Jr et al. (eds), *On the frontier of Adulthood: Theory, Research, and Public Policy* (Chicago, IL: University of Chicago Press, 2005), 225–55.

3 Data available from the Office for National Statistics, www.ons.gov.uk (accessed 06.09.19).

4 Ulrich Beck and Elisabeth Beck-Gernsheim, *Individualization: Institutionalized Individualism and its Social and Political Consequences* (London: Sage, 2012).

5 Jeffrey Jensen Arnett, *Emerging Adulthood: The Winding Road from the Late Teens through the Twenties* (Oxford: Oxford University Press, 2004), 9.

6 Dalal Katsiaficas, '"I Know I'm an Adult When … I Can Care

for Myself and Others": The Role of Social Responsibilities in Emerging Adulthood for Community College Students', *Journal of Emerging Adulthood*, Vol. 5.6 (2017), 392–405.

7 D. W. Osgood et al., 'Six Paths to Adulthood: Fast Starters, Parents without Careers, Educated Partners, Educated Singles, Working Singles and Slow Starters', in R. A. Settersten Jr et al. (eds), *On the Frontier of Adulthood: Theory, Research, and Public Policy* (Chicago, IL: University of Chicago Press, 2005).

8 In 2017, 52% of individuals had not participated in some form of higher education before the age of 30. 'Participation rates in Higher Education – 2006 to 2017', GOV.UK, www.gov.uk/government/statistics/participation-rates-in-higher-education-2006-to-2017 (accessed 06.09.19).

9 P. N. E. Robertson et al., 'Developmental Trajectories and Health Outcome among Emerging Adult Women and Men', *Journal of Emerging Adulthood*, Vol. 5.2 (August 2016).

10 'Ethnicity Facts and Figures', GOV.UK, www.ethnicity-facts-figures.service.gov.uk/british-population/demographics/age-groups/latest (accessed 06.09.19).

11 'Britain's Muslim Population is Relatively Young', *The Muslim Council of Britain*, https://mcb.org.uk/wp-content/uploads/2015/05/BMINBriefing1_1June15.pdf; 'Mid-year Population Estimate of the United Kingdom in 2018', *Statista* (accessed 06.09.19); G. Valentine, S. L. Holloway and M. Jayne, 'Contemporary Cultures of Abstinence and the Night-Time Economy: Muslim Attitudes Towards Alcohol and the Implications for Social Cohesion', *Environment and Planning*, Vol. 42.1 (2010), 8–22.

12 Jean M. Twenge, 'Have Smartphones Destroyed a Generation?', *The Atlantic*, September 2017, www.theatlantic.com/magazine/archive/2017/09/has-the-smartphone-destroyed-a-generation/534198/ (accessed 06.09.19).

13 World Health Organization, *Growing Up Unequal: Gender and Socioeconomic Differences in Young People's Health and Well-being* (Copenhagen: World Health Organization, 2016).

14 Noreena Hertz, 'Think Millennials Have it Tough? For Generation K Life is Even Harder', *The Guardian* (19 March 2016).

15 James W. Fowler, *Stages of Faith: The Psychology of Human Development and the Quest for Meaning* (San Francisco, CA: HarperCollins, 1995), 174–83.

16 Elizabeth J. Tisdell, *Exploring Spirituality and Culture in Adult and Higher Education* (San Francisco, CA: Jossey-Bass, 2003).

17 Paul Bolton, 'Student Loan Statistics (Commons Briefing papers SN01079)', House of Commons Library, UK Parliament Website, https://researchbriefings.parliament.uk/ResearchBriefing/Summary/SN01079 (accessed 06.09.19).

18 Mathew Guest and Kristin Aune, 'Students' Constructions of a Christian Future: Faith, Class and Aspiration in a University Context', *Sociological Research Online*, Vol. 22.1 (2017), 12.

19 Guest and Aune, 'Students' Constructions of a Christian Future'.

20 S. Sharma and M. Guest, 'Navigating Religion between University and Home: Christian Students' Experiences in English Universities', *Social and Cultural Geography*, Vol. 14.1 (2013), 59–79.

21 Marina Mendonça and Anne Marie Fontaine, 'Late Nest Leaving in Portugal: Its Effects on Individuation and Parent–Child Relationships', *Journal of Emerging Adulthood*, Vol. 1.3 (September 2013).

22 N. L. Galambos et al., 'Depression, Self-esteem, and Anger in Emerging Adulthood: Seven-Year Trajectories', *Developmental Psychology*, Vol. 42.2 (2006), 350–65.

23 C. J. Cockshott et al., '"Back to Square One": The Experience of Straddling Adolescence and Early Adulthood in Unemployed UK University Graduates with Common Mental Health Issues: An Interpretative Phenomenological Analysis', *Journal of Emerging Adulthood*, Vol. 6.4 (September 2017).

24 R. G. Tedeschi and L. G. Calhoun, 'Posttraumatic Growth: Conceptual Foundations and Empirical Evidence', *Psychological Inquiry*, Vol. 15.1 (2004), 1–18.

25 Aisha T. Asby et al., 'Living With Maternal HIV: Spirituality, Depression, and Family Functioning', *American Journal of Health Sciences*, Vol. 7.1 (2016), 15–22; M. S. Kopacz et al., 'Suicidal Behavior and Spiritual Functioning in a Sample of Veterans Diagnosed with PTSD', *Journal of Injury and Violence Research*, Vol. 8.1 (2016), 6–14.

26 José F. Domene et al., 'Change in Depression Symptoms Through Emerging Adulthood: Disentangling the Roles of Different Employment Characteristics', *Journal of Emerging Adulthood*, Vol. 5.6 (March 2017).

3

Relational Realities: Friends and Family

Having considered some of the economic and health demands Emerging Adults have to negotiate, we will now turn our attention to another core factor in their identity development – relationships. It is widely acknowledged that one of the key tasks of becoming an adult is exploring new forms of relationship. In the individualized Western world, becoming independent of one's family and renegotiating the amount of influence parents and siblings have is central to adult identity formation. Likewise, forming friendships and experimenting with romantic and sexual relationships are part of the same process. For some, that results in a stable partnership and parenthood – although these often come significantly later than in former generations (or indeed not at all). Active Affirmers undertake all these negotiations within the added framework of religious faith and the social expectations of faith communities. This means their attitudes, choices and lifestyles can often look markedly different from those of their secular peers. This chapter will explore the ways in which core relationships with friends and family were experienced by participants. They were always significant and sometimes a dominant part of the narrative they described of their twenties and inevitably their faith development.

The Significance of Friends

All those involved with teenagers and very young adults are well aware of the power that peers exert on their identity formation. One of the challenges facing those from religious homes or who have come to faith at a young age is that so few of their peers share their worldview or religious beliefs (or indeed have even a basic knowledge of what they are). Chapter 1 mentioned the pattern of certain churches attracting large cohorts of young people and Emerging Adults – functioning as 'plausibility shelters' – while many others have none. This is unsurprising given that friends are so important in reinforcing the legitimacy of religious belief in this life stage, and almost all the participants spoke about the centrality of friendships during their twenties.

Some described the relief of finding other young Christians when they began university, having been one of very few young people in their childhood church. Others mentioned the significance of attending religious holidays and festivals in their teens. Many had developed close groups of like-minded friends as students. Several used familial language to describe those: 'band of brothers'; 'they became like sisters'; 'we still meet for dinner like a family'. Typically, they had lived in shared housing, attended the same church or campus group, and some described close, even insular groups – a 'bubble'. These friendships had been highly significant in providing emotional and spiritual support through the ups and downs of early Emerging Adulthood. Several spoke nostalgically about how much they now missed those days; although others were more reflective about the emotional intensity of living in such communities. A decade or more later, some still met regularly or stayed in touch through technology to talk and pray, continuing to be each others' closest friends.

It was interesting that several of the men spoke at length about male friends who had significantly shaped their faith in those formative student years. Craig had two very devout friends at different points who 'pushed my faith hard', pressing him into theological discussion and 'keeping me accountable'. He was unequivocal: 'They are the reason my faith is still going.' Laura spoke about a group of graduate friends who had 'done a Bible study before we went to the pub quiz every Monday'. She described them: 'trying to work out together how to do this "living as a Christian thing" in modern-day life'. Matt's idiosyncratic selection of intellectuals, theologians and 'free thinker' friends strongly influenced his faith – although he recognized that sometimes that has been destabilizing rather than constructive. Nonetheless, being exposed to their ideas had been stimulating.

Having such influential (often slightly older) Active Affirmer friends was not always helpful though. Sally spoke of a highly charismatic 'leader' in their devout and insular friendship group. He had mentored some of the younger men (reading the Bible and praying with them) and when he began to 'wobble' and move away from his evangelical beliefs, it was unsettling for the cohort who were so strongly influenced by his faith.

These intense friendships with other Active Affirmers were often formed as the result of feeling like outsiders among their secular peers. Craig had shared a house with non-religious friends as a student (in part to evangelize them). Although they didn't pressure him to engage in activities that conflicted with his values, he still found the experience isolating and subsequently chose to live with other Christians. Olivia's closest friend found her change in lifestyle difficult when she began to embrace her former faith and no longer wanted to 'go partying all the time'. The friend took this as a personal rejection and the friendship became strained. The tension in lifestyles, particularly around alcohol consumption and sex, was raised on several occasions, a number commenting on the incredulity of their non-religious friends at their lifestyle choices.

Laura had spent some time with a foot in each world. She described having two lives as a student: her non-Christian partying friends and those who belonged to a religious campus group. She eventually felt that this was disingenuous and that she needed to have a life with more integrity. She 'picked a side' – in her case her religious faith. By contrast, Deborah did the opposite and found that her churchgoing friends did not stay in touch when she stopped attending. Only a few described a diverse combination of religious and non-religious close friends. For most, their friends were largely religious – or not. Shared values and lifestyle choices meant they had gravitated towards and maintained relationships that reinforced their belief system.

In terms of the longevity of close-knit friendship cohorts, the typical pattern was two or three years when they functioned as tight pseudo-family units. These were remembered as halcyon days – 'a lot of fun'. They often occurred during university or shortly after graduation (particularly among those with geographically distant families). Subsequently, most dissolved as people moved away or married. There were exceptions – Penny's largely gay non-religious cohort continue to spend much of their social time together. However, even if they remained close, most no longer lived in communal houses. Pairs of same-gender friends might rent or buy property together for longer, but typically they eventually separated for the same reasons. Loyalty to her closest friend had prevented Nicola from accepting a job offer in another city. Both were single and it was clear that the emotional support they gave each other was highly significant as their peers gradually married. Penny had what she described as a 'fake husband', a gay friend with whom she had a non-romantic but intimate friendship. For some who had not become romantically involved, a very close peer had provided companionship and emotional intimacy that militated against their sense of being 'other' among the young marrieds. However, when circumstances changed, or those pairs parted, individuals described experiencing isolation and loneliness.

Miriam spoke at length about the subject of Emerging Adult friendship groups within church contexts. Her observations (having led young adult ministries for several years) were that very young Emerging Adults wanted an extensive peer group to socialize with but that as people got older and had other demands on their time and energy, their social needs changed. Instead, they tended to stick with a smaller group of close friends. This could make it difficult for new individuals to 'break in' since those in more stable life stages needed fewer new friends. Others experienced this, commenting on how difficult they found it to form close friendships as they got older or relocated. In some cases, Emerging Adult communities within congregations were experienced as exclusive and insular. Some described never really having replaced their close student friends, their current relationships being superficial in comparison. By contrast, for both Maggie and Deborah the effect of being welcomed into a friendship group in a slightly older life stage was transformative; the beginning of their re-engagement with Christian faith. Deborah recounted:

> I had made friends with a girl on my [postgraduate] course who was interested in [the same area of research]. We arranged to have a coffee and she said, 'Have you found a church here? I thought you might be interested in this ecumenical service that we do once a month.' I remember walking in, and she said, '[Debbie] it is great to see you!' I thought, *That's the first time I've been welcomed in church in years!*

It was rare for participants to talk about conflict with their friends. Penny Edgell Becker writes about conflict avoidance within churches; Mary Pat Baumgartner identifies how middle-class attitudes exacerbate this and Kate Fox notes it is further accentuated by English cultural sensibilities.[1] My own findings are that the churchgoing Emerging Adults will tend to steer clear of potentially controversial subjects, using silence as a mechanism for non-confrontational disagreement.[2] The few episodes of acute conflict that were narrated to me tended to be described by participants from lower socio-economic backgrounds. Others described friendships 'drifting', something that, given the rate of relocation during Emerging Adulthood, happens easily. What did become evident, though, was that for those who rejected their former faith or left faith communities, friendships drifted very quickly. It was unclear how far this was intentional rejection and how far it was merely the result of not being in the same location on a regular basis. When asked, Samantha became emotional: 'I think [we've lost touch] more because of me feeling that they won't want to see me again now.' This may or may not have been true, but it was an assumption she had made; that in friendships based on shared faith the rejection of one meant losing the other. Clearly operating under a similar assumption, Charlie recognized the effort one couple within his former church had made to maintain social contact. He too became tearful describing it:

> I don't know why that's making me emotional, but that was really kind of them. I don't know if they would have been aware or conscious of the fact that pretty much every one of our close friends left in the same year, but I had had a couple of conversations with [name] about faith struggles. I think it was a clear decision by them in response to try to keep me involved in some sense. I was very conscious back in my time at university [that] the key thing for a good Christian to do when they see somebody straying from their faith is to try to keep them in the flock. I would have thought it would have been their motive. I could see myself during university wanting to do the same things, even if it wasn't someone I was particularly close with.

This may be the case in principle, but it was evident that most Active Affirmers do not remain in close contact with apostate or de-churched friends. The causes are diverse. For those with close bonds formed around strong religious beliefs, the rejection of those beliefs clearly causes tension in the friendship, particularly if individuals then embrace conflicting lifestyles. When identity is profoundly tied up with their faith (as it tends to be for Active Affirmers), a rejection of the latter can be experienced as a rejection of them as a person. Tolerance of an individual's choices and conflict avoidance seem likely to be causal factors too; not wishing to offend or get into difficult conversations. However, the simple fact of not being in the same space on a regular basis during a busy and pressured life stage undoubtedly contributes to a drifting apart rather than a sharp relational break.

In conclusion, it is well documented that friendships are significant in the faith of adolescents (and several individuals in this study spoke about that), but it is also clear that they are highly significant and influential throughout the twenties. They validate and encourage minority religious beliefs, reinforce related lifestyle choices and provide emotional support and intimacy. One of the key developmental tasks, and emotional challenges, of negotiating these relationships is their fluidity. Romantic, professional and geographic circumstances change frequently for many Emerging Adults. They can go from a strong group of close friends to social isolation very quickly, and although technology militates against this to some extent, instability is emotionally demanding. For some, loneliness pushed them to engage in personal religious activity (prayer, Bible reading etc.), deepening their dependence on God. For others it had caused them to question their beliefs since it felt like even God had abandoned them. For a generation caught between the desire for authentic relationship and 'the façade of connectedness that social media gives' (as one commented), churches with cohorts of peers are highly attractive. Whether those cohorts are inclusive of newcomers or insular and exclusive makes a genuine difference in their faith journeys.

Family Relationships and Faith in Emerging Adulthood

Parents

Although friendships are a central part of Emerging Adult identity formation, Millennials often maintain close relationships with their parents. (Indeed, 'helicopter parenting' is frequently cited as the root of their alleged deficiencies!) Their happy-midi narrative focuses on the well-being of 'friends and family' and, aided by technology, many are reported to be in daily contact with parents (and up to three or four times a day for some young women).[3] Research has also shown that they are likely to seek (and accept) parental advice and support throughout the period of Emerging Adulthood.[4] It is unsurprising, then, that among these participants, family was repeatedly mentioned as significant in the narrative of their twenties and influential in their faith development. One of the central developmental tasks of Emerging Adulthood is to create an independent adult identity. At the heart of that process is working out how to interact and relate to one's family – including their religious beliefs.

Positive parental relationships

Many of the participants in this study spoke in highly positive terms of their ongoing relationship with their parents and the support they had given through the demands of their twenties. All three African participants painted a picture of the strongly matriarchal culture they had come from and described at length their maternal relationships as pivotal to their faith and well-being. Closer to home, Felicity's mother was now her 'holiday partner' and Miriam's had been her rock through severe mental health problems. Others had received financial and professional help and all five who were divorced or separated described their parents as a primary source of support through that experience.

Seven of the sample were engaged in 'yo-yo housing'. Three divorcees had returned to live with parents and four others were doing so – none reporting relational strain. Despite findings from the early 1990s that those living with their parents felt that they were treated in an infantile way, these participants did not express the same sentiment; most were content with the arrangement, financial and relational support existing alongside autonomy.[5] It may be the case that the greater extent to which British Emerging Adults now live at home means that parental attitudes have changed and they are more inclined to accommodate their children as independent adults. For these participants, living with their parents had been a pragmatic decision with a positive outcome (though they all saw it as temporary). The attachment to their childhood home continued to be strong for a number. Despite not having lived there for some time, without permanent accommodation of their own, parental relocation made individuals feel unsafe and rootless. It was striking that for several this was an important event in their twenties, which they described in detail.

Several others had or wanted to relocate to be geographically closer to their parents – particularly once they had children themselves. As will become evident in later chapters, the desire for parental support with early childcare was significant for a number of the young women. However, men also described wanting their children to have good relationships with their grandparents, or the type of upbringing they had experienced. It was striking how close those born in the North East continued to be to their families, particularly their mothers. Indeed, strong attachment to one's family and choosing to live among them is a well-recognized regional pattern. Many of those born in the North East have fierce local loyalty, not just to the region but to their specific hometown. Several described themselves as 'home birds' who loved the location they had grown up in – even with the challenges it faced. Only two spoke about the political causes of regional issues – 'the closing of the mines' and 'a decade of systematic underinvestment'. Rather than critique the causes, others spoke about how they and their churches were endeavouring to address social problems.

A Catholic chaplain told me that among those he ministered to, many held the attitude that, 'To get on is to get out', and one participant described how his friends had done this – either to university or the military. However, most of the locally born participants had no intention of leaving. Their family, community and life were here. Some had remained or returned to the church they had grown up in and now much of their social network was formed of extended family or childhood friends. Their adult identity was not separate from their childhood community but integrated into it. These close and warm relationships with parents were often (though not always) rooted in a mutual faith. Claire explained the situation for her and her husband:

> We've both attended that church all of our lives. That's where our friends and family [are], Dave's side of the family all attend it and my parents did until [recently]. If we took church out of our life, there wouldn't be a lot left. It would be starting from scratch ... our hobbies are built around what we do with our friends and family through church. Our spare time is absolutely through what we do with our church. Everything we live is massively built on the foundations of the church that we are in. Take that all away and there wouldn't be anything left. It would be starting again.

She described one of the most difficult experiences of her twenties as being when her parents felt called to relocate to a town 40 miles away.

Challenging parental relationships

Not all parental relationships were positive, though, and several spoke at length about the challenges of negotiating complex interactions. Parental divorces, affairs, criminal convictions and mental health problems had been destabilizing and distressing. For some, caring for their parents in some way had been necessary; 'Being the grown up' as one put it. The challenge of developing their own sense of identity was exacerbated by their parents' dependence. Negotiating boundaries is a complicated task when parental behaviour is challenging. One woman had withdrawn from her church because her mother had joined and it no longer felt safe. She said, 'I didn't feel able to cry at church anymore, even though I was going through so much. I felt like I had to watch everything I said and did.'

Frankie's family was highly dysfunctional as a result of his father's alcoholism, and much of his twenties had been spent managing the resultant effects on himself and his siblings (several of whom died). He understood his faith as having liberated him to some degree from him past; however, he had been pleased to be reconciled with his father shortly before his death. Similarly, Diana's strongly religious family had collapsed during her early twenties due to her father's behaviour. She explained that most of her Emerging Adulthood had been spent trying to recover emotionally and spiritually. Having finally rediscovered a faith of her own, she was still anxious and emotional, unsettled in her sense of identity and security.

Negotiating boundaries with in-laws was particularly complex. Helen's were unreliable and demanding, 'a bit like a roller coaster'. After a decade of wrestling, she and her husband had established strong boundaries and low expectations of the relationship. The tensions around family comprised much of her narrative. Similarly, Charlie's in-laws had lent him and his wife money to buy a house. This had subsequently become a source of control and the conflict had been detrimental to his mental health and marriage. He said:

> I decided not to see [my wife's] family. Some hurtful things [had been] said and denied. It meant that I wasn't comfortable spending time with them. We reached a point where I felt very emotionally unsafe. Now I think we are at a point where all these boundaries in the relationship need to be redefined so that it has led to lots of insecurities and struggles over who gets the say on what.

Faith as a familial resource

It became evident from their accounts that religious beliefs created challenges in negotiating a sense of self as independent from parents for some. It was common for participants to talk about the problem of reconciling the biblical instruction to 'honour your parents' with the reality of their actions. Like-wise, the mandate to forgive was in tension with the need for self-protection and the risk of being drawn into the dysfunction. However, their faith also provided resources for negotiating those challenges. Hannah had used her Pentecostal framework to understand and resolve her complicated maternal rela-tionship. She spoke of unhealthy 'soul ties' that had shaped decades of negativity and how she had experienced a form of divine psychotherapy allowing her to re-form the relationship positively.

> The Holy Spirit showed me that when I was eight years old, my mum had said: 'Your dad is feeling really low and that we don't love him. When he comes home tonight let's just give him so many hugs and kisses and shower him with love, because we really appreciate him.' I remember being really sad that my dad felt that way. I thought to myself, *We all favour Mum because she's at home with us and looks after us, no one favours my dad.* I just made a declaration to myself that my dad would never feel unloved again. It started this negative relationship with my mum that lasted for 20 years. The Lord said, 'You are believing a lie, that if you love your mum, it doesn't mean that you don't love your dad.' My poor mum. I told my mum when she came to visit after the baby was born. She cried and said, 'I always wondered why my baby didn't love me.' The Lord is so good!

Like Frankie's faith-inspired reconciliation with his father, Adam explained that God had given him grace to forgive his father-in-law's infidelity (although his wife was still struggling to do so). A number were highly self-aware with regards to the interaction of their faith and parental relationship. Diana considered that her human father's actions had affected her view of God as divine father, something she was trying to dis-entangle. Pete believed that his parents' aloofness had been a factor in his joining a small charismatic church and marrying young. He believed that he had been looking for affection and had been pulled into what he now considered a 'cult-like' congregation and unsuitable marriage.

Much is written about the effects of parental faith on children and young people. This evidence suggests that this influence continues throughout Emerging Adulthood. Some participants were critical of what they saw as their parents' religious hypocrisy – their inauthenticity to what they claimed to believe. However, others were explicit that at times when they had considered rejecting their faith, anxiety at parental disapproval had caused them to reconsider. Many spoke of the ways in which their parents had encouraged their faith, particularly in praying for them. However, a few also spoke of hostility to their religious beliefs.

Hannah's father-in-law had been verbally aggressive towards her husband about his faith. She described an episode when 'He nearly kicked us out of the house at two o'clock in the morning. I was asleep in bed with the baby, but he was like, *You need to leave with your wife and my grandson!*' Matt's parents were bemused by his conversion – although his grandfather was supportive. Even some of those with religious parents had struggled. Danny's traditionalist parents opposed his involvement with charismatic Catholicism – although they had subsequently followed the same trajectory. Rachel described tension when she wanted to change career into ministry. She had deliberately broken the news in the presence of a supportive third party. 'I hardly ever go home, but my mum and dad had the Curate round and I said to Dad, in front of the Curate, that I wanted to quit my job and I didn't want to be a teacher. I felt a sense of letting everybody down [because] my mum and dad were thrilled and proud at the fact I was teaching.'

In short

It is well recognized that parents play a significant role in identity formation during childhood and adolescence, but it is evident that they continue to be a key factor in well-being during Emerging Adulthood. Psychological research provides evidence that 'high-quality relationships with parents (for example, those high in emotional support or attachment security) are associated with better social and psychological functioning in Emerging Adulthood, which suggests that parents can support their children's well-being beyond adolescence. However, parents also can undermine Emerging Adults' adjustment through negative parenting behaviours, such as low support, hostility or punitiveness.'[6]

Participants with positive parental relationships continued to want their support and advice. However, they appeared willing to forgo that if it clashed with what they believed God wanted them to do, or if their parents' behaviour was destructive. Theological resources and a supportive faith community or spouse enabled them to do this even if their parents were not convinced. Faith, then, provides both incentives to retain parental relationship and resources to separate and make independent choices. Balancing those can be challenging but it seems likely that this valuing of parental support in part explains Millennial interest in establishing friendships with those from older generations. Despite the cultural narrative of individualism, Emerging Adults seem to be seeking guides who will support and help them work out how to negotiate transitions and challenges. Whether secure, warm and supportive or not, parental relationships clearly continue to be highly significant to Emerging Adult faith and identity formation.

Siblings

Although grandparents, aunts and cousins were mentioned occasionally, many participants mentioned their siblings as important players in their Emerging Adulthood. Of course, establishing oneself as an independent adult is not just about renegotiating relationships with parents but also the family unit. To date, limited research has been done into the effects of siblings on identity development and even less on religious faith. However, there is evidence of the unique influence of siblings in contributing towards life satisfaction.[7] These accounts made it clear that siblings can continue to have influence on identity, particularly for younger siblings and women. Participants' reflections primarily fell into two categories: the effect of older siblings in influencing their faith; and the anxiety they had experienced around challenges their siblings faced during their own Emerging Adulthood.

Influencing faith

For several participants their faith had grown in parallel with their siblings' and had continued to be a source of mutual comfort and support during their twenties. Some used the word 'inspiring' to describe their siblings' faith. Mike was one of these, although he also recognized that he had established his own place in their church more fully after his elder brother relocated. The effects of proximity and distance from siblings was also experienced by Will. The rejection of their parents' faith by his elder brothers had impacted him as a teenager. Once away from them at university he established a faith. Others embraced older siblings' advice to pursue faith once they had left home, their common beliefs creating a stronger familial bond despite the geographic distance. Particularly for those whose parents were not religious, siblings were a source of guidance and stability. The support of Tania's brother gave her confidence to leave her abusive marriage despite her concerns about how her parents would respond.

> He said, 'If you are scared to [leave] don't be, because I am here, Mum's here and Dad's here.' Nobody had ever said that to me before. So, I said to myself, *Right, next time [my husband] does it [I'll leave]*. As it happens it was the next day. So, I left the next day, and never looked back. My life has changed in so many ways since then.

This conversation had evidently been a pivotal event in Tania's Emerging Adulthood, empowering her to leave her violent husband. Her former faith, inactive during her marriage, became a significant resource in re-establishing her life. By contrast, given the sense of stability the faith of siblings can provide, Helen had been shocked and theologically challenged by her older brother's decisions.

> I did struggle when my brother came out. Looking back now, I think part of that is me feeling that my world was rocked. Because my parents were divorced when I was young, and my brother was the main guy figure [in my life]. He was two years older and I was very close to him. He was a very committed Christian when I was growing up and he was quite influential. [When] he came out as being gay I found that really hard to deal with, partly because we had already drifted apart. Living in different cities meant we didn't see a lot of each other, but I knew emotionally we had drifted apart [too]. That was partly because his lifestyle was entirely changed. What he does when he socializes and his level of drinking, how promiscuous he might be. All of that has changed.

She has done much soul searching, reading and thinking about sexuality, and is pragmatic in her response at present. However, it was evident from the amount she spoke about it that her brother's loss of faith and subsequent disparity in their unified value systems was painful. Her own faith has not been shaken per se, but she has been forced to reflect on it.

Samantha's story was the opposite, of being the sibling to reject her faith, in part at least because of her brother's expectation that she would embrace his conservative evangelical tradition. She said:

> It felt oppressive, almost inescapable. I didn't feel like I belonged to it, but that was what I was surrounded by. My brother still is very much a part of that, as is a cousin of mine, who was a large presence in my life. Both these older male

figures felt that they needed to guide me and make sure that I didn't go astray. I was terrified about telling my brother [I was no longer a Christian]. I went to dinner and told him. He said, 'You will always be my sister and I will always love you.' Actually, he's never brought it up since. I feel in some ways our relationship has been better since then. Before, he really did see himself as being some kind of godfather to me and having to keep me in line and guide and instruct me. Because his Christianity was different to my own spirituality, I felt that I couldn't talk about what I thought – that he would think it was heretical, or dodgy.

Clearly, these accounts are unique and part of the ongoing negotiation of an adult identity. What they illustrate though is that, particularly for younger siblings, establishing a religious identity not only involves responding to their parents' belief system but those of older brothers and sisters. How far they admire or seek the approval of those individuals is highly significant in their choices and personal faith. Emerging into adulthood can involve significant reordering of family dynamics.

Siblings and trauma

The other subject that was raised by many of the participants with regards to their siblings was traumatic events. These included addiction, imprisonment, serious mental health challenges, deaths, road accidents, miscarriage, infant death and domestic violence. It is important to remember that Emerging Adults' friends and siblings are also experiencing the volatility of Emerging Adulthood themselves. Thus, individuals are not just dealing with their personal challenges and the theological issues they raise, but also trying to support those they love and make sense of their experiences. Marie's emotions were hugely conflicting; her pregnancy was healthy while her sister was devastated by her miscarriage. Wendy had endeavoured to shield her parents from the reality of her own domestic abuse because her sister was also suffering physical violence in her marriage. Penny had discovered that she had a half-sister from her father's former relationship. The sister's issues had spilled over into Penny's own life in a demanding and emotionally exhausting manner. It is evident that despite individualization, Emerging Adults belong to interweaving relational nets, which are facilitated by ease of communication via modern technology. Challenges experienced by their families, particularly parents and siblings, can be lived out in real time by that constant communication and can have significant impact on their own emotional well-being.

In Conclusion

It is evident that friends, parents and siblings all continue to be important forces in the lives of many Emerging Adults. The negotiating of differing value systems and expectations is part of the process of establishing their own beliefs and lifestyle. It is also worth considering the impact of not having these networks, for example for those in the care system, or displaced and isolated in some way. It is striking, as someone who never entertained the idea of moving home for more than a holiday after university, that so many Millennials have made that choice. Certainly, there are financial factors involved in that but also cultural shifts and an extended dependence on parents. Relationships with family and friends make a vast difference in how individuals experience their twenties, but they also influence their religious beliefs for much longer and much more significantly than might have been formerly anticipated.

Questions for Discussion

- How far have close friendships with peers been instrumental in shaping your own faith? Where and how were they formed and why have they been so significant?
- What do you consider the advantages and disadvantages of being a religious minority as a young Active Affirmer? What mechanisms do you observe individuals using to cope with that? What support or encouragement do they receive in your faith community?
- What are your reflections on the continual relational changes of Emerging Adulthood and their consequences?
- Why do you think that Active Affirmers lose touch with apostate friends so quickly?
- How far are you surprised that parents and siblings continue to be particularly influential in the faith of their Emerging Adults? What theological and structural resources do you think might be helpful where those relationships are absent, geographically distant, conflicted or dysfunctional?

Notes

1 P. Edgell Becker, *Congregation in Conflict: Cultural Models of Local Religious Life* (Cambridge: Cambridge University Press, 1999); M. P. Baumgartner, *The Moral Order of a Suburb* (New York: Oxford University Press, 1988); K. Fox, *Watching the English* (London: Hodder & Stoughton, 2004).

2 R. H. Perrin, *The Bible Reading of Young Evangelicals* (Eugene, OR: Wipf & Stock, 2017).

3 Aimee E. Miller-Ott et al., 'Cell Phone Usage Expectations, Closeness, and Relationship Satisfaction Between Parents and Their Emerging Adults in College', *Journal of Emerging Adulthood*, Vol. 2.4 (2014), 313–23.

4 Cassandra L. Carlson, 'Seeking Self-Sufficiency: Why Emerging Adult College Students Receive and Implement Parental Advice', *Western Journal of Communication*, Vol. 80.3 (2016).

5 C. Flanagan et al., 'Residential Setting and Parent–Adolescent

Relationships During the College Years', *Journal of Youth and Adolescence*, Vol. 22 (1993), 171–89.

6 Jamie L. Abaied and Chelsea Emond, 'Parent Psychological Control and Responses to Interpersonal Stress in Emerging Adulthood: Moderating Effects of Behavioural Inhibition and Behavioural Activation', *Journal of Emerging Adulthood*, Vol. 1.4 (2013), 258–70.

7 Christina Rogers Hollifield and Katherine Jewsbury Conger, 'The Role of Siblings and Psychological Needs in Predicting Life Satisfaction During Emerging Adulthood', *Journal of Emerging Adulthood*, Vol. 3.3 (2015).

4

Relational Realities: Romance and Parenthood

The last chapter explored the relational realities of Millennial Christians with regards to friends and biological family, particularly parents and siblings. This one will engage with the other types of relationship they reported negotiating during their Emerging Adulthood – romantic relationships and parenthood. For most, the former was a dominant part of the narrative of their twenties and it had significant effects on their religious faith. However, for some, fertility and parenthood had been profoundly influential on it too. At one level the participants were divided into those who had 'achieved' the tasks of finding a partner and/or having children and those who had not. For many, these journeys were complex. This included those who had been teenage parents, those who were divorced, those who were perfectly content to be single, and those whose fertility struggles had defined much of the decade. Understanding the impact of these journeys is vitally important in understanding both their identity development and their Christian faith.

The Romantic Lives of Active Affirmers – A Dominant Narrative

Jeffrey Jensen Arnett, in his seminal work *Emerging Adulthood*, argued that one of the central activities of the developmental phase was to explore romantic options before establishing a stable adult partnership.[1] Writing more recently,

Brian Willoughby argues that in the United States, Millennial Emerging Adults live in a paradox when it comes to marriage. Most want to marry one day and 'are bombarded with messages of eternal bliss through finding a soul mate'. However, fearful of divorce they postpone marriage until they feel mature enough and have accomplished career aspirations. Willoughby found that marriage, in Millennial eyes, was the ultimate romantic expression and thus many were unwilling to make the commitment until they were certain they had met 'the one' (ideally at first sight!). In the interim, relationships can take myriad forms ranging from one-off hook-ups to long-term monogamous cohabitation. The exceptions to this pattern of delayed marriage in his findings were those with conservative religious beliefs and those in the military, who continued to follow historic heteronormative familial patterns.[2]

In the UK, much of this also rings true. In 2017, 7.7 million people lived alone (half being over 65) and the number of cohabiting couples has doubled to 3.3 million over the past twenty years. The average age for first-time marriage was 30.6 for women and 32.5 for men – the highest since the 1970s.[3] However, the evidence is that Active Affirmers are likely to marry younger and prioritize starting a family. Among Christian university students, Mathew Guest and Kristin Aune found:

> A number of our interviewees, when asked about their plans for the future, emphasized their goal of getting married and having a family (with the raising of children in the Christian faith). This was frequently described either with no mention of careers or alongside a more dismissive comment about career choices, side-lined as relatively unimportant in comparison with having a family.[4]

This pattern of early marriage and subsequent family was true for half of my sample. The average age of marriage for Western participants was 23 for women and 24.3 for men. Half had done so before, or within two years of, completing their education, having met their spouse at, or prior to, university. Of course, wider Western cultural values are also at play. However, the evangelical, charismatic and Pentecostal Active Affirmers tend to cluster in typically espoused traditional Christian teaching on sexual abstinence before marriage. Equally, shaped by various cultural and theological assumptions, they articulate or simply model heterosexual marriage as the norm. Whether Emerging Adults conform to teaching on abstinence or not, they are affirmed by their faith communities for marrying – particularly other Active Affirmers (marrying non-believers is considered less than ideal in many such communities).

This is not the place to track the evolution of Western Protestant attitudes to marriage, but it is worth noting that it is rooted in the teaching of Martin Luther. In reaction to failures of Catholic clerical celibacy, he wrote, 'A married life is a paradise', honourable compared to 'that unhappy state of a single person', because it is 'celibacy in which one is a prey to devouring fires and to unclean ideas'.[5] Of course, over 500 years other social and economic factors, such as the rise of romanticism, the industrial and sexual revolutions, have been major factors in reshaping attitudes towards marriage. It is no longer an economic necessity, way of achieving social cohesion, or a pre-requisite for having children. Rather, it is an individual choice, based on romantic inclination, with the aim of achieving personal fulfilment. It is central to the happy-midi narrative.

Penny Edgell notes that this complex evolution has resulted in the (largely unreflective) sacralization of the 1950s nuclear family in the mind of Western Christians (although even in 1950s America only 43% of households followed this pattern).[6] However, this has continued to evolve during the late twentieth and early twenty-first centuries. Among Millennials, education and professional employment continue to rise among women and domestic activity likewise among men. Even among conservative Christians who espouse the doctrine of male headship (and many do not), 'soft patriarchy' is the norm and Millennial marriages are functionally egalitarian.[7] Edgell also identifies the endorsement of a 'stretched' version of nuclear family in many churches as they try to hold together 'what is right' with 'what is kind'. This creates space for divorcees, single parents, the unmarried and childless, and in some cases LGBTQi families. Nonetheless, in evangelical and charismatic churches the 1950s hetero-normative nuclear model is still idealized and encouraged, whether in rhetoric or practice.

Of course, there are legitimate theological discourses that value singleness, community living and non-nuclear family structures, but they are rarely articulated in many of these churches. This creates a clear tension for those who, for whatever reason, remain single or childless. Particularly for single women (who outnumber potential male partners), those who are same-sex-attracted individuals practising abstinence for theological reasons, and divorcees or single parents, churches can be socially isolating. Within those communities they are often 'other'.[8]

The drama of dating

Although Millennial Active Affirmers negotiate conflicting secular and religious narratives around sex, marriage and romantic relationships, finding a partner remains a priority. Almost all the participants in this project spoke about their romantic journey. For a few it had been of nominal significance, but for others it had been volatile, dominating their narrative. Most described some sort of relational breakdown causing varying degrees of disappointment and heartbreak.

The impression participants gave was that relationships were something they took seriously. A number described protracted reflections as to whether they should enter into or end a relationship; trying to discern God's will. They believed God was concerned with this choice and potentially steering them towards a particular individual – a sort of divine matchmaker. Rather than dating or having casual experimental relationships, many aspired to meeting 'the one' as soon as possible and establishing a stable committed relationship that would result in marriage. Some spoke about teenage assumptions that they would marry their first boy or girlfriend. Robbie said:

> I was in a relationship that ended quite messily. That, I think, was a crisis point for me. I just assumed that being in a relationship with someone who was also from church, there was only one outcome and that was that we would end up being in a relationship for ever, we'd get married because that's what people in church did. I was very naive.

Similarly, Samantha explained:

> I had started a relationship that didn't last very long. Most of the next year I was suffering the effects of the break-up and heartbreak. It was my second relationship and second break-up, having grown up with the idea that you are only going to go out with one person. I didn't expect to go through one, let alone two, relationship endings.

Her religious boarding school had instilled that idea. 'All the kids at school just thought they were going to fall in love with someone and get married at eighteen or early twenties. A lot of the kids' parents had done just that.' In the current cultural climate this attitude seems quaint and is certainly in conflict with wider relational patterns. Robbie and Samantha recognized this as naive but the overall trend for young marriages suggests that many Active Affirmers continue to believe in and aspire to 'true love' at a young age, ideally orchestrated by God.

The experience of relational turmoil was acute for some. Several young women described, at length, dysfunctional or multiple short-term relationships during their twenties. Three experienced relationships that were controlling, abusive or violent. All of them described a long process of trying to resolve those problems and make the relationship work (two were marriages). Though ultimately all had ended, the emotional and psychological damage had long-lasting consequences, including guilt and shame. The stigma of divorce was particularly acute for one who feared it would militate against her aim of ordination.

Another single woman wryly said of herself, 'I attract guys that have mental health issues or are complete weirdos. I have a beacon, it would appear, for attracting men that are "special" on a scale that is off the map!' Another explained: 'I was seeing this guy and then he died. I was young and my way with dealing with lots of things was not incredible then. I just kissed boys all the time and got drunk!' A second serious relationship ended when she discovered her boyfriend had been two-timing her for months. A third young woman described an incident when, abandoned by her boyfriend in a nightclub, her drink was spiked. 'I woke up two days later at my house. I don't think anything sexual happened, but it was a traumatic experience. My friend had come around and said that the house door was wide open. That was a significant enough event that I've never put myself in that situation again!'

These women were now reflective and self-aware about their behaviour and boundaries, a number having undertaken counselling. They described growing up into a more measured romantic expectation, greater personal confidence and self-esteem. One reflected on a relationship that devastated her at the time: 'I now look back and see that God really helped me dodge a bullet!'

Singleness and gender imbalance among Active Affirmers

Although this sample does not claim to be representative, it may be that the well-established pattern of higher religiosity among women and consequent gender imbalance in churches contributes to young women's participation in volatile relationships. Similarly, since they outnumber men, some female Active Affirmers look for partners beyond the church, consequently engaging in less conservative sexual behaviour (more like their secular peers) while maintaining religious identities. Several women spoke of sexual relationships, but given family or social disapproval these had tended to be secret – and something they came to regret. Equally, it may be that they are less likely to end dysfunctional relationships because they are anxious about finding an alternative partner. Indeed, one described remaining because 'Basically I had got to a point where I thought – I don't think I'm going to meet anyone [else]!'

Interestingly, none of the men described similar levels of romantic volatility. Instead they tended to describe singular relationships, many of which had resulted in marriage or alternatively an absence of romantic partners. Occasionally some hinted at incidents but did not go into detail; for example, 'I made some choices [then] which ended up having repercussions for future relationships. I made a bit of a mess at that time.' Another said, 'there were a couple of mistakes along the way, some immaturity from myself'. It is interesting that the male participants were much less likely to disclose the details of their relationships. This may be a result of societal pressures on British men to be private in such matters, or that they did not wish to disclose them to a female researcher. Alternatively, it seemed possible that social anxiety had prevented some from forming romantic relationships. Three of the five single male participants spoke about mental health problems and some measure of social isolation within their church; for single men there are also pressures.

Gender imbalance in churches that specifically promote internal marriage creates a range of problems for Emerging Adults. Kristen Aune found that single women in churches often felt marginalized, inferior, a failure; even deviant in some way.[9] Nicola spoke to me about this at length and in detail. She observed that:

[Although] my church would teach that singleness is good; biblical. They also recognize that it's a massive issue. [There is] a culture of Christian men who are almost paralysed by too much choice. There are so many girls that are beautiful and intelligent and godly women, that they almost feel that they have to make a decision that they will marry someone before they ask them out! There have been cases of people who have dated several girls and then have been named as players. I think Christian guys think, 'Oh, I don't want to ask too many girls out because I don't want to get a reputation.'

It appears that the social standing of Emerging Adult men within a congregation may depend on their dating behaviour and the responsibility not to exploit their minority status. This raises the stakes on any romantic involvement, the assumption being that going out with someone is a serious commitment rather than an exploratory friendship (which perhaps explains why so many were devastated when those relationships ended). Again, this illustrates the seriousness with which devout Active Affirmers take romantic relationships and their desire for approval – both from God and their religious community. Nicola also explained that, 'It can create conflict between the girls. One of my friends said when she joined our church, "I felt I had to go to the back of the queue [to date the guys]". I just thought, we shouldn't have that in a Christian community. But there are so few eligible guys that girls are almost competing to get their attention. It's probably the same in non-Christian cultures as well.'

As well as social and emotional pressure, dating and single-ness raise theological questions for Emerging Adults. If God – the divine matchmaker – is good and loves them, then why was he not answering their prayers in providing them with a partner? Why had they been excluded from the ideal hetero-nuclear lifestyle they had been taught is preferable to other lifestyles – even sacred? Nicola reflected on the effects of this conundrum:

A few girls that I know have not met someone [at church] and they've started dating a non-Christian and then they've just fallen away [from faith]. Or their friends have all got married and they've stopped coming to church and then met a non-Christian. That kind of thing. I think they are maybe bitter at God. [They] have done all this stuff in service and he's not given them what they want, or think they deserve. They get to a point where they think, I'm thirty and I want to get married and want babies, so I'm going to go out with the [non-Christian] guy who is asking me.

Not all the single women felt that pressure (indeed some were frustrated by the assumption that they did), but a number said similar things to Nicola. They felt a point came when being single became acute; when they moved from being part of the young unmarried majority to an older unmarried minority – the 'left behind'. That appeared to be around the age of thirty. Then they began to feel the need to choose between obedience to a life of chastity and (probably) childlessness, congruent with conservative theology, or finding a non-religious partner which was at odds with their own and/or faith communities' values. This explains (in part at least) Aune's findings that young women are leaving the Church at three times the rate of men.[10] Embracing (or enduring) celibacy and abandoning motherhood are costs too high for many Emerging Adult women when both church and secular culture emphasize that they should achieve both.

In fact, several participants said that the pressure they felt to meet 'the one' had not come from church. The cultural pressure to find a partner (whether that is a heterosexual spouse or not) is not exclusive to religious communities. They spoke of family members, colleagues and non-Christian friends who provided unsolicited advice. One described her friends' confusion as to why she did not use Tinder to 'widen the pool of men to fish from'. Another spoke of her grandmother's relentless comments about her 'running out of time' to have babies and how hard being single made family events.

It was somewhat surprising how few mentioned Internet dating. Given that there are dating websites specifically aimed at Christians and that there is an overall greater acceptance of meeting people online, I had anticipated that these Millennials might have used them. Almost none said they had. Anecdotally, I am aware of couples who have met online but also dating horror stories from those using such websites. Clearly there is a need for further research to explore attitudes among Active Affirmers to using this sort of technology. However, it is possible that there are theological values underpinning their choices. For those with a strong sense of divine providence it seems likely that their expectation is that God will provide them with a partner – rather than that they need to be pro-active in that search. Alternatively, it may be that a lack of confidence underpins that decision. Or, given how seriously they appeared to take engaging in relationships, that going on what is effectively a blind date was something they were unwilling to do.

Faith as a resource for resistance

By contrast to the pressures many felt within faith communities, there were those who were using their faith as a tool for resisting the narrative of singleness as failure. Many described learning how to make sense of their experience and status in theological terms. The process of making peace with singleness or childlessness was typically lengthy and painful. Older single or divorced women in church had provided a different perspective and with hindsight one said: 'I sometimes look back and wish I hadn't spent so much of my twenties worrying about [getting married].' She did reminisce though: 'There was a lovely guy who wasn't a Christian and who really pursued me. Sometimes I wonder, had I not been a Christian would I be married by now? [But] I know that God is good. I know that God's plan is better than my plan.'

Miriam believed she had 'dodged a bullet' by not marrying any of the dysfunctional men she had been attracted to. She understood her single state as divine protection from the worse fate of an unhappy marriage. Similarly, another told a story of a friend's unhappy marriage to a non-believer and said, 'As my friend puts it, [better to be] on the shelf, [than] locked in the wrong cupboard!' Nicola, Laura and Felicity all had a sense of God's calling on their professional life. The energy they would have put into a marriage had gone into vocational or religious activity and they enjoyed the flexibility to travel or embrace opportunities that they believe God had given them. This had not been ideal for any of them, but they had reconciled the tension and remained committed to their belief that God loved and wanted good things for their lives – even if he had not done so in the way they had anticipated.

Will and Harry also spoke about how 'other' they felt, given that all their male Active Affirmer friends were married. Church gender imbalance worked in their favour but still they had not met a partner. The impression they gave was that this made them feel inadequate in some way, although Will expressed confidence that he would marry eventually. Again, looking to make theological sense of his singleness, he said:

> It will stand me in good stead to be a better husband. I've had to learn to wait, to be patient. God has broken things off my life that I was scared of and struggled with. Out of my friendship group I am the only one that is single. All my friends have got married and have kids. [Sometimes] I think, why am I not? But then I think, God has a different path for me, a different journey. In the scheme of things, I'm still young. I'm twenty-nine. There are days that I think, *I'd like a wife*, but there are days when I'm thinking, *I'm able to do all these other things, like travel the country.*

Following the hetero-normative narrative

By contrast to those whose dating and singleness had been a challenge, for others the idealized relational pattern had been relatively straightforward. They had followed the expected trajectory of meeting, going out with, getting engaged and married to another Active Affirmer. Many had begun such relationships in secondary school or as undergraduates and married as they began to establish adult responsibilities. A few had married before graduating and moved into a distinctly different life stage from their peers, which had been challenging; often socially isolating. Some described their parents' reservations at the speed of their marriage, or their age (particularly if their parents were not religious). Others described the 'battle' to resist engaging in sexual activity prior to marriage but wanting to 'do it right' and marry before becoming sexually involved. Milly embodied a number of these factors, she explained:

> When I finally got together with Tim, it was for both of us our first proper relationship. That became quite serious quite quickly and we decided that we would get married three months in, partly to do with sex – we were quite committed to not having sex before we were married. So, we got engaged ten months into our relationship and shocked our parents. He had just become a Christian and he was twenty-one at the time, I was twenty-three. He moved here and we were doing long-distance [dating] while planning a wedding as I was finishing off my degree.

The positive consequences of marrying young

The effects of marrying very young were varied. Some had established stable relationships that a decade on were flourishing. They, like Willoughby's religious participants, had grown together and had experienced marriage as a central part of the transformative process of identity formation – they had grown into adulthood together.[11] Several spoke at length about how their spouse had caused their religious beliefs to develop and flourish. For example, Robbie said:

> Rachel's impact can't be overestimated. I think if I hadn't met her, I'm not sure where my faith would be now. She'd

grown up with really strong [Bible] teaching and an idea of what church should look like. I hadn't had any of that. She just gave me a whole new view of what the world could look like. She wasn't scared to challenge things that I was doing, or attitudes that I had. I liked that. I was like *Right, what do I need to do to marry this woman? What does she need from me to convince her?*

Others described how their spouse had kept them anchored to a church when they had wanted to leave, or the roles they played together in the community – for example as youth workers or worship leaders. They spoke about how processing frustrations, doubts and challenges together had helped them both develop robust theology, or about the importance of prayer to their relationship.

Religious faith was not only central to their individual identity but at the core of their relationship; informing the decisions they made about all aspects of their lives. They spoke of freedoms and opportunities they had had for holidays, home buying, enjoying time together both as unencumbered young couples and later parents. Equally, negotiating employment and financial challenges, working out how to cope with complex parental relationships and fertility difficulties were part of their marital journey. Some had made choices to follow vocational callings together, exploring Christian missions or church leadership. Others had worked as a partnership supporting each other's career development and/or juggling that with parenthood. In short, following this lifestyle had had its challenges but had worked for them.

It was interesting to note that those who had struggled spent more time talking about that than those whose marriages had been largely happy. Indeed, overall participants were more likely to describe the challenges of their twenties than the joys. This became noticeable when I interviewed the American participant. She was so positive about her Emerging Adulthood that I had to ask if anything difficult had happened at all. Of course, it had, but she chose to describe the narrative in positive terms. By contrast, many of the British participants tended to focus on the difficult things and so those whose marriages had been challenging spent considerable time reflecting on that.

The challenges of marrying young

A number described how marrying in their early twenties, before they had established their own adult identity, had been problematic. Four described extramarital affairs that they attributed, in part, to immaturity. In two cases the affairs were indicative of a marriage that was already failing. The others described two factors that they understood to have saved their relationship. First, that they were young enough to move forward and rebuild trust, and second the intervention and support of their church leaders. Miranda explained that her husband had been 'naive and unwise': a series of small decisions having a 'domino effect' in creating an 'unhealthy relationship' with a colleague. From her point of view, 'It was very intense at the time, but we recovered quite quickly' because '[The church leaders] worked us through it. I think had we walked away from the church it would have been much harder to work on the marriage because we wouldn't have had people around us to help with that.' Her husband's version of the same process was less positive. He felt that one of the leaders had:

> made it his goal to make sure I would never flourish in that church again. We were asked not to socialize with people, not to attend any groups, but we could go on Sunday, and we were encouraged to do so. At that point in time it was incredibly hard. Not only did I have to eat tremendous amounts of humble pie, deal with disappointment, deal with significant issues of forgiveness – mostly with myself – but I was seemingly without purpose, no longer with any responsibility in church.

For them both this had been a major event of their Emerging Adulthood. Although their relationship had recovered and Miranda was positive that they had moved beyond it, it was significant that Adam perceived this misdemeanour as affecting his long-term standing within their faith community and derailing his hopes at leadership.

Given the close-knit nature of evangelical and charismatic church congregations it was not surprising that the failure of marriages had wider social and spiritual implications. It was evident in all four cases that the ending of their marriage would also have meant one or both parties leaving their church and thus support network. In Claire's case her whole identity and belief system were at stake, her relationship with God and her husband being closely related.

> I had an affair with a guy that I worked with. It was very short. I always put it down to [the fact that] I left [my parents'] home, had my independence and that's when I lost my way. From there was when I had to decide if I was going to have a relationship with God or not. I told [my husband] and we worked through that horrendous time. We spoke to our senior leader [at church] and [my husband] gave me an ultimatum of, *Leave your job and we will work through this or stay at your job and [we split up]*. We wanted to make it work and put things back together, so I handed in my resignation. I used that couple of years to start putting my marriage back together. We had a lot of counselling through that time. It never became public knowledge in church, which was really important. It meant that I could deal with the guilt and everything else that was going on without thinking that the whole congregation were aware. In lots of ways we were still young and naive enough to put things back together again.

She also recognized that her decision to rebuild her marriage had included moral, spiritual, social and familial dimensions because they were all integrated:

Being completely honest, I knew that if I walked away then I didn't just walk away from my marriage, I walked away from everything. In my head my decision was to leave everything and go with this guy and I've lost my family. Or I stick with it and work through this and I keep them. So, if I'm honest, my decision was probably because I would lose my extended family as well. That might not have happened, but at the time I knew that it would be a massive disappointment for my parents. They never said that, but that's how I felt and that is how I made my decision. I felt that God honoured me in coming back, making the right decision and being able to say to people at work, 'Yes, I've messed up, but I wasn't just going to throw it all away, I was going to work at it.' So many people on the work side that were saying, 'It doesn't matter, just leave and start again.' I felt God saying, 'We can make this work [but] it's not going to be easy.' I would say it has taken a good ten years to work through a lot of those issues.

It is evident from her account that Claire was negotiating conflicting cultures: the colleagues who viewed her marriage as disposable, and her family and faith community who considered it profoundly significant. In her late twenties she found herself needing to decide for herself which belief and value system to embrace. She also recognized that both options were personally costly but ultimately chose to retain the spiritual, familial and social network she grew up with along with her marriage. Her faith, she believed, was stronger as a result and she mentioned several times that she believed God had 'honoured' her choice, helping them to resolve their issues.

By contrast, three of the divorcees had made the opposite choice. They had chosen to leave their spouse, social network and in two cases their religious identity entirely. All of them had married young and described how the pressures of work, infertility or sexual problems had driven a wedge into their marriages. These pressures and disappointments were compounded by communication issues and theological doubts. Some had sought support, including counselling, but this had not proved helpful. All had struggled with their mental health as a result and ultimately had chosen to leave the marriage. Although they had received parental support (indeed, two had moved back in with their parents), they had each become socially isolated by that choice. Chris had intentionally isolated himself. A mixture of shame, anxiety and introversion meant he went to work, went home and occasionally saw one friend. Deborah's refusal to conform to how friends believed she should behave also contributed.

> I remember meeting with them and talking; them praying for me. They said that they would really love to see me back in church with [my ex] and that they could help us fix it. I said, 'I don't want to come back to church. I've been struggling with it for a long time and I just can't be there. I definitely don't want to get back together with him, I don't think it is good for either of us.' I remember [name] saying, 'Well, there's nothing more we can do for you, you should just go.'

She had sought comfort in an affair. 'I felt so precious and spoilt and loved and cared for and treasured. He was married so that was ridiculous and stupid and messy; selfish and horrible. At the time I thought I was head over heels in love with him. He was older and I was just so grateful not to have to organize everything for once.' She was now highly critical of the heteronormative narrative of her church.

> I finished university and got married straight away because that's what adult Christians looked like for me. They were all married, and I wanted to be an adult married Christian. I wish somebody had said, *Actually, we dated and we lived together.* I wish somebody had said, *I didn't get married until my thirties.* But none of those narratives were around. Everything was, *Yes, we got married at twenty-two. Look at us now, five kids and really happy. It's been tough at times, but it has really worked out in the end.*

Similarly, Pete had fallen in love with a colleague and embarked on an intense, guilt-ridden relationship that ended his unhappy marriage. He too is highly critical of conservative Christian sexual ethics: 'I think some parts of it are dangerous. If you tell young people that they can't have sex before marriage you set up a system [where] getting married is like roulette. If teenagers are told they've to figure out the big wide world in a certain way, then they end up making decisions like I did. If I wasn't a Christian I wouldn't have married [my wife]. If I had [had] more experience in relationships I would have known that she was not the one.'

Some conclusions

It is evident from these accounts that romantic volatility is almost ubiquitous for Emerging Adults, and the gender imbalance in most churches compounds that in a variety of ways. It is also clear that marriage is held in high regard and thus romantic relationships are taken seriously by many Active Affirmers. They are not for fun or sex, but to explore a potential lifelong partnership. Consequently, there are social consequences for those of both genders who embark on too many.

The tendency in this sample was also for many to have married young. For some this meant their Emerging Adulthood was closely entwined with their spouse, their identity and faith forming in tandem. For others, perceived (or actual) pressure to marry had been detrimental to their well-being – including their mental health and faith. They simply hadn't been ready, or the challenges they faced in their marriages were beyond their emotional capacity to deal with. Clearly, there are both benefits and risks to meeting 'the one' and marrying young.

Parenthood in Emerging Adulthood

Although the twenties are often a decade of continual change, few things impact Emerging Adults like parenthood. Whether or not they find a partner and/or begin a family in the time-scale they hoped for, having children is often emotive, always demanding and in some cases traumatic. In the UK the average age for first-time parenthood is at its highest since the mid-1970s – 29.5 for women and 33 for men. Current birth rates suggest that 1 in 5 women will currently remain childless.[12] The number of those struggling with fertility issues and seeking assistance has also increased. One in seven heterosexual British couples struggle to conceive and in 2016, 20,000 children were born using IVF and donor insemination treatments.[13]

Given the age of the participants in this study, it was a subject frequently raised by them. Although (as already discussed) Millennial Active Affirmers tend to marry younger than their secular peers, they often still delay beginning a family until their late twenties. Of this sample, 70% were or had been married, but only half had children. Excluding one teenage mother, the average age of having their first child was 27.25 for women and 28 for men.

Parenthood as normative

Although limited research has been undertaken to date, it is unsurprising that becoming a parent (or not) has a dramatic impact on the identity and faith of Emerging Adults. As has been mentioned, in the UK most belong to church traditions that, whether in rhetoric or practice, advocate a hetero-normative pattern of family as the ideal. Within this, the expectation of men as breadwinners and women as taking primary responsibility for nurturing children has a long and enduring heritage. Writing in 2002, Elisabeth Beck-Gernsheim noted that with increased education and financial independence, women typically aspire to 'A bit of life of their own', yet 'the desire to have children does not simply disappear in the individualized and thoroughly rationalized societies of the West. To some extent, in fact, it acquires new importance as a search for content and meaning in life, for closeness and warmth, for a counter-world of roots and familiarity.'[14]

Just as they still aspire to marriage, many Millennials also aspire to parenthood. Willoughby reports many Emerging Adult women saying they want a family – one day, after they have explored other lifestyles. For young Christians, regardless of gender, this is often compounded by the expectation in their faith community that parenthood is a normative role they should expect to take up. However, as previously mentioned, many evangelicals combine conservative views on sex and relationships with contemporary patterns of family life.[15] This means that even if they advocate traditional views on family, employed mothers and emotionally engaged fathers are common, paralleling wider British middle-class values.[16]

Motherhood and faith

With regards to how parenthood affected their faith, it is not surprising that among 47 participants, experiences were diverse. One described it as 'utterly transformative'. Others spoke of remarkable adoptions, prophetic visions given months before a child's conception and miraculous survival of desperately ill children – all of which they attributed to God. Such experiences had profoundly strengthened their faith. One described how the anxiety of an unexpected pregnancy had been transformed through prayer, and their subsequent confidence that the conception had been divinely orchestrated.

Much of the historic religious discourse around motherhood paints it in an idealized manner but more recently attention has been paid to 'maternal silence' and how rarely the voices of actual women are considered in describing the effects of children on their religious identity.[17] Although not questioned directly about the subject, it was noticeable that women were far more likely to raise the effects of parenthood on their faith than men, illustrating the ongoing norm of mother as primary caregiver in British culture.

They also held a diverse range of attitudes towards employment and parenthood. Although actual or functional egalitarianism was shaping their choices about family life, it was noticeable that all those at home with their children were women, and only female participants raised the tension of employment and childcare. Half juggled motherhood and their career. Some voiced intentional feminist principles of wanting to model professional success to their children. Others worked to fulfil a sense of vocation or for financial necessity. None of them articulated any sense that this was at odds with their religious beliefs. Their decisions were personal or pragmatic rather than theologically principled.

In contrast to the traditional conservative narrative that mothers should stay at home with their children, some full-time mothers were apologetic for that choice. More than one stated: 'I know it's not very feminist of me, but I just want to be a stay-at-home mum.' They seemed to believe that educated women should be pursuing a career, and experienced guilt for wanting to stay at home with their children. Chloe described weeping at her mother's insistence that she should return to work, and Suzie was at pains to explain that her decision to walk away from a successful career was not based on her religious beliefs. 'I got married at the beginning of my PhD and it was immediately obvious that female academics are single or married without children. I wanted to have children, but you don't have children and stay in academia.' The extent to which she repeatedly justified her choice throughout her interview gave the impression that she was expecting to be criticized for it.

Others had no compunction about being full-time mothers. Mandy said: 'When Janey was born, she just felt like an absolute gift. She gave me a purpose in life.' Similarly, despite a traumatic pregnancy and mental health problems, Marie described her daughter as 'Just the best thing ever!' For these women motherhood had been hard, but what they had hoped it would be – personally rewarding.

The key to maternal thriving appeared to be the combination of their desire for children and their support network. This ideally included other mother friends to empathize and pray with and a wider support group, including biological or church family. Being at a distance from their own mothers was hard, and a number spoke about missing that support at this crucial time, particularly in the strong matriarchal culture of the North East. Others had relocated back to the region precisely to be close to grandparents. However, participants often described the social capital and sense of community provided by their church. Emotional support and advice, as well as practical functions like cooking meals, cleaning the house and taking the baby so they could sleep were described. This had been profoundly influential on their faith and sense of God's provision; some were now doing the same for others.

Many also explained how motherhood had given them opportunities to build relationships they might otherwise not have had, particularly with those from other socio-economic and cultural backgrounds. For some this had created opportunities for them to share their faith, and one had intentionally become pregnant in order to make contact with other women in a new location. Life was busy, demanding and stretching, but they largely found motherhood personally fulfilling and it had provided them with social capital.

Fatherhood and faith

Although it was striking how much more women talked about the effects of children on their life and faith, they did not have a monopoly on enjoying their children. Pete was effusive: 'Rosie was born, and it was just incredible. I love being a dad. It is my favourite thing. I have two beautiful girls and they are just amazing. Life is messy when it comes to marriage, but there is zero regret about becoming a dad. I love them to bits and getting to spend time with them. [It's] challenging at times because they are little kids, but [they are] beautiful little girls.' Illustrating soft patriarchy, imminent fatherhood and a traditional view of that role had inspired Robbie to take his relatively new faith more seriously: 'I really felt convicted and wanted to be the Christian head of the family and be better than I had been. I felt that I needed to get baptized. I attended an Alpha course after that. By that time I wasn't challenging religious things [anymore] I was more re-affirming what had been said. I think the birth of my daughter was a really big push for me to re-assess a lot of things like prayers, reading the Bible to her at night, even when she couldn't understand it.'

Robbie was unusual in articulating this view of male headship. Catherine Redfern and Kristin Aune argue for gender equality as a given for Millennials, and my own earlier findings are that British male Active Affirmers are often reticent to voice any views on gendered issues.[18] It seems probable that even if they did hold conservative views, most would be unlikely to volunteer that information. Many of them were living out the traditional breadwinner role, suggesting that historic expectations continue as a lived reality even if they are not defined by theological principle.

Shaping their children's faith

The most frequently articulated effect of parenthood on Emerging Adult faith was shaped by the consideration of their children's spiritual development. Anna Strhan writes about the contrasting emphases placed on how to raise children within conservative and charismatic evangelical traditions. Order, discipline and obedience on the one hand and a greater democratization, agency and desire for spiritual intimacy on the other.[19] Although coming from a range of churches, those who spoke about it wanted to encourage their children's theological curiosity, autonomy and faith development. They did this by providing resources that would help children understand prayer, the Bible and develop a relationship with God. Most had infants or very young children but were still considering how they wanted to achieve this. They wanted their children to develop a positive and personal faith.

Greg and his wife had withdrawn from church, in part at least to protect their children from what they perceived as its dysfunction. Instead they were having 'Sunday school at home', reading the Bible and talking to their children about faith. Wendy was concerned about the influence conservative attitudes on sexuality might have on her daughter, and one of Tim's greatest regrets about rejecting his faith was that his children would grow up without the social capital and benefits of a faith community.

Some had changed church, embracing a form of spirituality they did not find particularly fulfilling for the sake of their children. Others had taken over leading the crèche or a children's ministry themselves to ensure the quality of spiritual input their children received. One young doctor spent most of his (limited) free time running a dads' and kids' outreach group, mirroring Strhan's observation of children's groups as a mode of evangelism.[20] Reflecting on how to engage with their children's spiritual development by looking for theological resources, considering how to pray, worship and read the Bible with them had significantly impacted participants' own faith. More than one commented on how their child's faith inspired them. Wendy said of her daughter:

She's probably more spiritual than I am sometimes. She's quite open about what she thinks about God and Jesus. We have some really in-depth conversations. She's a very thoughtful little girl. We have some big conversations about God and why he lets bad things happen. She's only six but she comes out with some crackers and you have to really think about how you answer.

Parenthood as detrimental to faith

However, not all the effects of parenthood were positive for Millennial faith and some were candid about that. Unsurprisingly, the strain of sleep deprivation was widely reported. At least two participants attributed it, in part, to the failure of their marriage. Reflecting on her faith journey, one woman commented, 'Oh those years were lost in babyness – it was so all-consuming!' A number described the strain of exhaustion, loneliness, and post-natal depression on both their relationships and faith. With spouses working long hours in high-pressure jobs, many women described feeling anxious and overwhelmed. This was particularly acute for those who had recently relocated and were isolated without established social and spiritual networks.

Many described having had little spiritual input since their baby was born. Previous devotional patterns had become untenable. 'I needed to sleep so badly that I don't think I picked up a Bible for months' was how one woman explained it. Another talked about how much she missed the intellectual stimulation of 'a good sermon' and how banal she found all-age worship. Others expressed the challenge of being unable to worship or pray as they once had, although the discovery of liturgy had helped at least one.

> When the kids were really little, I found that [liturgy] was really good, because you don't have the brain capacity to think of a prayer sometimes. I wasn't even in a position to be able to form sentences [so] just to be saying words and thinking, *Yes, I do believe that [helped]*.

Ultimately, she was sanguine about the effects of early motherhood on her faith.

> When the kids were really little, I felt like life was just crazy and I was firefighting, but it wasn't that I felt that God wasn't there. I barely brushed my hair. There were no long periods of prayer or worship, or anything else, because they both just

cried a lot. That is definitely a change in how you relate to God at that point in life. I have felt like [my faith] has gone up and down in terms of the emotional intensity with which you feel connected to God. [But] as I've got older, I've realized that really it is not all that important, that experiential feeling.

Several described the lack of provision at their church. 'You are lucky if you get to church to shush your children for twenty minutes before you all go off to crèche. It is hard to keep up that momentum of being really heavily involved.' Another explained that a mum's Bible study was her sole source of spiritual input for several years: 'I actually found the church really difficult since becoming a parent. They don't have a supervised crèche, so parents have to go in. I don't mind it because you get to chat, but you don't get any spiritual input at all and that's really hard.'

Theresa was already on the fringes of church, her faith in a liminal place. For her motherhood was even more demanding.

I got unexpectedly pregnant and got a baby who did not sleep, and I was rootless with my faith. I didn't have any new practices to carry me. I'd shed everything. I didn't have my old quiet time. I didn't enjoy going to normal church. I don't listen to those authors anymore. I don't like these podcasts. I'm going to find a new ... Oh, I don't have any time to do that! All the flippin' contemplative explore your soul thing ... I don't get any time to do that shit either! Basically, I've been drifting. There is no spiritual sustenance when you have small kids. Pre-schoolers and church is ridiculous. I'm not really in a community and it is a bit crap. I listen to great stuff, or read great stuff, but nobody is picking me up on it. It is just drudgery. It literally feels that they are saying, rejoin church properly when you are out of this phase. The nicest thing they can offer is not to hassle you to go on a rota. I literally don't see the point of going to Sunday church with really small children.

Of course, early parenthood has always been demanding, but for geographical reasons Emerging Adults are often doing it with limited family support. Likewise, juggling two careers with childcare costs creates logistical and financial strain. Millennial women appear to experience the tension of career and motherhood in a different way from former generations. They seem to feel pressure to return to work and have to choose intentionally to remain at home. Although often continuing the hetero-normative breadwinner role, Millennial fathers appeared highly involved with the nurturing of their children and concerned about their spiritual well-being. However, even for those with a strong church community and an established faith, their capacity was stretched by what is often the most demanding responsibility they had yet experienced. Unlike most other aspects of their lives, this is something that cannot be changed to re-form a happy-midi narrative; there's no giving back a baby! As will be discussed in Part 2, the effect of parenthood on many in the longer term was to turn their youthful religious enthusiasm into something more moderate and pragmatic. The energy they once put into spiritual activity was often channelled into family life.

Sam summed up the demands well: 'Around the time Charlie was born, [I had] work and exams and when you are not sleeping, and life is stressful ... I don't think I've ever seriously doubted [my faith] but at that point it was just, *Life's rubbish! Why God? Where are you?*'

Infertility and childlessness

Of course, the challenges of parenthood for Emerging Adults contrasts with the experiences of those who were not following that 'normal' narrative. This included those who were ambivalent or had wanted children but did not or could not have them. Of the participants, 47% did not have children at the time of interview. Of the five who were married, most said they were not ready yet or were waiting for circumstances to change in some way. The assumption seemed to be that they would have children – eventually. The rest were single, divorced or in long-term relationships. It was clear that they believed marriage pre-empted children and thus without one the other was not possible. Even among the three who were cohabiting (including an ex-Christian), two were adamant that marriage was a pre-requisite to starting a family. For Active Affirmers the traditional perspective on family construction is clearly still dominant in their value system; a stark contrast to their secular peers.

Single and child-free

Paralleling the gendered pattern of comments from parents, of the ten childless men only three spoke about the issue and then only briefly. Two were single, and part of their struggle with that was that they wanted to be fathers. One was hopeful that it would happen 'in God's timing'. In the meantime, he was putting his energy into religious activity.

By contrast, all the twelve childless women spoke about the subject. There were those who were content not to have children. Some felt there was still plenty of time. Others had never particularly wanted them or explained that close relationships with nephews, nieces and godchildren were a sufficient alternative. They often described being fulfilled by professional and spiritual rather than parental roles, and in some cases were irritated by the assumptions of others that they must want children. Dawn Llewellyn draws attention to those who have intentionally chosen not to have children. She highlights some of the ways in which that 'rub[s] up against Christian ritual, teaching, scripture and practice'.[21] However, in this sample most who spoke in terms of being content in their 'child-free' state appeared to have accepted or become resigned to their current status rather than having actively chosen it. Part of their faith journey had been developing tactics to manage both their own expectations and those of others. Some spoke in terms of the opportunities and freedoms they felt God had given them as childless women being a compensation for not being mothers, or how church community had helped in managing their childlessness. Nicola said:

> I think if you had asked me when I was 20, or even if you had asked me at 24, where I would be now, I always thought I would get married in my mid to late twenties and have a baby by the time I was thirty. Obviously, that's not how it has panned out. Sometimes I look back and think that if I had married, I wouldn't have been a registrar or researcher. I would be a GP because I would have thought that would be more conducive to having babies – and I would have hated being a GP. I am so pleased that I didn't do that. My attitude throughout it all has always been to glorify God in my situation and trust him. It is hard sometimes. You need to stick in a church and grow as a Christian. It's not necessarily peers [that help], but people who are ten years older than you or who have got families and just welcome you into their life. Probably the thing that has helped me most is the fact that families have welcomed me in.

Several spoke of 'being closer to God' because they had fewer distractions and responsibilities. A number had poured their energy into children and young people in professional, ministerial or voluntary capacities. The attitude of these non-voluntary childless women appeared to depend on several factors. These included whether they had a sense of professional vocation and whether they felt their skills and contributions were valued within their church context. Or, similarly, whether they had peers who were also childless and the health of their relationships with friends who were now parents. The sense of not being the only one, excluded or 'left behind' meant their social network continued to be supportive. Being valued in church and having something of spiritual significance to invest in provided self-esteem and consequent emotional resilience. Typically, those who were thriving had found that their faith provided a theological resource to reinforce a sense of purpose and value as non-parents.

This was not true for all the childless participants though. Llewellyn notes that even the language of 'childless' implies that to have a child is the norm; those who do not are implicated as deficient in some way.[22] A number spoke about the struggle they had experienced as they moved from being like their peers in their early twenties to being 'other' as non-parents. Those with strong non-religious friendships were somewhat insulated since their friends were typically marrying and beginning families later. However, many expressed the challenges they faced within the church. Rachel and Penny described joining new congregations in their mid or late twenties and feeling that the community and leadership didn't know how to relate to them as single, childless women. Making friends with peers (who were all mothers) had been almost impossible since they were at work when those women were free, and they felt that they had been denied opportunities to serve because they did not fit the typical category of women their age. Although Rachel had stayed, finding a supplemental spiritual community elsewhere, Penny typifies the single Christian women who are leaving the Church in large numbers.

Infertility

As well as those who were single and childless there were those for whom struggles with fertility had been a – if not *the* – defining experience of their twenties. Deborah's multiple reproductive losses were a major factor in both the failure of her marriage and her isolation from her faith community. She said:

Pregnancy loss broke us. It really did, because he couldn't handle it, church couldn't handle it, and I couldn't handle it. We just had no resources, physically, emotionally, health-wise, we had nothing to help us deal with it. Everybody we knew had [a baby] and went on to have children. I had people prophesy that next Mother's Day I would be holding my own baby. [Those were] from women that I really trusted and had a real track record of making good prophecies. I believed them and hung on to it. That was so damaging and so painful. I wonder if they even remember, and the damage they caused from it? I don't believe it was malicious, or anything like that, they just wanted that to happen as much as I did. They used the spiritual resources they had to articulate it.

It was clear from her account that, theologically, her reformed charismatic house church were at a loss about how to respond. They understood biological family as God's intention for all – and infertility threw the whole community into theological turmoil, providing her with little support or alternative theological resources. After a long struggle with faith and still childless, she identifies as a liberal Anglican having discovered those resources herself. Her understanding of divine sovereignty has dramatically changed. She concluded, 'I have never not believed in God. I don't know why I would get pregnant so many times and lose each time in really horrible ways, but I think I've come to the conclusion that God is just not in control of the world like that. That is neither his fault, nor could he have stopped it. It is probably the only way that it can make sense to me moving forward, or to be able to move forward.' The experience of infertility in a church so focused on traditional family had been profoundly traumatic, almost costing her faith.

For Maggie and her husband Matt (who now have children) their miscarriage was also a major part of their faith journey. Again, the responses of their evangelical communities were significant. As the situation with her pregnancy deteriorated, Maggie said of her large Anglican church:

I had a lot of people praying for me and none of the prayers were working and that really knocked my faith. Quite a lot of the foundations of my faith were built on prayer and now prayer wasn't working. At every point we were praying, and every time we went back to the hospital it was one step worse than we thought was possible. There were quite a few other people who I had heard similar stories of – they'd gone in for the first scan and loads of people had prayed for them and gone in for the second scan and the heart was beating. That was something that part of me thought would happen – if we prayed hard enough.

For a variety of unrelated reasons, she and her husband were moving away from their congregation. She admitted: 'If I had stayed within my network at that church, I would probably have ridden the storm a little bit [better].' However, eventually relocating and joining a smaller Baptist church had helped.

The pastor is very gentle and the two other mothers with young families had also both miscarried. They were like, *Aw that happened to me*, and a tremendous amount of healing happened. Miscarrying was the first time in my life when I'd had something happen that was really bad, that I didn't have control over. Other things had happened that I had found hard, but that was something that really shook both of us. That was the first time I'd had to wrestle with the tough questions of faith, like what happens when a prayer doesn't get answered. It obviously happens loads, but it hadn't happened to me.

This is a stark contrast to Olivia's experience: empathy, gentle support and a recognition of fertility problems as common within the context of a faith community helped her to make sense of her experience. However, it should also be noted that she has other children. The miscarriage was an episode in her fertility history, not the entirety of it. Ultimately, she fits the hetero-nuclear norm and found support and theological resources among her peers.

Some conclusions

These stories highlight several important considerations. They include the challenge of experiencing traumatic experiences and profound disappointments – possibly for the first time. Active Affirmers are typically trying to make sense of them in a framework that anticipates God to be intimate, compassionate and all-powerful. However, they often have limited theological resources or narrow frames of reference. Also significant is the ability (or inability) to share those experiences with a partner, family and/or faith community. The responses they receive can make a huge difference to their well-being and capacity to continue to pursue their faith.

Ultimately, Maggie reflected on her experience of miscarriage as something 'God can work within but that doesn't mean he wanted it to happen'. It had caused her continuing evangelical faith to become 'grounded', 'richer' and 'more complex'. She concluded, 'Someone said it in church on New Year's day, that you realize as you get older that really hard things happen, people die and people are born, there's joy and there's heartache and there is love and arguments, and actually it is finding God within it and walking through those years with God, and praying and talking to God and keeping that open. I think I hadn't quite got that.'

Of course, Millennials do not have a monopoly on the challenges of romance, marriage, singleness, parenthood or infertility. Those have been true throughout human history – something both Christian tradition and the biblical text acknowledge. In many ways social change since the 1960s has created a fluidity and plurality in how family units are created, which makes it much easier for those not following a hetero-normative pattern. Alternative lifestyles are increasingly acknowledged and valued. On the other hand, both wider culture and church community still often idealize a version of the 1950s nuclear family. Some Millennial Active Affirmers access theological and social resources to militate against that script, but many struggle on that journey. Whether they experience validation, encouragement and community that supports them in their singleness, relationship, childlessness or parenthood, has significant influence on whether their identity and faith thrive or flounder.

It is easy for those who walked these developmental journeys some time ago to forget how intense and demanding they are. In a generation that have so often experienced parental divorce, many are anxious to 'get it right' for their own children yet are unsure how. Like other aspects of their lives, Millennial parenting requires the creating of a self-biography from myriad conflicting sources. Similarly, the Internet exacerbates both the joys and anxieties of this season. Whether it is a newsfeed full of cooing baby posts or fabulous adult social activities they are unable to attend, Emerging Adults can experience the same negative impact depending on whether they are struggling with or without children. Religious faith can provide resources that help negotiate identity formation among these transitions, but equally the expectations in religious communities can compound the sense of 'other' or fail to recognize the challenges Emerging Adults face.

Finally, although maternal silence is beginning to be broken, there are questions around how far young men feel able to express their hopes and struggles around fatherhood and how far gender stereotypes continue to shape and, in some cases, prevent that. As Olivia's story illustrates, infertility can be devastating for men too. Millennials are far more likely to be 'hands on' fathers than former generations and are concerned about the faith of their children. Whether following egalitarian or 'soft patriarchal' patterns, only a few voluntarily reflected meaningfully on their fatherhood (or lack of it). There is considerable scope to explore both maternal and paternal silence. Ultimately, parenthood and fertility are core factors in emerging into adulthood. Expectations around it as a marker of adult identity come from many sources and, as one of the most demanding transitions, it inevitably influences religious faith in both positive and negative ways.

Questions for Discussion

- How far do you agree that the Western Church has made the pattern of the nuclear family 'sacred', rather than embracing a broader definition of family or honouring singleness in the way the biblical text does?
- In what ways do you view that as positive and/or problematic?
- What does your faith community consciously/unconsciously communicate about family to young people and Emerging Adults?
- To what extent were you surprised by the finding that young Christians aspire to marriage and parenthood and seem to take romantic relationships very seriously? What have your experiences/observations of that been? Again, do you see that as positive or problematic?
- How far do you recognize the benefits and challenges of Active Affirmers marrying young in comparison to their secular peers?
- Theologically, how might young people and Emerging Adults be helped to make sense of disappointment, or develop emotional and spiritual resilience – particularly around these relational issues?
- In both its espoused and practised theology, how far is your faith community honouring and inclusive of those who are:
  - Single (for whatever reason)
  - Dating
  - Married (particularly recently married)
  - Divorced
  - Childless
  - Parents (including single parents).
- How might you develop strategies for supporting those who are minorities in your context?

Notes

1 Jeffrey Jensen Arnett, *Emerging Adulthood: The Winding Road from the Late Teens through the Twenties* (Oxford: Oxford University Press, 2004).

2 Brian J. Willoughby and Spencer L. James, *The Marriage Paradox: Why Emerging Adults Love Marriage yet Push it Aside* (Oxford: Oxford University Press, 2017).

3 'Families and Households: 2017', Office for National Statistics, www.ons.gov.uk/peoplepopulationandcommunity/birthsdeathsand-marriages/families/bulletins/familiesandhouseholds/2017 (accessed 06. 09.19).

4 Mathew Guest and Kristin Aune, 'Students' Constructions of a Christian Future: Faith, Class and Aspiration in University Contexts', *Sociological Research Online*, Vol. 22.1 (February 2017), 12.

5 Merry Weisner-Hanks, 'Martin Luther on Marriage and the Family', *Oxford Research Encyclopaedia of Religion* (Published online June 2016).

6 Penny Edgell, *Religion and Family in a Changing Society* (Princeton, NJ: Princeton University Press, 2006).

7 W. Bradford Wilcox, *Soft Patriarchs, New Men: How Christianity Shapes Father and Husbands* (Chicago, IL: University of Chicago Press, 2004); Sally K. Gallagher, *Evangelical Identity and Gendered Family Life* (New Brunswick, NJ: Rutgers, 2003).

8 Wesley Hill writes extensively on this in *Spiritual Friendship: Finding Love in the Church as a Celibate Gay Christian* (Grand Rapids, MI: Brazos, 2015).

9 Kristin Aune, 'Singleness and Secularization: British Evangelical Women and Church (Dis)affiliation', in Kristin Aune, Sonya Sharma, Giselle Vincett (eds), *Women and Religion in the West: Challenging Secularization* (Aldershot: Ashgate, 2008), 57–70.

10 Ibid.

11 Willoughby and James, *The Marriage Paradox*.

12 'Have kids, settle down', UK Parliament website, www.parliament. uk/business/publications/research/olympic-britain/population/have-kids-settle-down/ (accessed 06.09.19).

13 www.hfea.gov.uk/media/2563/hfea-fertility-trends-and-figures-2017; 'Fertility problems: assessment and treatment', National Institute for Health and Care Excellence, www.nice.org.uk/guidance/cg156/chapter/context (accessed 06.09.19).

14 Elizabeth Beck-Gernsheim, *Individualization: Institutionalized Individualism and its Social and Political Consequences* (London: Sage, 2002), 120.

15 Wilcox, *Soft Patriarchs, New Men*.

16 Gallagher, *Evangelical Identity and Gendered Family Life*.

17 Dawn Llewellyn, 'Maternal Silences: Motherhood and Voluntary Childlessness in Contemporary Christianity', *Religion & Gender*, Vol. 6.1 (2016), 64–79.

18 Catherine Redfern and Kristin Aune, *Reclaiming the F-Word* (London: ZED, 2010); Ruth H. Perrin, *The Bible Reading of Young Evangelicals* (Eugene, OR: Wipf & Stock, 2016).

19 Anna Strhan, 'Children in Contemporary British Evangelicalism', in A. Strhan, S. Parker and S. Ridgley (eds), *The Bloomsbury Reader in Religion and Childhood* (London: Bloomsbury, 2017), 51–60.

20 Ibid., 60.

21 Llewellyn, 'Maternal Silences', 64–79.

22 Ibid.

PART 2

Changing Shape:
How Emerging Adult Faith
Develops

5

Emerging into Adult Faith: What Shapes Millennial Belief?

Let me begin with a story, not about a Millennial, but rather a member of Generation X.

It is the story of a girl raised going to church and Sunday school in an unremarkable part of the UK. As a teenager none of her friends had faith and she had (many) theological questions. The doctrine of pre-destination taught in her Reformed Baptist church sat uncomfortably with her, as did their policy on women's leadership. Much of her teens and twenties were a tussle between her faith and the ongoing angst of relationship dramas and a party lifestyle. As a student and young adult, she spent many Sundays in church with a hangover. Student workers – she would have been the ongoing thorn in your pastoral flesh!

And yet something happened along the way. She is now writing this account after two decades of Christian ministry as a pastor, preacher and now faith researcher.

I share this account not to blow my own trumpet (far from it!) but rather to make the point that faith development is unpredictable. None of my youth leaders nor student workers would have guessed the trajectory mine would take. Several years ago, I met someone I hadn't seen for 20 years. When he heard what I now did his incredulity turned into uncontrollable laughter. I couldn't blame him. No one, including me, could have seen my faith journey coming when I was 20 (honestly, had I done so I would probably have been horrified!).

This is my story so far, but in middle age I am more aware

than ever of the partial nature of my spiritual formation and theological understanding. The truth is that Christian faith is not static, it continues to evolve and develop over a lifetime, shaped by experience, environment and personal choice (and, people of faith believe – divine activity). This is what the New Testament writers anticipated. Many of their metaphors are agricultural, embracing concepts of growth and pruning, declining and flourishing. The examples provided by the often hapless disciples of Jesus are of understanding and transformation emerging from confusion and failure. Theologically speaking, Christian faith is not simply assent to doctrine or a belief system but also the dynamic formation and re-formation of the believer's identity and relationship with God.

We are all a work in progress. Much of my ministry has been motivated by a desire to help others navigate those volatile young adult years better than I did. I have been privileged to work with hundreds of young adults in that time. Some of the least likely have become devout, mature Active Affirmers while others have rejected religious belief entirely. In contemporary Britain, as we recognize decline in church attendance, rise of the 'Nones' and the existence of a small, highly devout minority, there are pressing questions. One is why religious faith flourishes or declines. A second is whether today's young adults are really so different from former generations.

This second half of the book will look explicitly at the Christian faith of the 47 Millennials who took part in the changing faith research project. The subsequent three chapters will consider the journeys of those who no longer have a faith; those whose religious belief is now practised on the edge of or beyond a church congregation; and those who continue to be Active Affirmers – remaining within established faith communities. By way of introduction, this chapter will consider wider trends within Millennials' faith formation and factors that play a part in that during the volatility of Emerging Adulthood. First, by considering how faith development models (in particular Fowler) interact with Emerging Adulthood, including the impact of biological, cultural and familial influences.

Second, observing some of the factors reported to be key in faith formation for those specifically aged 17–22, which has historically been considered so pivotal. Then the diversity of spiritual and theological resources Active Affirmers access will be examined. Finally, this chapter will consider some of the ways in which they negotiate tensions when cultural and theological values conflict.

Faith Development Models and Emerging Adulthood

Within the Judeo-Christian tradition, practices to encourage spiritual development have existed for millennia. However, the advent of the Social Sciences in the twentieth century created methods for the empirical study of religious belief and faith development. The best-known faith development theory was developed by James Fowler in the 1970s.[1] He described six stages of faith maturation that individuals might sequentially pass through in a lifetime, three of which applied to adulthood. According to Fowler, not all individuals would make this journey: some would get 'stuck' in lower developmental phases. However, the implication was that one should aspire to reach the highest level of human faith development – 'universalizing' faith. This he defined as total altruism and a transcending of belief systems to achieve a sense of one-ness with all things (though he believed that few would achieve this).

Criticisms of Fowler have come from many sources. Some accuse his model of being rigid, hierarchical, reductionist and overly simplistic. Others have been critical of its lack of supporting empirical data, of its valuing of individualism and liberalism over communal, traditional or evangelical forms of belief. Feminists argued that his model was based on privileged, male patterns of identity and faith. A number presented alternatives for women's faith development, typically arguing that relationality and experience were central to women's faith rather than individualism and rationality.[2] They too have been criticized for focusing predominantly on white, Western women. However, what all these models had in common was the assumption that between the ages of 17 and 22 was when most people became adult in their identity and thus owned or rejected a religious faith – which they would probably continue to hold.

The aspect of Fowler's theory that is pertinent to this discussion centres on the transitions that he anticipated might happen within the first half of adulthood. The first was a move from 'Synthetic-Conventional' faith (Stage 3) to 'Individuative-Reflective' faith (Stage 4). The former he considered to be an unexamined faith determined by one's circle of influence in which others held authority on truth. The latter sees a relocation of authority to the self, the discovery of one's own beliefs, often resulting in black and white thinking. Fowler argued that this transition would take place from the late teens as individuals transitioned from dependence on parents to independent young adulthood. He considered that a further transition might occur into 'Conjunctive Faith' (Stage 5) when one was an established adult, secure in one's own identity and worldview. Involving as it does the ability to critique oneself and one's values objectively and develop the capacity to hold multiple views in tension, he considered it rare before the age of 30.

Although Fowler's work is probably most well-known, there are alternative models of faith development that conceptualize it as a spiralling process (rather than occurring in linear stages). These argue that learning is an active process in which individuals construct new ideas or concepts based upon existing knowledge; spiralling round and modifying former knowledge rather than simply discarding it. Developmental psychologists argue that: 'Through daily activities such as prayer or participation in a religious community, individuals acquire a religious consciousness. Through such religious experiences, they formulate a religious judgment, which then contributes to the formation of a deep mother-structure involving whatever beliefs and values relate to religious issues.'[3] As they are exposed to new experiences and ideas, individuals reflect on those in the light of this existing mother-structure and modify their beliefs and actions accordingly, adapting their cognitive schema.

Rather than sharp breaks or radical changes this model argues that faith development is typically an ongoing journey of assimilation, adaption and rejection. As opposed to rigid levels, faith development is more like flowing waves that overlap – with individuals often reverting to former patterns in times of crisis. Elizabeth Tisdell notes that in middle and older age some individuals spiral back to reconsider their childhood religion and remember or reinterpret the life-enhancing parts of it. Thus 'faith development is a process of revisiting what is already known, but moving forward, integrating old understanding into new ways of understanding, rather than rejecting and adopting something new outright. Ways of organizing experience are not just replaced but subsumed into more complex systems of mind.'[4]

Faith Formation, Emerging Adulthood and Twenty-First-Century Britain

Given cultural and social changes since Fowler and other theorists wrote, it is legitimate to ask how far these patterns are applicable to contemporary younger generations. Do the same transitions still take place, and if so at the same times? Jeff Astley, writing in 2000, commented that despite the criticisms, many did experience something akin to Fowler's model of transition from conformist to individuative faith, and Jane Loevinger's feminist version presented gendered variation, but parallel age patterns.[5] Sharon Parks, writing in 1986, also called the ages 17 to 22 the critical years.[6]

For middle-class Baby Boomers and Gen Xers, 17 to 22 *was* the age when many began the journey of independence from their parents, often leaving home to study or starting in employment. Few had experienced extensive travel or multiculturalism and other religions; most of their friends were like them. Exposure to new ideas and worldviews did happen at that age in a pre-Internet, largely mono-cultural world. Likewise, most in those generations expected to be fully established in their adult identity with partners, families and careers well before 30. Their period of early self-discovery was much shorter. Consequently, Astley was right: many people did follow something akin to Fowler's model. However, as we have already established, those patterns are not the ones many Millennials (and presumably younger generations) will follow. Emerging Adulthood has stretched those processes.

So how does faith develop today?

Biological factors in faith formation

In recent years, neurobiology has revealed much about age-related processes in brain maturation that allow for cognitive development. In the early teens these processes allow for the shift from concrete to abstract thinking, which is clearly significant for faith formation. As youth workers well know, the early teens are pivotal for faith journeys, and many of the participants in this study reported the ages of twelve to fourteen as important. Some had stopped going to church while others reported making a religious commitment – even if that waned through their teens. However, it is now widely recognized that the process of brain maturation continues well beyond the legal age of adulthood, on average until the mid-twenties. Typically, from the ages of 18 to 25, maturation of the prefrontal cortex allows for the development of 'executive functions'. These include:

- The ability for greater focus of attention and logical, organized thinking.
- The ability to anticipate outcomes creating greater capacity for: risk assessment; impulse and emotion control; decision-making; goal-setting.
- Increased self-awareness and capacity to self-evaluate.[7]

Essentially, these adult cognitive abilities mean that individuals gradually become more able to analyse, critique and make decisions about ultimate questions – including religious faith.

Since the process of adult brain maturation can take a decade or more, it is likely that the journey to own one's own faith might stretch for that entire period, on average from puberty to at least the mid-twenties. Although it may continue to develop, spiralling as new information, experiences and ideas are presented throughout life, this period of brain formation is significant in shaping that essential mother-structure. Ian Gutiérrez and Crystal Park argue that: 'As adults grow older, belief structure changes in increasingly minor ways. In Emerging Adulthood, however, worldviews remain in flux: determining one's worldview contributes a key developmental task of Emerging Adulthood.'[8]

Of course, this process of brain maturation and worldview formation is not exclusive to younger generations, but what is unique is the culture within which they are experiencing those biological changes.

Cultural influences on faith formation

As in other liberal democracies, since Fowler wrote in the late twentieth century, cultural change in the United Kingdom has been dramatic. Almost no aspect of social, cultural, political or economic life remains unchanged. Transformations that began with two World Wars and accelerated in the 1960s have now become so rapid that, as stated in the introduction, the term 'liquefaction' can be used to describe Western society.[9] Patterns of religious belief have inevitably been reshaped by these changes. In a pluralized and multi-cultural society with access to global travel and the Internet, the social and institutional forces that once reinforced a dominant Christian worldview have largely been eroded. Secularism has replaced religious belief as the norm for much of the population, and religious belief has become an option rather than obligation, often defined by subjective personal conviction or experience.[10]

Christian Smith, researching in the United States, coined the phrase 'Moralistic, Therapeutic Deism' (MTD) to describe the form of religious faith he believed most American Millennials held. In this 'misbegotten cousin' of orthodox Christianity, he argued, God was viewed as a 'divine butler and cosmic therapist' and the main purpose of faith was perceived as being to 'stop people being jerks' and ensure they had a comfortable life.[11] Things are somewhat different in Britain. The faster pace of secularism means that few young people have Christian parents or experience of church or Sunday school, and despite legislation around acts of worship there is little Christian education in most schools. Where previous generations had a basic understanding of Christian beliefs, the chain of religious knowledge passed from generation to generation and reinforced by institutions and social norms has been broken; young people are 'memory-less' in religious terms.[12] Although Mathew Guest et al. found, five years ago, that many university students still self-designated as Christian in some way (particularly young Catholics), the memory-less teens have grown up to be a significant proportion of the 51% of British adult 'Nones'.[13] Rather than assenting to active, nominal, cultural or natal Christianity (or other religions), 70% of those under 30 describe themselves as having no religion at all.[14] As already mentioned in the introduction, this does not mean younger generations are necessarily hostile to Christian faith. Half of British Emerging Adults have almost no contact with it and many more are indifferent; religion is simply not of any interest.[15] Grace Davie explains generational attitudes towards a Christian heritage and worldview:

> Broadly speaking, those born before World War II will respond most easily to vicarious religion. Those that follow – the Baby Boomers – are less convinced. Generation X reacts even more sharply against the inherited model but retains at least some knowledge of what went before. Generation Y does not. But Generation Y has lost the rebellious hostility towards formal religion that was characteristic of earlier

decades, for the obvious reason that there is nothing to rebel against. Religion, vicarious or otherwise, is very largely an irrelevance in their day-to-day lives.[16]

In addition to this vacuum of knowledge, scepticism about all forms of authority extends to religious leadership and the Bible. Tensions around gender and sexual orientation, sexual abuse across denominations, the rise of radical Islamic groups, and American Evangelical support for the Trump presidency – all mediated by the press – have contributed to negative attitudes towards conservative religion. Today's young adults are more likely to be 'pre-religious' (vaguely curious), have no engagement with religion at all or to create their own eclectic forms of spirituality.[17] Based on pragmatism, superstition and uncertainty, these spiritualities are often an unreflective mix of habits and attitudes. Practising (quasi-Buddhist) mindfulness, lighting a candle, tattoos and roadside or online memorials for the dead are all common examples of attempts at making meaning. Rather than, 'Is it true?' many Emerging Adults are more likely to ask, 'Does it help?' Sylvia Collins-Mayo summarizes:

> Young people are charged with the responsibility of finding their own way through life in an increasingly uncertain world, using whatever cultural resources they can access. Religions are cultural resources which young people may – or may not – draw upon as they work out their identity and lifestyle, but they are treated more as an object of consumption than obligation.[18]

Owning religious belief in a secular society

Fowler (and others) argued that Stage 3, Synthetic-Conventional or conformist faith (associated with adolescence), was largely defined by the beliefs of others; an external locus of authority. For older generations in the UK this was typically some form of Christian worldview. Belief in God, the Ten Commandments,

Heaven and Hell, and the Lord's Prayer were all part of public consciousness (even if actual adherence was nominal or negligible). However, younger generations are bombarded with multiple worldview options almost from infancy. This inevitably raises the question of *which* others are the *loci* of external authority.

It could be argued that the 'maybe, doubter and don't know Nones' described by Linda Woodhead represent a pluralist/ secular version of Synthetic-Conventional faith. Family, friends and wider society say that there probably is no personal God (although there might be spiritual forces), therefore individuals should feel free to create a mosaic of whatever spiritual activity (or none) is personally useful. Just as Fowler argued, many remain in a belief system defined by others, so 95% of those brought up with no religion currently continue with that designation.[19] By contrast, the minority of young people raised within actively religious families are fully aware that their family's faith is at odds with most of their peers and wider society. Nick Shepherd's teenage research participants described how difficult it was to have a Christian faith at school; their youth group was a refuge where they would not be ridiculed for it. Religious festivals, holidays and large gatherings provide reassurance to young people that Christian belief is legitimate because large numbers of others also hold it; they function as 'plausibility shelters'.[20] Yet if faith is formed in relation to authoritative others, then in a generation sceptical of authority and strongly valuing self-determination, it is hard to anticipate how young people and Emerging Adults will decide what to believe. Are their parents, religious siblings, church leaders and friends (if they have them) the dominant 'others', or the wider secular culture and their other-religious or non-religious peers? Currently the split is 50/50: half of those raised in Christian homes continue to have faith into adulthood, half do not.[21]

Given wider secularism and the plurality of worldviews they are exposed to, it is inevitable that Millennials from religious homes have experienced pressure to make choices around religious identity earlier than Fowler et al. anticipated. Findings are that those who have strong attachment to their family and for whom religious activity is a positive experience are far more likely to continue following that belief system than those with weaker attachment or who felt compelled to attend very conservative churches.[22] Similarly, the ways in which parents model their own faith has been shown to be strongly significant in whether teens and young adults view those beliefs as credible. Christian Smith argues:

> Parents are mistaken if they think they do not influence the faith of their teenage children. The evidence is clear that attitudes to faith and religion in the household make a significant difference; the most important social influence in shaping young people's religious lives is the religious life modelled and taught to them by their parents.[23]

By contrast, parental divorce, religious nominalism, erratic participation and perceived hypocrisy are well documented as reasons why children reject Christianity.[24] Research from the United States (which continues to have much higher levels of religious adherence) reports that only 12% of churchgoing children and teens have meaningful conversations about faith with their mother, and only 5% with their father.[25] It is not unreasonable to assume that the statistics are lower in Britain. Whether parents authentically live, model and speak about their faith with their children is hugely significant in creating a Christian mother-structure at a young age. Similarly, although during adolescence and Emerging Adulthood friends and romantic partners take on a more influential role, it is also evident (as Chapter 3 demonstrated) that attachment to parents continues to be significant for religious belief.[26] Technological advancements mean that contact between parents and Emerging Adult children is frequent. Many speak to a parent or family member daily or turn to them for emotional support on a very regular basis.[27] Considerable numbers continue, or return, to live amicably in their parental home during their twenties, which encourages intimacy and ongoing reliance on parental advice and values.[28] Therefore, despite the dominant wider culture and other relationships, family is potentially a powerful ongoing influence for many Emerging Adults. Where families are close (emotionally or geographically) and parents' faith meaningful, congruent and open, they may have influence on the religious socialization of younger generations for a longer period than might be expected.

Aged 17–22: Still Significant for Faith Formation

Although I am arguing for a reshaping and extending of how faith develops among contemporary young people and Emerging Adults (starting younger and extending later), there is still considerable evidence for how important the late teens and early twenties are in this process. As will become evident in subsequent chapters, many of those whose faith was established in their thirties described their student (or equivalent) years as profoundly foundational. They included those who had left home to attend university, those who had remained at home while attending a local institution and those who had not attended tertiary education. They also included a number who had taken that Millennial rite of passage – a gap year.

Leaving home – or not

The effects of university experiences on faith will be explored in greater depth in subsequent chapters, but decisions made around this transition significantly affected faith development. Matching Tim Clydesdale's 'identity lockbox' theory, some, liberated from parental expectation, abandoned church and/ or faith.[29] By contrast, others were delighted to find vibrant churches and Christian friends whose passionate faith inspired and influenced their own. A number had spent much of their student life involved in church and faith-based campus activities. Others found alternative forms of Christian spirituality disconcerting, even disturbing. However, for most, being exposed to a diversity of worship styles and theological perspectives was helpful in the long run. There were longer-term, often negative, consequences for those who did not have exposure to alternative faith traditions at this age. Those who had started work, or were young parents, often described feeling 'left behind' and unsupported. With the costs of tertiary education having escalated dramatically in the past decade, increasing numbers of students opt to study from home. This is particularly common in certain geographic regions – London for example, and the North East. Of these participants, 20% had remained within the region to study, a number living at home while doing so. As will become evident, they too can lack exposure to alternative forms of Christian spirituality. This can leave them with the impression that Christian faith simply looks like their own congregation; something that may become problematic in the longer term.

Gap years

Gap years, although not universal, have become a norm among middle-class Emerging Adults, and many young Christians undertake religiously orientated ones. Most large churches and Christian charities have (often unpaid) internships, while smaller ones may offer year-long opportunities for service. Debates have raged as to whether these schemes are exploitative or beneficial, but there is limited research into their effects on the spiritual development of those who participate. Rob Haynes, investigating short-term mission trips among young American Methodists, has argued that although billed as opportunities for practical or evangelistic service, they function as pilgrimages, a journey through which individuals anticipate a spiritual encounter that will transform them.[30]

Short-term trips and gap years (including study years abroad), according to my participants, are transformative – though not always in a positive way. Half had spent a period in their late teens or early twenties involved in some sort of international service or mission. Notwithstanding the West Africans who had all done a year's national service (which was also highly formative), 13 nations across five continents were mentioned, plus five whose gap year had been in the UK. All of them had been working with children, young people or impoverished and vulnerable communities. Almost all commented on the profundity of those experiences, a number identifying them as foundational in subsequent career choices.

Whether the long-term effects of being exposed to culturally alien and emotionally or spiritually intense environments strengthen or damage faith appears to depend on a combination of personal resilience and the support individuals receive. Some reported coming home with a stronger faith, shaped by inspirational individuals and experiences of divine intervention. They used language like 'precious', 'humbling', 'a major eye-opener' and 'a cross-cultural baptism of fire'. Penny said her gap was an 'amazing adventure because I was terrified, but it completely built my trust in God'. Sam said: 'It taught me how God works, but also how it takes time for things to change. It was foundational in giving me a different perspective.' Indeed, that challenge to their perspective was the most frequent comment on the long-term effects of their trip. Two specifically commented on the impact the sacrificial ministry of Catholic nuns had on their decision to embrace Christianity. Here were women demonstrating authentic faith in the most desperate of circumstances; it had profoundly inspired them.

However, not all had positive experiences. Others returned burned out, confused and struggling. 'Really traumatic', 'exhausting', 'a rocky time for my faith' were some of their comments. Isolated by the language, Harry had 'seriously started to doubt my faith' and Suzie considered she had been 'too young and a bit depressed' for the situation she was placed in. Theresa came home angry from 'seeing poverty for the first time and thinking about colonialism'. She was among several who described struggling to fit back into British church contexts and being frustrated at their lack of engagement with prayer or social justice. For most of this sample, ongoing life had allowed them to process those intense experiences into something that was a formational part of their faith journey. As Frankie said, despite having subsequently found a different theological tradition, 'bits of [that organization] made me who I am'. However, it would be interesting to know how many Emerging Adults come home and cannot reintegrate into church community, or reject faith altogether as a result of their experiences.

In summary, then, although Guest et al. found little evidence of large-scale religious change among undergraduates during their university years, my findings are that the ages between 17 and 22 do still function as critical for the critiquing and/or consolidation of a mother-structure of Christian faith among Active Affirmers.[31] One fifth of participants described themselves has having converted or become Active Affirmers during this life stage. Therefore, there is still validity in the argument for it as a pivotal age in faith formation, particularly among those for whom significant life changes occur.

However, given the secular environment they are living in and the process of Emerging Adulthood, forming an independent faith identity is more complicated than it once was. Religious 'self-biographies' for Millennials are complex, diverse and take longer by virtue of exposure to spiritual and cultural alternatives previous generations never experienced. Pew Research Center findings suggest that the age of 24 marks the end of this early adult developmental season, but David Kinnaman found that faith-switching in the United States is most likely to occur between the ages of 18 and 29 (71% of those who had significantly changed faith views did so before 30).[32] Kinnaman's position is affirmed by the six apostate participants in this study who had rejected their Christian faith in their mid to late twenties. Likewise, a small number described re-conversion or discovering meaningful faith for the first time well into that decade. These often lengthy journeys had led to them becoming devout believers by their early thirties. In short, adult faith formation not only starts younger, but it extends far longer than earlier models anticipated.

Resources for Millennial Faith Development

During their interviews the participants in this research spoke at length about their experiences of religious faith development. Before we look at them in detail in the following chapters, there are trends that emerged from their stories that match wider findings and are important to note. These are to do with the eclectic sources of theological input Emerging Adults access. The trends are: trans-denominationalism, diversity of religious resources, and contemporary pilgrimage in the form of conferences, festivals and religious holidays.

Trans-denominationalism

It is well documented that, among younger Protestants, denominational loyalty rarely exists. Beyond clergy and church leaders, few know the history or ecclesiology of the congregations they attend. Many house churches (established since the charismatic renewal of the 1980s) contain individuals from a wide range of denominational backgrounds.[33] This results in an interesting mix of doctrinal and ecclesiological views within any given congregation and a pragmatic tolerance for the sake of unity. Given mobile lifestyles and a wider culture of consumer choice, most British Christians (and particularly evangelicals) choose their church based on personal stylistic preferences rather than the historic parish system. Worship and teaching styles, pragmatic factors such as location, provision of childcare, or a peer cohort are likely to determine their choice. Indeed, a 2013 Evangelical Alliance survey found that only 8% of its members considered denomination to be an important factor when selecting a church.[34]

Millennials, as a hyper-mobile generation, are typically influenced by this diversity across multiple congregations during their twenties. Of course, individuals do tend to be drawn to congregations with certain obvious values (for example, their position on women's leadership, use of charismatic gifts or doctrinal emphases). There are also some networks that strongly encourage members to remain within that tradition (typically Reformed or very conservative congregations). But in general, although denominational heritage may have some influence, a hybridization of doctrine and praxis appears routine and many Christians (not just Millennials) unconsciously adopt theological positions from an eclectic range of sources.

Within this sample just six individuals (13%) had consistently remained within the same denomination or tradition throughout their lives; the other 87% had switched, in many cases multiple times, with some making significant theological transitions.

A pattern that did emerge from the sample, though, was that there are trends when it comes to Active Affirmer church attendance. In short, regardless of their childhood faith background (and they were extremely diverse) the vast majority had embraced a personal faith identity sometime in their teens or early twenties within an evangelical, charismatic or Pentecostal context. Some had made professions of faith as young children, but still within these denominational settings. A number described how, having grown up in traditional denominations, they were taken to church or a youth group by a friend, and heard Christianity explained in a way that made sense to them. The pull of a peer group had been part of the attraction, but lively worship and clear, practically applied Bible teaching had made religious faith coherent. All of those in this sample therefore had some aspect of evangelical, charismatic or Pentecostal spirituality in the mix of their religious identity.

Subsequently, not all had remained within these traditions. Some were apostate and others de-churched but there were also those whose faith had become more liberal or liturgical, often in reaction to experiences within evangelicalism. Grace Davie notes that beyond charismatic evangelicalism the other form of Christianity that is increasing in the UK is cathedral attendance. The attraction of an individual, even anonymous expression of religious commitment (which she suggests this provides) is borne out by my participants. Some were withdrawing from conservative ethical values or what they considered was narrow, overly simplistic theological teaching. Others did not want any social or volunteer demands made on them (often having been heavily committed in a previous context). This will be explored more fully in subsequent chapters, but it is worth recognizing that traditions that are intentionally conversionist and activist, but also experiential in their spirituality, appear to exert the greatest pull on young people and Emerging Adults, even if they do not all remain within those settings as they age.[35]

Global diversity of religious resources

In addition to this post-denominational trend, Millennials have emerged towards adulthood with unprecedented access to a diversity of religious resources. Via the Internet they can access religious teaching, worship, spiritual resources and online faith communities from around the world. They can live-stream a service from their favourite mega-church or use Benedictine meditation practices from apps on their phone. Certainly, they may read Christian books, but blogs, podcasts, conferences and festivals also feed into their spiritual formation. Given their post-denominational outlook, the background or theological positioning of certain speakers or resources is of limited concern to most. Emerging adults are typically pragmatists and whether something is helpful to the issues they are facing is far more likely to be the deciding factor in whether they access it. Previous research with British Millennials showed that they widely access resources from across the transatlantic charismatic and evangelical spectrum. Although, typically, their favourite writers or speakers come from their preferred tradition (for example, Reformed, progressive evangelical, Pentecostal), some were highly eclectic, accessing a diverse range with seemingly little awareness of their contradictory theological positions.[36]

Among this sample the majority spoke of accessing resources

from beyond their church congregation. Well-known evangelical writers were regularly cited: Richard Foster, John Piper, Rick Warren and Tim Keller. Some were more charismatic or Pentecostal, like Pete Greig, Nicky Gumbel or Bill Johnson, and others more progressive, such as Brian McLaren, Rob Bell or Richard Rohr. One woman had received all her theological education from podcasts and CDs from international Pentecostal ministries. Although a committed member of her Anglican congregation, she said: 'I don't hear any of that in church. I don't learn that much in church to be honest. I don't go to church to really learn – I go for other things.' Others were gaining theological input from their churches but supplementing it with apps and podcasts. Bethel, Mars Hill, Hillsongs and Holy Trinity Brompton were all mentioned as such sources. Similarly, others had pursued academic theology to supplement their spiritual journey. Tania said her course was providing '[t]he kind of nourishment that I would like, that I don't have [in church]'. Another articulated her realization: 'These people are really Christians. I was meeting really committed Anglo-Catholics and thinking, *Oh, you are really keen and committed, you just have a whole different way of looking at it!*'

Of course, sometimes these resources did create tensions. Deborah was explicit about her dissatisfaction with the church she had attended in her early twenties and her desire to attend the sort of congregation she saw online. 'We would watch live stream. I guess at the time we were probably massively influenced by the kind of churches that we would see on the Internet, like Mark Driscoll – Mars Hill, or the Hillsongs stuff. It just seemed so amazing and appealing. We were stuck in this little country [church] ... there were a hundred people, so not small, but very rural.' Craig also described having been an enthusiastic listener of Mark Driscoll, a now largely disgraced American neo-conservative, famous for his hyper-masculine version of evangelical Christianity.

I listened to Mark Driscoll quite a lot. I don't listen to him any more. I found him guiding my views on women, on role of women in the Church, of being a manly man. There were a group of CU lads who really moved that way. [But] I was challenged by my dad about the role of women, and he said that some of the most important people in your Christian life were women. Some of your guiding lights in terms of junior church and Sunday school were women.

He went on to articulate his subsequent support for women's ministry but recognized he and his friends had been strongly influenced by Driscoll's teaching because he had been dynamic, speaking about something they were interested in, and they had been theologically unreflective. During previous research I discussed this phenomenon with the leader of a charismatic church with a large Emerging Adult cohort. She expressed her frustration at the influence that dynamic, but extreme teaching had on members of her congregation, something she had to address frequently. Enthusiastic young Active Affirmers are clearly supplementing the theological input they receive in church, but their ability to discern its influence and significance are not always very developed, particularly if their peers are equally enthusiastic about it.

Contemporary pilgrimage – religious holiday, conferences and festivals

In addition to written, musical and online resources almost all the participants in this study had, at some point, attended conferences, festivals or religious youth holidays and events. These are popular and formative among young British evangelicals. Most frequently cited were Soul Survivor and Spring Harvest, but Scripture Union camps, CYFA holidays, Crusader camps and others were also mentioned. All evangelical and often charismatic, these provided inspiring theological teaching, lively worship and a sense of being part of something bigger than their local church. Since its inception in 1993, Soul Survivor had grown exponentially to 25,000 young people and Emerging Adult attendees in 2015. Maggie, from a non-religious background, described taking the youth group she led for the first time. 'All the kids absolutely loved it and I was just, *Oh my goodness! This is just overwhelming!* Soul Survivor has been significant to me over the years and has impacted me a lot.' The size and atmosphere of the festival was something she had never experienced before, a religious subculture she did not know existed but found highly attractive.

Suzie, currently attending a non-charismatic Anglican church, summarized the ongoing role of Spring Harvest in her faith:[37]

> I like that in times of worship when you do feel connected to God and full of the Holy Spirit. One way that we seek that is that we go to Spring Harvest most years. I do feel that's a time when there is more lively worship than there is at [our church] and there's just more time. Four days when you can spend a lot of time seeking God, which is more difficult in everyday life. I guess at Spring Harvest you do get very talented people and it is a longer period. I think that is something that is useful to go to, because it gives you that space and it is a holiday as well. It's fun and useful to hear what is happening in the world.

These sorts of events appear to function as a form of pilgrimage, a time annually devoted to religious activity in a context that provides large-scale, high-quality Bible teaching and spiritual experience. The sense of being connected to other Christians also appeared to be an incentive to attend and many spoke about going with their family or youth group as young people. The mixture of pragmatic relevance to contemporary issues for their life stage and spiritual encounter were a large part of the attraction. A number gave accounts of prophetic words, or ways in which they believed God had spoken directly to them at these events, shaping their identity. Rachel said:

I went to Soul Survivor and someone was talking about the parable of the sower and about people who have been so crushed, or the ground has been so crushed, that the seed can't fall on it and that God wanted to come along with the rotavator. I was like, *That's me!* I spent about three days crying and God really healed me.

These intense emotional experiences had profound effects on several but despite their significance at the time, some of those who were apostate had reinterpreted them, reflecting with scepticism. Charlie felt they had been hyper emotive, no different from the euphoria football fans experience at a game, while Tim said:

All of them had the same format in that they had big worship bands, very atmospheric music and then whoever was speaking would say, 'God is saying that you've got this going on in your life.' There were occasions when I felt (as I imagine many young men do) [that I] had pornography [issues] going on [and] constantly felt like I wasn't good enough, and only through going to church and these events and purifying myself ... I am quite cynical about the way that that is all framed and pushed to young people. I don't think there was any systematic abuse, not that I experienced anyway, but that structural set-up, there was something to be gained in going forward and confessing and then feeling rubbish about yourself, and some sort of purification.

Whether they continued to understand these experiences as the presence of God or had become sceptical that it was merely hype that their vulnerable younger self had been drawn into, the influence of these events on young people and Emerging Adults should not be underestimated. The experience of practical teaching, worship and large-scale religious community are a dynamic part of faith development for those who regularly attend them.

It is clear, then, that Emerging Adult Active Affirmers draw on a wide range of resources to form a religious identity: family, friends, a range of churches, online resources, literature and large events. Exposure to other cultures, setting and traditions contribute, as do formal and informal studies. They have access to a veritable smorgasbord of spiritual resources and may well try out different ideas and theologies before deciding whether to add them to the mosaic of their own beliefs or reject them. What is important is to understand how that process of belief selection works.

Negotiating Cultural and Theological Tensions during Emerging Adulthood

One of the central challenges young people and Emerging Adults negotiate in forming a religious identity is the tension between religious claims of exclusivity and wider cultural values of tolerance and inclusivity. Typically, what appears to be fair underpins Millennial ethical decisions rather than external standards of right and wrong. Thus, religions (like Christianity) that claim an external source of moral authority or exclusive doctrines of salvation are problematic. Millennials have been described as the 'great agreement generation' – likely to avoid anything divisive. Kinnaman notes:

> Tolerance has been the cultural north star for most of their up-bringing. Inclusiveness, diversity and political correctness are ideals that shaped this generation. Young people are growing up with peers who are more ethnically, religiously and relationally diverse than the peers with whom their parents came of age. Egalitarianism, hypersexuality and sexual orientation are simply part of the scenery.[38]

What is meant by tolerance is of course interesting. There is a difference between civility or respectful disagreement and indifference or religious universalism. The churches that are attracting converts (including Emerging Adults) in the UK are conservative rather than liberal, but doctrinal exclusivity claims are problematic to many. Recent UK findings are that (to researchers at least) young people from a multi-cultural context were keen to emphasize what those from all ethnicities and faiths had in common. They repeatedly articulated 'We are all the same!', and were reluctant to ask questions that might have been perceived as divisive.[39] Likewise, Nicola Madge et al. found that 'a multicultural value set is normative for young people. Dissent from that, if it takes place at all, takes place in private.'[40] However, research into the beliefs of young Muslims suggests that they value their religious heritage and clear belief systems precisely because they do not change and thus provide a sense of security and identity.[41] This may explain the pull of charismatic evangelical forms of Christianity that 'epitomize firm commitments, strong fellowship and conservative teaching, balanced by the warmth of charismatic experience'.[42] Certainty and clarity continue to be attractive despite being in tension with liberal values espoused by wider culture, although as will become clear, not all of those attending such churches personally hold conservative views.

Part of the problem with negotiating such tensions is the tendency for public dialogue to take place in soundbite form. Few individuals (of any generation) take the time to thoughtfully weigh up or critique the credibility of religious ideas, or to engage with nuance within them. Grace Davie argues that many in public life do not have the conceptual framework or appropriate language to engage in dialogue with religious groups and that much of the public education on religion comes from media reporting of religious controversy.[43] Thus, rather than reflectively assessing belief systems for their internal coherence, young people have typically been taught to attribute equal validity, or non-validity, to them all. Of course, the current rise of public vitriol via social media and hate crime call into question how deep tolerance actually runs in British society. Nonetheless, young people and Emerging Adults find themselves trying to form religious identities between often conflicting, yet sometimes also overlapping worlds and value systems. Given its complexity, it is no surprise that this can be a lengthy process of spiralling around beliefs and uncertainties where they need to reassess, consistently, 'Do I still believe?', and thus convert, de-convert and reconvert multiple times over an extended period.

Sexuality and faith development

Perhaps nowhere is the current tension between a liberal society and conservative religious values more acute than in the arena of sexuality. The legalization of same-sex marriage in 2014 across most of the UK stands in tension with traditional Christian teaching on sexual activity between members of the same gender. The internal struggles of the Church of England on this subject have been widely reported by a liberal press to a largely uncomprehending secular society. To a generation whose worldview is based on a happy-midi narrative and the right of individuals to be true to themselves, conservative religious values appear not only unfair but intolerant, repressive and homophobic.

Millennial Active Affirmers negotiate this tension in churches where leaders are often also conflicted on the subject. As Penny Edgell found, many churches are trying to balance what they consider to be morally right with what is pastorally kind.[44] Some are explicit in their teaching but given the tensions, many rarely address the subject, essentially leaving their Emerging Adult members to draw their own conclusions. Linda Woodhead argues that many individuals retain affiliation with Catholic and Anglican churches while disagreeing with official teaching on moral issues.[45] Undoubtedly that is true for more conservative Protestant congregations too. In faith communities that emphasize traditional biblical ethics and a hetero-normative narrative it is more difficult to belong if one holds differing views or is defying social expectations on sexual behaviour. For young gay Christians this is particularly acute, given that most spend at least part of their faith journey within charismatic, evangelical and Pentecostal churches that are often most conservative. Their options are: joining a (usually) more liberal pro-gay church; following a 'Side B' lifestyle of embracing their sexual identity but refraining from sexual activity; leaving church but continuing their faith in private; or rejecting their religious identity altogether.

Although none of the participants in this research presented themselves as LGBTQi+, without any prompting approximately one-third raised the subject of faith and sexuality as something they were concerned about and that had informed their own faith journey (I suspect that had they been directly asked it would have been an issue for the vast majority).[46] The topic is a good illustration of the process of cultural and theological negotiation they undertake. Attitudes were diverse, at one end of the spectrum was a West African participant, Ade, who described his experiences of discussing sexuality with British people.

> Because of the place I come from, I come across quite strong with something against being gay. The person told me that I was homophobic. He also said that I was being rude. I told him that it is not proper for a man to be married to a man, or a woman to be married to a woman. He told me that I can't say it. He said I had a right to my opinion, but I couldn't say that I was against it.

As a non-Westerner he did not feel compelled to tolerance and inclusivity. Instead he was quite certain that this was a moral issue on which there were clear boundaries established by both God and Scripture. What he was confused about was that holding a view was acceptable, but articulating it was not. He also described other conversations that had led him to think that liberal inclusiveness was not 'a true picture of British values. Even though the press and the laws are pushing it, I've had discussion with people, and they say that it is not a true picture.' Given the ongoing reporting of hate crime aimed at the LGBTQi+ community, he may be correct. He also expressed concerns over other behaviours he had witnessed, particularly around sexual activity and alcohol consumption. There were many things about Britain he was enthusiastic about, but the morality, particularly of young people, was something that disturbed him. For him, such things were clear cut – they were right or wrong because God said so in the Bible.

His was a unique voice in the wider sample. Others described the tension of juggling conservative theology with cultural tolerance and inclusivity. Most of these were informed by personal experience. As mentioned in Chapter 3, Helen described an extended process of trying to reconcile her evangelical brother's de-conversion, coming out and pursuing a promiscuous gay lifestyle, with her own faith. She had done this by seeking the opinions of those around her. She concluded:

> I still don't know exactly where I stand. I spoke to a lot of people at that time because I really struggled with that. Some people have a very hard line, very much, *It's wrong and that's a big issue in his life*. Someone [else] might say about him that [promiscuity] it is a big issue and that he needs to abstain from that. Other people might say that that is one sin alongside other sins that anyone else might have in their life; that we all have some sin in our life, so that's not so much of an issue.

She added: 'I guess I'm feeling more like that [third option] now. We have one other family member who is gay and who got married to his partner. Again, previously I would not have known what to do with that, but we went along – he is part of our family. Personally, I think supporting them in that is a better witness rather than making some judgement – it is not my place to judge.'

Helen's concern to be able to continue to witness to her faith and evangelize her gay family member is indicative of the tension many Millennial Active Affirmers find themselves in. Their conversionist value is in tension with what they know are unpopular conservative sexual ethics. A desire to be non-judgemental and inclusive conflicts with what they have been taught (and may or may not believe) are moral boundaries. Given that so many have friends and family members who are gay, this is not an abstract discussion for Millennial Active Affirmers, it is a lived reality that they must negotiate on a regular basis. Helen's comments reveal a pragmatic response but ongoing personal conflict. They also illustrate some of the diversity of attitudes among older evangelicals. None were enthusiastic about her brother's sexuality, although there were varying degrees of acceptance. However, his promiscuity was a problem for them all.

Wendy epitomized the tension for many Millennial Active Affirmers and another way of resolving it. She articulated personal moral conservatism, although mediated by her own conscience rather than doctrinal authority. However, it went alongside liberal non-judgementalism, moral relativism and frustration at the absolutist attitude of older members of her congregation.

> I worry about what [my daughter] is taught in organized church. Not so much what is said from the front but some of the other things that are said, or the prayers. I struggle with the intolerant 'Can we please pray about stopping whatever', whether that is abortion, or gay rights, or whatever. I don't know if it is because of my job, or just because I don't believe that I have the right to make choices for other people. I know what I would or wouldn't do for myself, and what I believe my relationship with God tells me what is right for me, but I'm not sure I have the right to dictate what that should or shouldn't be for anybody else.

She was self-reflective about this, recognizing the intergenerational tensions and cultural shifts but, like Helen, was also concerned for the evangelistic mission of the Church and not alienating the LGBTQi+ community.

I'm probably too tolerant, and people would probably say that it is people like me that have eroded Christianity and stopped it from being the more moral high ground, and that it has become too soft. They are probably right in some senses, but at the same time I want [my daughter] to learn, through church, to love everybody. I think we should be the epitome of loving everybody. I feel that she needs to be a little bit older to understand some of the dynamics and tensions and some of the different things that you have to hold together.

This well sums up the tone of those who spoke about this subject. Traditional teaching was the preferred option for practising believers, and personally they were happy to accept historic Christian sexual ethics. However, imposing them on others was problematic. The sense was that everyone had to decide for themselves how best to conduct intimate relationships. Given that the Bible did not address specific contemporary patterns, that there were a variety of views from within the faith community, and that they wanted friends and family to convert, participants were not confident that traditional readings of Scripture were universally authoritative. Like Anna Strhan's conservative evangelical research participants, they were aware of and conflicted by the ways in which traditional Christian doctrine clashed with contemporary sensibilities of personal choice and inclusivity.[47]

Whereas Ade was holding a position of moral absolutism, Wendy and Helen were in various stages of negotiating the tensions, there were also individuals who felt that intolerance of LGBTQi+ lifestyle was itself immoral. One was Penny, whose close friends (from before her Christian conversion) were largely gay. She described how accepting, hospitable and kind they had been to her, adopting her – a young heterosexual woman – into their community. She had not attempted to negotiate any theological tension but instead had left her charismatic house church, in part at least because she believed her friends would be unwelcome given its conservative theology. She was currently attending a liberal congregation

where she knew they would be welcome but couldn't imagine
that they would want to come given its traditional worship
style. More extreme was Pete. He had become apostate for a
range of reasons, but one was the treatment of a lesbian friend
and the theological journey he had been on as a result.

> She went through so much horrific stuff when she was
> coming out. She got involved with a pastor's daughter and
> was essentially excommunicated and prayed over, and
> demons prayed out of her and all that stuff, because she was
> a lesbian. [Another friend] that was a Bible scholar, he came
> out. I thought, *Right, I need to deal with this. I've been told
> for years that the Bible says that it is wrong.* I went back to
> it and thought, *Jesus didn't say anything about it for a start.*
> The other instances that are in [the Bible] are to do with de-
> praved sexual activities like rape. I thought that if the Bible
> can be used like that – like a flexible document that someone
> can go, *Here it says that slavery is alright, this says that sexu-
> ality is abhorrent …* I'm going, *It doesn't say anything about
> it really.* It is talking about the rules at the time and homo-
> sexuality is not mentioned because they didn't have such a
> rigid view of relationships. Obviously, it wasn't on Jesus'
> radar at all, or he would have gone on about it.

His compassion for his friends had pushed Pete to seriously
consider both his hermeneutics and how the Bible was used in
his tradition. Ultimately, however, he did not follow Penny's
route towards liberal Christianity. Instead this issue combined
with other concerns to undermine his conviction about religion
entirely: 'I realized that if God really was God who oppressed
people that were homosexual and all that kind of stuff, then I
didn't want to be any part of it.' For him, in the culture clash
there had been no accommodation; liberal secularism was the
morally correct choice.

This spectrum is indicative not just of Millennial Active
Affirmers but the Church more widely. What it does illustrate,
however, is that theological reflection does not take place in

abstraction, it is stimulated by lived experience – of friends, family and other cultures. It is also complex and painful. Younger cohorts are exposed to issues of sexual orientation and gender fluidity far more than any previous generations. They find themselves suspended between a culture in which liberal inclusivity is the oxygen they breathe (and is thus self-evidently moral) and conservative Christianity that espouses external sources of morality. Many are also conversionist – they want their church and beliefs to be palatable and accessible to their friends. Most are trying to form their own identity and religious beliefs in a complex and conflicting set of circumstances – often with limited help in how to do so from religious leaders. These are not hypothetical theological discussions but pressing personal and relational issues. Essentially, British Emerging Adults are at the sharp end of cultural shifts and have to negotiate a way to either hold them in tension or – like Pete – to reject religion altogether.

In Conclusion

It is clear from these findings that there are some circumstances that are unique for Millennials and the generation following behind them in forming a coherent adult religious identity. Formerly, British young people had limited exposure to alternative religious beliefs and Christianity was the de facto worldview (in culture if not in praxis). John Hull, writing in 1985, argued that widespread spiritual passivity within the Church was the result of professional adults wishing to embrace a childlike spirituality under the theological expertise of clergy. He suggested that the Church had become a refuge from reality, where people wanted comfortable homilies rather than challenge to take responsibility for their own faith.[48] Today's Emerging Adults do not have the option to hide from reality in church. In a secular, pluralistic society with access to global information they are fully aware of their minority status as Active Affirmers and therefore have little choice but to take responsibility for owning or disowning a religious identity. With all the options, changes and pressures they face, the process of achieving a stable adult identity (be it religious or not) is a far more complex task than previous generations faced. Inevitably, it (like other aspects of their adult identity and lifestyle formation) takes longer. My previous findings suggested that many evangelical Emerging Adults are still tentative about significant theological questions well into their mid-twenties. It was not just recent converts who were exploring basic Christian doctrines, but those who had been part of faith communities their whole lives. It was not until their early thirties that confidence in those beliefs appeared to be established.[49] The stories of the Millennials in this project suggest that that has been true for many of them too.

Questions for Discussion

- How might the fact that younger generations are uninterested or sceptical but not hostile towards religion influence the ways in which you engage with them?
- How far do you agree that younger Christians have to make decisions about their faith earlier, but take longer to form a coherent religious identity than formerly? What are your reflections on the reasons for that?
- To what extent do you think religious belief 'spirals' rather than develops in clear stages? What are the implications of that for theological education in faith communities?
- How far are you convinced by the argument that 17–22 continues to be a key age in faith development? If you agree, what might that mean for both ministry and mission in your context?
- What do you identify as the benefits and challenges of creating a 'mosaic' form of Christian faith drawn from diverse resources and contexts?

- How far do you recognize that Emerging Adults are at the 'sharp end of the wedge' when it comes to cultural and theological tensions? How do you negotiate them yourself? How far is your faith community a place that allows and supports others as they learn to do the same?

Notes

1 James Fowler, *Stages of Faith: The Psychology of Human Development and the Quest for Meaning* (San Francisco, CA: HarperCollins, 1995).

2 E.g. Carol Gilligan, Carol Oseik and Maria Harris cited in Nicola Slee, *Women's Faith Development* (Aldershot: Ashgate, 2004); Mary Field Belenky et al., *Women's Ways of Knowing* (New York: Basic Books, 1986).

3 Carolyn McNamara Barry et al., 'Religiosity and Spirituality During the Transition to Adulthood', *International Journal of Behavioural Development*, Vol. 34.4 (2010), 311–24.

4 Elizabeth J. Tisdell, *Exploring Spirituality and Culture in Adult and Higher Education* (San Francisco, CA: Jossey Bass, 2003).

5 Jeff Astley (ed.), *Learning in the Way* (Leominster: Gracewing, 2000); Jeanne Stevenson-Moessner, *In Her Own Time* (Minneapolis, MN: Fortress, 2000), 27–9.

6 S. Parks, *The Critical Years: The Young Adult Search for a Faith to Live By* (San Francisco, CA: Harper & Row, 1986).

7 M. R. Levenson et al., 'Religious Development from Adolescence to Middle Adulthood', in R. F. Paloutzain and C. L. Parks (eds), *Handbook of the Psychology of Religion and Spirituality* (New York: Guildford Press, 2005), 147.

8 I. A. Gutiérrez and C. L. Park, 'Emerging Adulthood, Evolving Worldviews: How Life Events Impact College Students' Developing Belief Systems', *Journal of Emerging Adulthood*, Vol. 3.2 (2015), 85–97.

9 Zygmunt Bauman, *Liquid Modernity* (Cambridge: Polity Press, 2000).

10 Grace Davie, *Religion in Britain: A Persistent Paradox* (London: Wiley & Sons, 2014).

11 Christian Smith and Melinda Lundquist Denton, *Soul Searching: The Religious and Spiritual Lives of American Teenagers* (Oxford: Oxford University Press, 2005).

12 Sylvia Collins-Mayo et al., *The Faith of Generation Y* (London: Church House Publishing, 2010).

13 Mathew Guest et al., *Christianity and the University Experience: Understanding Student Faith* (London: Bloomsbury Academic, 2013).

14 Stephen Bullivant, *Europe's Young Adults and Religion: Findings from the European Social Survey (2014–16)* (St Mary's University, London: Benedict XVI Centre for Religion and Society, 2018).

15 Linda Woodhead, 'The Rise of "No Religion" in Britain: The Emergence of a New Cultural Majority', *Journal of the British Academy*, 2016 (4), 245–61.

16 Davie, *Religion in Britain*.

17 David Tacey, 'What Spirituality means to Young Adults', in Sylvia Collins-Mayo and Pink Dandelion (eds), *Religion and Youth* (Farnham: Ashgate, 2010), 67–71.

18 Collins-Mayo and Pink Dandelion, *Religion and Youth*.

19 Woodhead, 'The Rise of "No Religion" in Britain', 245–61.

20 Nick Shepherd, *Faith Generation: Retaining Young People and Growing the Church* (London: SPCK, 2016).

21 David Voas, 'Religious Census 2011 – What Happened to the Christians? (Part II)', *British Religion in Numbers*, www.brin.ac.uk/religious-census-2011-what-happened-to-the-christians-part-ii/ (accessed 06.09.19).

22 Carolyn McNamara Barry et al., 'Religion and Spirituality During the Transition to Adulthood', *International Journal of Behavioural Development*, Vol. 34.4 (2010), 311–24.

23 Smith and Lundquist Denton, *Soul Searching*, 56.

24 David Kinnaman, *You Lost Me* (Grand Rapids, MI: Baker, 2011).

25 Chap Clark and Kara Powell, *Sticky Faith: Everyday Ideas to Build Lasting Faith in Your Kids* (Grand Rapids, MI: Zondervan, 2011).

26 McNamara Barry et al., 'Religion and Spirituality During the Transition to Adulthood'), 311–24

27 Caroline Marchant and Stephanie O'Donohoe, 'Edging out of the Nest: Emerging Adults' Use of Smartphones in Maintaining and Transforming Family Relationships', *Journal of Marketing Management*, Vol. 30 (Nov. 2014), 15–16.

28 Karen L. Fingerman et al., 'Coresident and Noncoresident Emerging Adult's Daily Experiences with Parents', *Journal of Emerging Adulthood*, Vol. 5.5 (2017), 337–50.

29 He argues that many young Americans put their faith in an identity 'lockbox' for a year, in order to explore other lifestyles, before deciding whether subsequently to return to it or not. Tim Clydesdale, *The First Year Out: Understanding American Teens after High School* (Chicago, IL: University of Chicago Press, 2007).

30 Robert Ellis Haynes and Laceye C. Warner, *Consuming Mission: Towards a Theology of Short-term Mission and Pilgrimage* (Eugene, OR: Wipf & Stock, 2018).

31 Guest et al., *Christianity and the University Experience*.

32 Michael Lipka, 'Millennials Increasingly are Driving Growth of "Nones"', Pew Research Center, www.pewresearch.org/fact-tank/2015/05/12/millennials-increasingly-are-driving-growth-of-nones/ (accessed 06.09.19); Kinnaman, *You Lost Me*.

33 Philip Richter, 'Denominational Cultures: The Cinderella of Congregational Studies?' in M. Guest et al. (eds), *Congregational Studies in the UK* (Aldershot: Ashgate, 2004), 169–84.

34 Greg Smith (ed.), *21st Century Evangelicals* (Watford: Instant Apostle, 2015), 22.

35 Davie, *Religion in Britain*.

36 Ruth H. Perrin, *The Bible Reading of Young Evangelicals* (Eugene, OR: Wipf & Stock, 2016).

37 At its peak in 1991, 80,000 attended the Spring Harvest Conferences. It has, however, suffered from the instigation of multiple similar events and festivals over the subsequent years. Rob Warner, *Reinventing English Evangelicalism, 1996–2001* (Milton Keynes: Paternoster, 2007).

38 Kinnaman, *You Lost Me*, 171–2.

39 Phoebe Hill (ed.), *No Questions Asked: The Findings of a Qualitative Study of 16–19 Year Olds in Luton* (2018), available from http://Youthscape.co.uk (accessed 06.09.19).

40 N. Madge et al., *Youth on Religion: The Development, Negotiation and Impact of Faith and Non-Faith Identity* (London: Routledge, 2014).

41 L. Ryan, 'Islam Does Not Change: Young People Narrating Negotiations of Religion and Identity', *Journal of Youth Studies*, Vol. 17.4 (2014), 446–60.

42 Davie, *Religion in Britain*, 8.

43 Ibid.

44 Penny Edgell, *Religion and Family in a Changing Society* (Princeton, NJ: Princeton University Press, 2006).

45 Woodhead, 'The Rise of "No Religion" in Britain', 245–61.

46 Mark A. Yarhouse addresses the experiences of those individuals in *Listening to Sexual Minorities: A Study of Faith and Sexual Identity on Christian College Campuses* (Downers Grove, IL: InterVarsity Press, 2018).

47 Anna Strhan, 'Discipleship and Desire: Conservative Evangelicals, Coherence and the Moral Lives of the Metropolis', PhD diss, University of Kent, 2012.

48 John M. Hull, *What Prevents Christian Adults from Learning?* (London: SCM Press, 1985), 5.

49 Perrin, *The Bible Reading of Young Evangelicals*.

6

Losing Faith:
'I Don't Call Myself a Christian Anymore'

I had a good friend at university who lost his faith. He was a few years older than me but we met through the Christian Union and became sufficiently good friends to share a house when we graduated. Neither of us was particularly devout at the time but we both identified as Christian and went to church. Some years later he got back in touch. I was now in full-time ministry having undergone some radical experiences of God in my twenties. He no longer believed that there was a God, personal or otherwise. He told me he'd always had doubts; now a scientific researcher, the idea of the supernatural was no longer credible to him.

I suspect most of us have stories like this. Sometimes those we thought were nominal in their faith become devout as they age; others drift away or intentionally reject what they were once committed to. Whenever I speak on this research, people tell me stories of those who fit this pattern of apostasy. Often they are distressed, sometimes bewildered, they usually have two questions: 'Why?' and 'Could I have done something?' For some this raises theological questions, but the purpose of this chapter is not to debate theology. It aims to provide some insight into those two questions. Why do some people reject their former religious beliefs and what might we do to support those experiencing loss of faith?

Apostasy across the Atlantic

Apostasy can be defined as 'The relinquishing of a set of religious beliefs', including not just faith loss but the rejection of a religious community as a basis for self-identification.[1] Only a small amount of literature exists about contemporary Emerging Adult faith loss and most of it is American. Statistics clearly show overall decline of religiosity among Emerging Adults but understanding why some decisively reject formerly held faith involves listening to their unique, individual stories. Having done so, Phil Zuckerman helpfully distinguishes different sorts of apostasy. Early apostates reject the faith of their family as part of the maturation process of identity formation in their teens or early twenties (statistics from the UK suggest that up to half of those raised in Christian homes currently follow this pattern).[2] Late apostates, who adopt religion as adults and later abandon it, are relatively rare. He also distinguishes between shallow apostates, who still consider themselves to be 'spiritual', and deep apostates (like my friend), who have made a total break from all religion and are convinced non-believers. Finally, he identifies the difference between mild apostasy, where individuals were not very religious anyway, and transformative apostasy, which he describes as a life-altering 'massive psychological reorientation'.[3]

David Kinnaman describes apostate young adults as 'Prodigals'. He estimates that one in nine young American Christians currently follow a prodigal trajectory and identifies causal patterns in their stories. These include overprotective churches that stifle their creativity, do not provide scope to explore doubts, or present a shallow form of Christianity lacking any sense of personal calling. Similarly, anti-scientific attitudes, exclusivity claims and 'repressive' rules (particularly around sexuality) are problematic for contemporary young people, 'shaped by a culture that esteems open-mindedness, tolerance and acceptance'.[4] Zuckerman too noted tensions around attitudes to sex and exclusivity claims in his sample. However, for those exposed to other cultures, higher education or with left-wing political views, conservativism within the American church can be alienating. Personal relationships also influence apostasy: parents with lukewarm or no faith, the influence of significant friends, colleagues or lovers, and the malfeasance of religious associates.[5]

However, despite the ongoing transatlantic influences, it has become clear over the past few years that the British and American Church (including in its evangelical forms) are culturally distinct. Whereas 80% of American evangelicals voted for Donald Trump in the 2016 presidential election, British evangelicals were significantly more likely than average to have voted Remain in the Brexit referendum. Indeed, English evangelicals and frequent churchgoers are spread along the political spectrum but tend to be politically centrist or left-leaning liberal-progressive, whereas US evangelicals are firmly conservative and Republican.[6] In the light of this it seems likely that at least some of the theological and cultural factors that drive young Americans towards apostasy may not apply in the UK.

What then causes young British Emerging Adults to renounce their faith? Andy Frost's short book *Losing Faith* written in 2010 is a helpful starting point in recognizing both the uniqueness and commonality of journeys of faith loss.[7] However, I hope this chapter will add to the understanding of these complex and often painful experiences.

British Journeys of Apostasy

Six individuals in this research sample described themselves as no longer Christian. Not all self-described as atheist (three still expressed a level of openness to spirituality) but all had rejected the charismatic evangelicalism of their teens and early twenties. Two had attended a local university largely motivated by commitment to their church community. Three more had held leadership roles within their university Christian Union, and one had been a student leader within his university church. For all of them, their faith in Jesus in their late teens had been sincere. Several described powerful conversion experiences in their early teens or spoke of how their faith had sustained them through adolescent difficulties. They had all clearly been Active Affirmers.

Interestingly, none described having previously rebelled against or seriously questioned their faith. Although not all from Christian families, they had been enthusiastic youth group and church attenders who were strongly socialized into, and conformed to, the expectations of those groups. Four reflected that their desire for approval – to appear as 'successful' believers – meant they had never really questioned any of the doctrines they had been taught. The approval of family, peers or authority figures meant that they performed their faith with enthusiasm. Certainly, it had been sincere, but the social capital, affirmation and identity they acquired had given them little reason to critique their belief system. Even at university, several had existed primarily within the previously discussed 'Christian bubble' with limited exposure to alternative worldviews.[8]

At some point in their twenties, this bubble had burst.

Clearly, the life and faith journey of any individual is unique, and that is true of these six. Individuals make choices, including those about their faith, based on a wide variety of factors. However, there are patterns that emerged from their stories, based around three themes:

- The process of faith loss.
- The price of faith loss.
- Some of the causes of faith loss.

The Process of Faith Loss

Faith loss is gradual

For all these participants their disillusionment with Christianity came over an extended period. This is typical; wider research shows that few people have a sudden de-conversion.[9] Instead, over several years, their faith became less and less convincing, a process referred to as 'acquired incredulity syndrome'.[10] Something may trigger a final decision to renounce belief but, typically, that is a final straw in an already long-term process.[11] As Sarah explained: 'There wasn't a moment where I was aware that I stopped believing, but there was a point that I realized I did not believe and had not believed for some time.'

For several of them this gradual journey would fit the definition of 'early apostasy'. Raised within a religious family or community, they began to question their faith as part of their adult identity development. Popular wisdom has it that starting university is the key point at which young adults question or reject their faith. However, Tim Clydesdale describes an 'identity lockbox' where American students frequently put their faith on hold for a year but later return to it, and Mathew Guest's large-scale British survey found limited evidence of faith change at university. He concluded that 'if changes to religious identity happen at university, all of the evidence points to them being, for the most part, gradual rather than dramatic.'[12] However, the phenomenon of Emerging Adulthood appears to mean that 'early apostasy' can happen much later than might have been previously anticipated. As mentioned in the last chapter, David Kinnaman found that 'faith switching is most likely to occur between the ages of eighteen and twenty-nine'.[13] That is also true of this small sample. Certainly, some began a journey of religious disorientation at university or shortly after graduation, but for others it came much later in their mid and even late twenties. Nevertheless, all described the experience of their worldview gradually unravelling until they could no longer maintain the façade, as one put it, 'of being a good Christian'.

The integrity of apostasy

For all six there came a point at which integrity demanded they acknowledge their lack of belief. None made this transition lightly, but all (again mirroring wider research) expressed some measure of relief that they were no longer having to pretend.[14] Three described conducting a form of experiment to try and find the truth. Craig explained:

> In my science head I thought, *I'll try the Christianity route and see if it works.* Then if the evidence was that it was working, it was worth believing in and living. My next thought was, *I need to spend some time not being a Christian, and see what the effect of that is.*

It is easy to question what 'working' means, or whether he was just looking for an excuse for a period of libertine behaviour, but Craig appeared to be sincere in wanting to find what was true and then live by it. Zuckerman argues that many apostates are strongly moral and 'need to be true to themselves and adhere to their own consciences'.[15] Charlie had tried 'clinging to it [faith]' and hiding his doubts for a long time, but eventually wasn't willing 'to fake it to fit in'. Similarly, after several years of struggle, Pete said: 'I find it [apostasy] releasing if I'm honest, maybe for the first time in my life I'm being totally honest with myself.' Mark compared it to breaking up from a dysfunctional relationship: a mixture of sorrow and relief.

Disaffiliating from church

The relationship between these six and church was complicated but, typically, leaving was a lengthy process, with a gradual distancing from the community as their faith waned. Most felt this had gone largely unnoticed, matching the experiences of church-leavers in Scotland, where '[people] were quickly forgotten, 92% reporting that no one from the congregation had talked to them about why they were not attending during the weeks after their church-going ceased.'[16]

Two participants had relocated several times during their twenties. With each move, their faith and commitment decreased as they struggled to find a church that felt comfortable for them in a new area. Eventually, they had moved again and simply stopped attending. It took more emotional energy than they had to engage with a new church when their doubts were so pronounced anyway. A demanding new job and/or young family meant Sundays were precious recovery time from a hectic week, and there was no one to notice they were missing. The drift of circumstances is often much more significant than a self-conscious cognitive decision to abandon faith, but in these cases the two interacted and compounded each other. Many churches intentionally support new undergraduates leaving home for the first time, but these older Emerging Adults, without any support structures and with highly mobile lifestyles, are potentially just as vulnerable, particularly if their faith is hanging by a thread in the first place.

As Steve Aisthorpe found, change within a church is also a time when those with doubts may withdraw.[17] Changes in leadership and ethos had discouraged Mike (whose faith was faltering) from re-engaging when he returned to his hometown in his late twenties. Pete's church was meeting less frequently, so his departure was less noticeable. Change in leadership, alongside his own doubts, meant Mark had been looking for an 'out' from his church for some time. Although he had withdrawn from services, he continued to attend his home group. 'I really valued the community and there was [some] stuff that I believed, but actually I didn't like the church services. There would be times that I would literally turn up in time for coffee at the end.' He had even considered moving cities so that he could leave without causing offence. In the end, moving to a new house created a sufficient break to justify leaving in his own mind – although he still described it as 'sneaking out'. He was surprised by people's responses, given that he had been an active member for many years.

I think at that point I was expecting to have to do a lot of explaining and a lot of dealing with people having a negative response. Actually, a lot of people didn't really seem to care. That really confused me because, in my mind, if you really believe this then it's the most important thing by a million miles. So, if someone stops believing, or starts moving away [then] that's a really big deal. It was weird to me that people were just, 'Yeah, OK.'

Many of his friends had already left, and those who remained appeared unconcerned or unaware of his doubts and departure. Eight years later, he still receives members' emails and cannot face asking to be removed from the mailing list.

Charlie had not experienced disruption in either location or church, but the relocation of many of his close friends left him socially isolated. He also described a process of gradual withdrawal: 'I would be in church to think about things I was processing rather than be engaged with what was being preached. It was space to reflect and part of my routine.' Eventually he stopped attending and commented, 'Church-wise, it's very easy to withdraw.' He became emotional describing an individual he hadn't known well who had worked hard at maintaining social contact. Clearly, he was touched that they still cared.

Certainly, several had made lifestyle choices that their evangelical faith would have been at odds with. For some that was before they rejected their faith, after a long period of doubt and struggle. For others, it was afterwards. But all their accounts show that apostasy among Emerging Adults is a lengthy, gradual and isolating experience. These individuals were unwilling to pretend any longer; integrity meant they had to be honest about what they believed, and several described having found a measure of peace in that honesty. Nonetheless, losing their faith had been costly, particularly in relational terms.

The Price of Faith Loss

The emotional and social cost of apostasy

For all these young adults, the process of losing their faith had been distressing. Some people experience mild apostasy –

the rejection of a nominal faith. This typically has few social consequences and little psychological turmoil. However, transforming apostasy such as these six experienced is a life-altering and traumatic event. Four of the six became tearful during their interview, even several years after their de-conversion.

Although more sanguine than most, Mike was sad that his children would now grow up without the positive aspects of a faith community. Pete was angry, considering Christianity to be dangerous and his church responsible for much of the emotional turmoil of his twenties. He profoundly regretted his conversion and the choices he had made based on what he had believed God wanted. Now separated from his wife, his apostasy had freed him from what he perceived as the destructive control of church but left him in pain, without any meaningful support network.

Several of the others talked about the anxiety they had experienced at how friends and family would respond, one using the language of 'coming out' to describe the process. Craig, whose faith and mental health had disintegrated, explained:

> That was the first time I told my parents I wasn't a Christian anymore. That was really tough; it was a really big step. I was really down ... I'd been trying to tell them for a while, because I had no idea how they'd respond [but] they were lovely – they just loved me. It was hard to believe, given the state that I was in. I thought I was useless at everything. Stupid as it sounds, I thought they would turn their back on me. It's ridiculous really, but it's what I thought at the time.

Although his family had been supportive, Craig is now divorced and, having intentionally isolated himself, maintains few relationships with his former church friends.

Sarah said: 'It was in [city] that I came out as not being a Christian anymore. I hadn't considered myself a Christian for several months before I told anybody. I was terrified about telling my brother. I went to dinner with him and told him. He said, "You will always be my sister and I will always love you." Actually, he's never brought it up since.' She also wrote a blog, explaining to her friends why she could no longer call herself a Christian. The responses she received were kind, although she too has little contact with them now. She became emotional explaining that she had distanced herself, believing that they wouldn't want to be friends now she had rejected their formerly shared faith.

It seems that few Christians stay in touch with apostate friends. I had assumed that snowball sampling would provide me with apostate research participants (namely Christian participants would be able to put me in touch with their ex-Christian friends). Almost everyone I interviewed had friends who had rejected their faith. Few of them were still in regular contact. Most did not report hostility in that loss of contact, more a drifting of relationship as they no longer saw each other at church. It appeared that to avoid conflict many had let those relationships become polite acquaintances or made assumptions that the other party would no longer want a close friendship with them. Either way, relational distance appears to regularly emerge if individuals become apostate.

Loss of meaning and framework

As well as social losses, there were also psychological costs. Although he reported being more at peace in himself now, Charlie reflected: 'My belief in God was such a positive thing for my well-being and how I felt. My life is less hopeful now. I don't approach it with the same purposefulness and meaning.' Change in belief and worldview has both freed and cost him.

Sarah, likewise, described feeling somewhat alone and adrift. 'I feel a bit of an anomaly, and a bit between worlds. A lot of my make-up as a person is very Christian, so I don't feel that I fit with the secular world and that standard.' Although now living with her boyfriend, she maintains a strong moral code rooted in her former faith, is profoundly humanitarian, and retains a deep hunger for spiritual truth. Other research has identified this pattern of keeping some of the values of a faith but rejecting the faith itself.[18] Sarah described how she reads Buddhist literature and had once attended a secular church – hungry for a community of people with a similar mindset.[19] Not having an outlet for her spiritual curiosity, a coherent worldview, or social framework to situate herself within was difficult. She explained:

> Christians are quite joyful people. Quite positive and accepting of things that happen in their lives. They see it as being part of [a] plan or as God being in control, which gives you a different way of approaching your life. Now I think, *If God isn't in control, if there isn't a path for my life, then how do I decide what to do? What am I going to use to steer myself?* Maybe what I miss is having a faith with other people around that.

It is hard not to feel compassion for these young adults whose lives have been turned upside down by their faith loss. Certainly, these are just the experiences of six individuals, but they show that for those who experience transformative apostasy, be it shallow (namely they still retain some form of spirituality) or deep (actively secular atheism), there are considerable costs. The journey is typically traumatic and often goes unnoticed by their church community.

What Caused this Faith Loss?

Kinnaman repeatedly reiterates the fact that every loss-of-faith journey is 'a mixture of unique and mundane reasons', and that would be true of these six.[20] However, he notes three distinctive factors that are the culmination of societal changes since the Second World War.

1 This generation has greater access to alternative worldviews than any previous group had.

2 Alienation from all forms of institution is at an all-time high.

3 Individuals are widely encouraged to reject authority, including that of spiritual leaders and the Bible.[21]

Zuckerman concurs, suggesting that personal morality and scientific learning are central to faith loss.[22] This sample illustrated that faith loss is indeed a complex process. However, there were three factors that had contributed to it. They varied in intensity or dominance, but were present in all six narratives:

• An existential reshaping of worldview;
• Experience of personal difficulty or trauma;
• Disillusionment or isolation from church.

An existential reshaping of worldview

It is true that today's Emerging Adults are exposed to a far wider range of worldviews than any previous generation. They are aware of the plethora of religious and secular perspectives on reality and morality and have grown up encouraged to be inclusive and tolerant of these. Likewise, valuing experience as authoritative (often over factual data) means decision-making is more complex that an examination of the data to which one then gives intellectual assent. Of course, there are Emerging Adults for whom logic, historical evidence and apologetics are central to their faith, but for many, personal experience is more important. Inevitably all this can make the creation of a stable worldview challenging. Which of the many options do they select, and on what basis do they do that?

Within this sample, exposure to a convincing alternative worldview caused participants to question beliefs they had never previously queried. Various things triggered this process: new relationships and professional environments or further study; a gap between their lived experience and belief system; or frustration at simplistic theological answers. The result was that eventually their faith no longer seemed credible. As Charlie said: 'The world made absolute sense to me up to 2010, and in a sense I consider that blissful ignorance because I hadn't appreciated or considered lots of what there is in the world that is real and exists. Life has gone from simple to complex – I have more information on the world. You can't unlearn things.' His understanding of Christian faith was that it was too simplistic for the complex world he was discovering. He no longer believes there is a God. Likewise, Craig concluded:

> I don't believe in God full stop. Whether it's a Christian god or any other religion. In my current thinking (although I'm not sure I'm happy with it – but it's where I am at the moment) I don't see the need to make up an extra construct to try and explain things, which is what Christianity was for me. There was this whole extra dimension that I ended up bolting on to my life as an add-on. I can't justify bolting on something that I don't think is true.

Some reinterpreted spiritual experiences within a rationalist framework. Charlie redefined his charismatic experiences as a psychological phenomenon of mass enthusiasm, similar to a football crowd, rather than a divine interaction. Mike likewise was sceptical of the emotionalism he had experienced at large youth events, considering it manipulative hype rather than the presence of God.

For others, new perspectives or relationships meant traditional doctrines presented ethical problems. As described in the last chapter, the experiences of Pete's own marriage and LGBTQi+ friends had caused him to reject Christianity as inherently oppressive. Sarah was concerned about the exclusivity claims of Christianity. While she very much liked Christian social activism, the doctrine of penal substitution and teachings on condemnation of the unsaved deeply troubled her. That God would exclude anyone was a problem that became more pronounced through her twenties until she acknowledged she couldn't believe in sin, judgement and Hell. Studying led Pete to reject his former understanding of the Bible.

You can't trust this! You cannot go into that [studying] and go, *This is what God says.* You just can't. It's a really interesting document, but it's not reliable in that sense whatsoever. I got really pissed off. People were saying, 'This is what it says in the Bible.' On top of all that [when someone preaches] you have got one person's view and all their cultural understanding. They read it and go, *This is what God is saying.* I could take the same passage and get something totally different. That was one of the starting points [in my faith loss]. I thought, *Actually I'm not sure how reliable this is and I'm really sick of people using it how they did.*

When asked whether they had considered pursuing a more liberal form of Christianity in the light of their ethical and theological concerns (as others within the research sample had), both Pete and Sarah had decided not to. Pete explained: 'Once I started down that line, the natural outcome is that God doesn't exist. It feels like double-thought to be more liberal about it; just believe certain bits of it and you don't have to believe that bit.' Sarah too felt that it was conservative evangelicalism or nothing. That was her definition of Christian – and she was not one. Craig and Charlie no longer believe there is a God at all, but Mike and Mark both explained that although they missed the community aspect of faith, they were comfortable in a place of agnosticism, liked not being constrained by religious boundaries, and had no desire to pursue any form of spirituality at present.

Although their journey had ended in different places, all six demonstrated some form of change in worldview – an existential and intellectual shift often shaped by dominant cultural narratives of pluralistic tolerance and rationalism. For half, it was towards a form of secular rationalism. While others were still open to the concept of a spiritual dimension to life, they were unclear as to what that might be. It was not, however, orthodox Christianity.

Experience of personal difficulty or trauma

Combined with this worldview reformation, all the participants described some form of profound personal difficulty.
Of course, for most people their twenties are a volatile and
unstable decade but for these individuals that struggle interacted with their existential questioning. Difficulties came in
various forms and differing intensities but included: mental
health struggles; family, relational or marital conflict (in two
cases divorce or separation); loneliness, social isolation and
difficulty with demanding workloads. For several this caused
intense self-reflection leading to counselling. This had resulted
in some cases in significant identity reformation and a move
away from the faith of their upbringing or youth. 'I realized I'm
just not that Christian person, not really. I've been pretending
to keep everyone around me happy' was how one phrased it.

Identity formation is well recognized as a central task of
Emerging Adulthood, and all the participants talked about
emotional problems in their twenties. However, for these six,
difficult events, along with intellectual and worldview reshaping, impacted how they understood themselves in a way that
undermined their faith. There is no obvious reason as to why the
faith of these individuals was negatively impacted when others
found that personal struggle caused theirs to deepen. Research
has shown that personal difficulties can inspire post-traumatic
faith growth as well as loss: 'In the most extreme instances,
highly stressful or traumatic events can lead people to over-
haul their religious beliefs, through rededicating themselves to
religious practice, adopting a new faith, or renouncing religion
entirely. Such dramatic shifts, however, are rare.'[23] However,
for these individuals, in combination with the profound worldview changes they were experiencing, their personal difficulty
was a compounding factor in their faith loss.

Disillusionment or isolation from church

The other significant issue that all these participants (perhaps unsurprisingly) described was a sense of isolation from a Christian faith community. Although not all were vitriolic about this (several said they missed the community), all six of these 'prodigals' expressed some sense of detachment, frustration or anger at the Church. Some were cynical about perceived abuses of power, financial priorities and neglect of the poor. They wanted churches to follow the example of Jesus and care for the poor more intentionally. Others were frustrated with changes of leadership and theological shifts and priorities that they felt neglected important doctrines or marginalized certain groups. Despite the attraction of large churches with significant numbers of peers, several identified the challenges of building meaningful relationships in those settings. Repeated relocation for work and the challenge of trying to find new faith communities left some isolated, processing their questions and struggles alone, or with equally sceptical friends.

There seemed to be a particular problem for those who had remained within small churches. The restrictive, insular nature of their faith community, and lack of exposure to wider theological perspectives as very young adults, gradually became claustrophobic as they got older and wanted more sophisticated answers to their questions. Similarly, the charismatic style that had once appealed to them gradually became problematic. Mark, who had long-term struggles with depression, found just attending a church that strongly emphasized prayer for healing destructive: 'They didn't really get the idea of lament. It felt like there was this whole group of people who were struggling with mental health issues, or their faith, or whatever, and the church as a community wasn't acknowledging that in the way they worshipped.' In the middle of mental health and marital problems, Craig 'put his faith on hold' in order to cope. He couldn't deal with the existential trauma of his doubts as well as everything else, and the emotive worship was too painful.[24]

Several of those who remained within their church community for quite some time, despite their doubts, described feeling unable to voice these doubts. Again, this parallels wider findings, and the question of whether individuals feel able, or are allowed, to do this is crucial.[25] Charlie's former church prides itself on its strength of community. It has a strong ministry to young adults, yet he still felt unable to speak up; there was no safe space to engage with his questions. Kinnaman comments:

> There is an isolating element to unexpressed doubt as well. When a person feels as though church is not a safe place to be honest, he or she feels compelled to pretend, to put on a show, which all too often results in a faith that is no more than skin deep. When young believers hang back, holding their doubts, concerns and disillusionments in private, they cut themselves off from leaders and peers who might help them deal with their doubts in a constructive, faith-building way.[26]

Some Conclusions

Kinnaman describes two types of prodigals:

- Head driven – those who have a rational, well-reasoned abandonment of faith.
- Heart driven – those whose deep wounds, frustration or anger shape their apostasy.[27]

That dichotomy does not quite match this sample. These individuals could all clearly and rationally articulate why they no longer believed in the God of the Bible or the Christian tradition of their youth, but they also had some sort of emotional pain that informed that intellectual shift. This was compounded by some level of disillusionment with church, either as a contributing factor or because it failed to help in processing the significant challenges and struggles of their twenties. These three factors were not equally weighted. For some, the intellectual reshaping of their worldview was the primary driver. For others, their negative experience of church was the dominant force. Ongoing personal struggle was the key issue in some cases, but nonetheless these themes were present in the accounts of all six participants.

However, to move from an apparently passionate adolescent faith to a place of apostasy is a long journey, and a frightening one. It often takes place in secret or at least among a very small circle of conversation partners. That two of these individuals are now divorced, and all of them are, to a large extent, isolated from their former networks, indicates the disorientation and social loss they have experienced. Indeed, at the time of interview, of the six, only one appeared to be completely at ease with their current circumstances. All the others were still trying to reform their identity belief system or life in some way.

It is easy to point fingers, and some participants did. They identified an individual or church community that they felt had failed or deceived them. However, it was also striking that often they chose not to look for help, or circumstances meant they were already isolated from potential sources of it. Other individuals in the project had also experienced some of these things and yet still maintained a faith. They had found a way to resolve their existential or theological concerns; had processed the struggle they experienced and found God with them in it. There is no obvious way to predict who will take which path. Temperament certainly plays a part, so do individual choices, circumstances and the health of relationships, but being aware of how that journey *can* commonly occur is helpful for those of us who are concerned about the spiritual well-being of young people.

Questions for Discussion

- How far do you recognize or identify with these stories of faith loss?

- What in them (if anything) strikes you as unique to this generation?
- How do you react to the evidence that it is often painful, lengthy and isolating to experience deep apostasy as an Emerging Adult?
- Why do you think it appears to be such a common occurrence that no one follows up on those who leave churches and that Emerging Adults often feel unable to voice their doubts in faith communities? How far would these things be true of your faith community?
- Given that disruptions (of location, relationship, leadership, etc.) appear to act as catalysts for faith loss and that change is frequent in Emerging Adulthood, how might faith communities help individuals to develop genuinely robust and resilient faith?
- Practically, what does loving those who choose to leave look like?

Notes

1 Phil Zuckerman, *Faith No More: Why People Reject Religion* (Oxford: Oxford University Press, 2012).

2 D. Voas and A. Crockett, 'Religion in Britain: Neither Believing nor Belonging', *Sociology*, Vol. 39.1 (2005).

3 Zuckerman, *Faith No More*, 5–7.

4 David Kinnaman, *You Lost Me* (Grand Rapids, MI: Baker, 2016), 130.

5 Zuckerman, *Faith No more*, 73.

6 G. Smith and L. Woodhead, 'Religion and Brexit: Populism and the Church of England', *Journal of Religion, State and Society*, Vol. 46.3 (2018), 206–23.

7 Andy Frost, *Losing Faith: Those Who Have Walked Away* (Milton Keynes: Authentic, 2010).

8 Mathew Guest et al., *Christianity and the University Experience: Understanding Student Faith* (London: Bloomsbury Academic, 2013), 119.

9 Alan Jameson, *A Churchless Faith: Faith Journeys beyond the Church* (London: SPCK, 2002), 32.

10 Zuckerman, *Faith No More*, 35.

11 Steve Aisthorpe, *The Invisible Church: Learning from the Experiences of Churchless Christians* (Edinburgh: St Andrew Press, 2016), 47.

12 Tim Clydesdale, *The First Year Out: Understanding American Teens after High School* (Chicago, IL: University of Chicago Press, 2007); Guest, *Christianity and the University Experience*, 90.

13 Kinnaman, *You Lost Me*, 29.

14 Zuckerman, *Faith No More*, 32.

15 Ibid., 38.

16 Aisthorpe, *The Invisible Church*, 11.

17 Ibid., 63.

18 Frost, *Losing Faith*, 73.

19 'Welcome to your London community', Sunday Assembly London, www.sundayassembly.com (accessed 06.09.19).

20 Kinnaman, *You Lost Me*, 91.

21 Ibid., 71.

22 Zuckerman, *Faith No More*, 35.

23 I. A. Gutiérrez and C. L. Park, 'Emerging Adulthood, Evolving Worldviews: How Life Events Impact College Students' Developing Belief Systems', *Journal of Emerging Adulthood*, Vol. 3.2 (2015), 85–97.

24 Frost also identified this in several of his participants, in *Losing Faith*, 6–7, 20–1.

25 Ibid., 127.

26 Kinnaman, *You Lost Me*, 193.

27 Ibid., 67.

7

The Disenchanted

'My faith in God is stronger. My faith in church has been blown to bits.'

These are the words of Greg, a young man who had chosen to remain in the town where he went to university because he was committed to serving the church there. Dynamic, with great people skills, compassion for the disadvantaged and a desire to see people meet Jesus, he had poured much of his time and energy into leading ministries to do that. A decade on, he still has a faith, but told me a distressing narrative of mistreatment and broken relationships. He wants a faith community, but admits to being sceptical that he and his family will be able to trust a church again. Honestly, given his journey, I don't blame him.

In 2016, Steve Aisthorpe described the experiences of considerable numbers of de-churched Christians in Scotland in *The Invisible Church*.[1] He built on work investigating the same phenomenon in New Zealand.[2] David Kinnaman refers to young Americans who fit this category as 'nomads' and James Bielo has examined those who he calls 'Emerging Evangelicals'.[3] He found their de-conversions are not a matter of jettisoning faith altogether: '[rather] they are a matter of self-consciously heightening religious devotion because they deem their religious lives wanting. They are still compelled by the hope and effectiveness of Evangelicalism; just not in the form they have learned it.'[4]

It appears that across the Western world there are significant numbers (including Emerging Adults) who are committed believers but for a variety of reasons do not affiliate with a church congregation. This research sample included ten young

English Christians who fit a broad category that might be labelled 'The Disenchanted'. It is not that they are disenchanted with God – far from it, what they are disenchanted with is church. Their stories are obviously unique, influenced by personal circumstances and individual responses to these, but they also show common patterns. Some describe their faith as 'more important', 'deeper' or 'stronger' than it had been aged 20; their disaffiliation matching Bielo's description above. Others used phrases like 'broader' or 'more liberal' to describe their faith having moved away from their evangelical roots. For some, faith is now deeply internalized rather than directed through religious activity, or else expressed in their professional life. Yet despite their complex relationship with organized Christianity, all of them understand their Christian faith as central to their identity and way of life. This chapter will explore their journeys.

Who Are the Disenchanted?

Given the prevalence of trans-denominationalism among younger generations it is not a surprise that there was no clear denominational pattern among the disenchanted in this sample. They came from a variety of backgrounds: Anglican, Methodist, Baptist, Conservative Evangelical and New Church. Three had come to embrace a meaningful faith in their early twenties but the others had been committed members of youth groups or student faith communities. Not only were they Active Affirmers as very young adults, but they had held leadership positions. Some had been salaried, others volunteered large amounts of time and energy. They had been youth workers, worship leaders, preachers and small-group leaders; in short, enthusiastic, core congregation members. Now in their early thirties, they fit three categories:

Withdrawing

Some were intentionally much less involved. One was 'taking a break' from church but thought she'd return at some point. Another had backed off, explaining: 'I'm not tired of God, but I'm tired of church; I feel invisible here and it's not impacting my life.' A third was returning after a hiatus, beginning to re-engage but cautious about overcommitting herself.

Disillusioned

Others, although still attending, voiced profound frustrations with church structures. One from a traditional denomination explained, 'I'm hanging on by my fingernails.' Some were still linked to a faith community by their spouse or endeavouring to reshape their church from the inside. Few had much hope they would succeed.

De-churched

A number had left altogether. Although they occasionally attended services, they did not see themselves as part of a worshipping community. Matching other research, their journeys of departure had been long and painful.[5] While sceptical about church structures, most still expressed a longing for a faith community in which they could feel comfortable.

Apart from their zeal as very young adults, the other factor that united all ten was how capable and articulate they were. Temperamentally, they were all influencers, initiators or leaders. Many were now in management roles and some had taken considerable professional and financial risks for the sake of their faith. A majority were pastorally concerned and had been (or still were) passionate about evangelism. In either academic or informal ways, they continued to wrestle with theological issues, question culture and structures – including ecclesiology.

It struck me that all could have been church leaders, although it seemed unlikely that many would consider that at this point. Instead, they were exerting what one described as 'kingdom influence' beyond the church walls.

All this raised two questions:

1 What had caused these able young leaders to become so sceptical about the churches they once served so diligently?
2 Why was it that they, unlike others, continued to maintain a meaningful Christian faith?

Detachment from Church

Much has been written about consumerist attitudes towards church, and Millennials are often accused of that (as they are of many things). Certainly, today's young adults rarely act out of a sense of duty as older generations might have, nor are they nominal churchgoers. However, many are deeply loyal to the values they do hold and people they care for. Obviously, these findings are not true of every Emerging Adult who has left church, but these participants had been strongly committed to their church congregations at one point; they were not consumerist church-hoppers or peripheral, occasional attenders. It had taken a lot to make them cynical about or detach them from that community. For none of them had there been just one event or issue. Typically, two or three factors informed and reinforced each other over a long period of time, pushing them towards, or beyond, the edges of their church. Among their accounts there were five recurring trends:

1 Aborted leadership;
2 Church conflict and resistance to change;
3 Relationship failures;
4 Theological tension;
5 Lifestyle conflicts and priorities.

Aborted leadership

As already mentioned, most of these young adults had held leadership roles of some sort. Several had understood themselves as being on some sort of informal leadership pathway. However, almost all described episodes that derailed that process, leaving them frustrated and hurt. One woman was asked not to make public contributions during charismatic worship because it upset her ex-boyfriend. Another stated: 'They said they valued me, but they didn't let me do anything. Because I was not a happily married couple, or into youth work, they didn't know what to do with me!' Others reported stories of mistreatment, miscommunication and even financial exploitation. These weren't single incidents, but rather patterns over long periods that eventually caused them to withdraw.

Neil spent several years working up to 50 hours a week for his church. He was committed and passionate but conflict over some of his more creative innovations, combined with the ongoing lack of a liveable salary, left him feeling exploited. Greg was being mentored for an eldership role after years of voluntary service. However, a change in leadership left him side-lined; his contributions were deemed superfluous to the new vision. Wendy became increasingly uncomfortable with the directive nature of small groups and was ostracized for asking challenging theological questions. Ed experienced a personality clash with the elders in his church. They shut down the ministry he had established, announcing it publicly to the congregation rather than discussing it with him first.

Unsurprisingly, these experiences made young adults sceptical of throwing themselves into further involvement. Of course, there are (at least!) two sides to every story and several reflected that their own behaviour had not helped. With hindsight, some could see why things had gone wrong and recognized that they had been hard to work with. However, at a time when they were exploring their identity and calling, these experiences had been deeply damaging. Their passion for Jesus meant they had wanted to bring positive change. Had they been better managed, or had communication been clearer, events might have turned out differently.

There are generational factors that might shine light on tensions like these. Where older generations rebelled against their elders, Millennials typically have a different attitude. More interactive forms of education and an egalitarian wider culture have encouraged their participation, and they are inclined towards collaborative engagement. Rather than dutiful obedience, they anticipate being listened to. Questioning, then, is not necessarily a challenge but a desire to understand. Typically, they want to work alongside elders to learn from them, but they also want to be taken seriously and to contribute. Thus, there is considerable scope for mentoring, mutual learning and partnership between generations.[6] However, if older believers feel disrespected or threatened, and respond by withholding opportunity or relationship, that rejection can cause young adults to withdraw. Certainly, they may be impulsive and immature – they are young after all! However, recognizing that young adult actions are often not rebellious may help older leaders to have grace and wisdom in engaging them constructively. Directing their enthusiasm helpfully, treating them fairly, and communicating well could have made a world of difference to these individuals. Indeed, one has found a church where he is being mentored, well managed, and his confidence is returning. It is taking effort on the part of those investing in him, but it is slowly rehabilitating his enthusiasm into something constructive.

Resistance to change and church conflict

Intergenerational conflict

There is nothing new about intergenerational tension within churches; younger generations have long been frustrated by the resistance of older people to change. What has exacerbated this more recently is the rate of change in wider society, which young adults – with greater brain plasticity – cope with better.

Their creativity, ability to think outside the box and willingness to try (and fail) are potentially helpful to the Church. Likewise, their understanding of technology and contemporary culture (which leaves many of their elders reeling) means they often recognize the need for new ways of engaging with unchurched portions of society.

A number of these participants described significant frustration at the reluctance of churches to adapt and thus be accessible to a post-Christian society. Explaining the realities of the 'memory-less' generation, who have little understanding of basic Christian doctrine, Penny explained:

> We've got so much on in life at this age. We are all trying to fill the jigsaw-shaped piece in our life that is missing. But [we] would never think of looking to the Church, or to God, because *I'm busy. Sunday morning I'm dealing with a hangover and even if I did come along, it is not at all relevant to me. I don't understand what you are doing.* My friends have told me, and I felt at the time [before I came to faith], that it was just an irrelevant tradition.

This desire for relevance causes much of the tension. Rick observed that small traditional churches are '[by] and large populated by people of grandparent and great grandparent generations, very small numbers [with] very little vision outside of the leadership'. He observed that older generations provide much of the finances and to his mind were 'paying to keep the status quo'. He considered that this creates:

> [A]n inertia that won't allow congregations to be challenged and changed. That's a massive disservice to an awful lot of faithful people who are so generous with what they have to give to the Church. I don't want to sound disrespectful, but there is an element that with that comes an expectation that this is *our* church. I'm not sure that is the clergy's fault. You see the guys who are going forward for ordination and they are by and large those who are really on fire for the Lord and

want to see change happening. They are committed to God's kingdom building and then they get put into a local church where it is, *This is how it has been for forty years; don't be coming in here with that idea!*

He, and another participant from a Methodist background, considered that New Churches were doing better because they were more likely to be 'permission giving'. They had friends who now attended them because of their willingness to try new things and allow younger people opportunity to lead. However, those in New Churches also described resistance to change. Diana reported the lack of enthusiasm, and extensive 'hoop jumping' required to instigate anything in her large New Church. Instead, she puts her energy into activity outside it. Ed had experienced older congregation members voting against his initiatives to evangelize local youth, and Neil's successful activities with young people had caused tension with older members. These frustrations were not, in themselves, deal breakers, but they were part of a larger perception that their vision and desire to reach beyond the Church were unsupported. Churches said they wanted to reach young people but weren't willing to be flexible to make that happen.

Church conflict

The other relational tension described was internal church conflict. Two individuals had experienced serious congregational division, which had done tremendous damage to their faith. Young adults within close-knit congregations often view leaders as spiritual parents, to whom they are deeply loyal. Church as family is a strong motif in many evangelical, non-conformist and new churches. Particularly if their own parents are geographically distant or don't have faith, this is deeply appealing to young adults, and church genuinely becomes a second family. Conflict within that is therefore experienced as family breakdown and church splits as a form of divorce. Of course, conflict within church is difficult for the whole community, but just because young adults are not directly involved doesn't mean they're not affected. For a generation that places such high value on authenticity of faith and is looking to their elders to see that modelled, seeing them deal poorly with conflict can profoundly undermine their attitudes towards church; even if they remain committed to God.

Relationship failures

Perhaps the two most commonly used words across all the interviews were 'authentic' and 'community'. 'Genuine', 'sincere' and 'relevant' also ranked highly. This prioritizing of mean-ingful relationships is widely reported across research into millennial values.[7] Repeatedly, individuals described groups of peers who were functioning as surrogate families, and older friends who they deeply appreciated. Christian young adults (who by virtue of their faith are a minority) long for a faith community that models hospitality and demonstrates sincere, life-giving faith outworked. They want to know how to be disciples of Jesus in their everyday lives, and many have not seen that modelled well in their biological family. For those in this disenchanted category, disappointment in relational areas was often a compounding factor in their disillusionment with church. Hospitality, pastoral support or genuine community had been lacking at crucial moments. Several described attend-ing traditional churches where there had been little community and no peers. Mel had subsequently found a church that had impressed her:

> Everybody was friendly and there were lots of families. The way they spoke about God, they were so open and spoke about their faith and what living it out on a day-to-day basis meant. It wasn't a case of stand up when you are told to stand up and sit down when you are told to sit down and sing a hymn in between. It was people coming to be fed and going out to live their lives. It was amazing; people were

really honest about their flaws and failings. The minister was a gentle, lovely man who supported me and my family.

Problems had started during an interregnum when she experienced a traumatic bereavement and serious work problems. For a variety of reasons, she felt unsafe expressing her emotions on Sunday and began to absent herself. No one from the church followed up on how her family were coping, leaving her hurt and isolated.

Penny, who was exploring faith at the time, described the following experience:

> A couple of times I'd gone to a church to try to find something. I went to the church near the end of my road to see what it was like. I walked in and they were already halfway through. Everybody looked at me. I sat down and then after the service nobody came anywhere near me. Eventually somebody came up to ask me if I was there to book a wedding. I was like, 'No'. They said, 'Aw, ok', and then just walked off.

The second time she attended a local parish church no one spoke to her at all. She eventually met someone at a social event who invited her to his New Church, where she came to faith. Even there, 'I really struggled because North East families are so close. The chat after church would be, *I've got to head off because the whole family is coming round for Sunday lunch.* I was putting something in the microwave because I don't have family up here.' Apparently, even in a family-orientated church she was rarely invited to join biological families. She is currently attending a traditional church but frustrated by missed opportunities to engage the unchurched.

> There's this lovely couple who are getting married. The other week we had a baptism of thirteen Iranians, the licensing of a Reader, a Eucharist, a Bishop, and a Partridge in a Pear Tree! The service went on for an hour and a half and it was just ritual after ritual after ritual. Don't get me wrong, I appreciate

the liturgy, but this guy had an Apple watch so he can be on Facebook without anyone noticing. I'm sat there thinking, *This is not what God is all about.* They've got massive issues going on [and] have to come to church for a year in order to get married there. We've got this amazing opportunity, and nobody knows how to engage with them. They say they are welcoming but if you are not over seventy or Iranian (and the Iranians welcome themselves) nobody even bothers!

Again and again these young adults told me stories of being ignored in all varieties of church. One couple, new to the country and homesick, described attending a New Church.

We were joking about it earlier; it feels as though we took an invisibility pill before the Sunday service. Everyone is friendly and would say 'Hello', but we needed [to build community] from scratch. People are nice to you but it doesn't go any deeper. It's been hard for us to make friends. We didn't understand what was wrong with us. We always needed to start the conversation; it was tough. Going to church, sometimes tired, you'd think, *For goodness sake people! Can somebody come to us rather than us going to them?* We felt like we were invisible in church.

This is a profound problem, particularly for young adults who have relocated. They are looking for meaningful relationship to sustain their faith at a vulnerable life stage. All these individuals wanted to belong and were willing to serve, but had left Sunday services feeling more alone than when they arrived. Even for some of those who were more socially integrated there was a frustration at superficiality. They wanted deep relationships rather than just meeting at specific church functions. Greg reflected:

I think the whole format of [midweek] groups doesn't work that well. My impression is that they are trying to be a discipleship/accountability sort of thing, but in groups like that, people don't want to open up. You're lucky if people will really open up to one person. It's a way of keeping an eye on how people are getting on, but actually you can sit in that group and make up whatever you want and not tell anyone the things you are struggling with. You are normally put in a group. There might be two or three [people] you really get on with. It's awkward. Those groups are so forced, so structured and rigid and never achieve what they want. Just scrap the structure, have half-and-half of just getting to know each other and then pray. Genuinely do life together!

That desire for space to talk about real joys, struggles and faith questions came up repeatedly. Rick wanted someone to care that he was struggling with depression, not just wonder when he'd be well enough to rejoin a rota, and Oliva described the pain of being the only childless couple in her small church: 'Occasionally new couples would join the church and we'd think, *Have they got children? Oh, damn it – they have!* We just felt like we desperately wanted friends who were like us. It was such a family-orientated church that we really struggled.' The pastoral support she received was less than helpful – exhortations that her prayers would be answered and prophecies of impending motherhood. When it got too painful and she began to absent herself, members questioned her husband – adding pressure to their already struggling marriage. Failure to support her after emergency gynaecological surgery was the final straw.

We were at a wedding and the church leader didn't speak to me. We'd known each other for a long time, and he didn't speak to me and he hadn't been to see me post-surgery. I felt that I had given all this time to his bloody church and he couldn't even be bothered to come and have a cup of tea. I spoke to him later that year and I told him I had seen him at the wedding, and he hadn't spoken to me. He said, 'I just didn't know what to say to you.'

These are young men and women journeying through one of the most demanding of life stages, trying to establish identity, family, career, a faith to live by in an aggressively secular society. Breakdown in relationship is at the core of their disillusionment with church. Had they felt supported, included and loved, then perhaps the other contributing factors would have been less pronounced.

Theological tensions

Being a young Christian in contemporary Britain is challenging. Most are very aware that they are a minority and considered odd for having religious beliefs at all. Not only are they trying to undertake the normal developmental tasks of identity and worldview formation, but they are doing so within a culture that is shifting in myriad ways at great speed. Inevitably this amplifies theological questions. Many participants talked about the theological tensions they experienced. Some had managed to resolve those, others had not. For the most part the disenchanted cohort had found ways to do so but this often involved moving away from their church tradition.

The attraction of certainty and challenge of complexity

Broadly speaking there were two noticeable trends in the theological journeys of the disenchanted. One was a move towards evangelical or charismatic forms of faith in their teens or early twenties. Half of these individuals had grown up in mainstream Anglican, Catholic or Methodist traditions but made this transition. It was usually because a friend had taken them to a youth event with lively worship where faith had been articulated in a way that made more sense than their traditional upbringing. As has already been mentioned, the pull of a peer group and involvement in a 'plausibility shelter' should not be underestimated but, within that context, they had found a faith they could understand, own and be enthusiastic about.[8]

The second pattern was that as they got older, and life became increasingly complicated, their teenage answers often no longer sufficed. Wrestling with mental health problems, bullying at work, fertility, bereavement, and family breakdown made them ask questions around God's sovereignty and benevolence. As Sharon Parks comments: 'Faith must stand up under the test of the truth of lived human experience.'[9] As prayers appeared to go unanswered and they recognized complications around Scripture, several began to doubt what they had been taught about divine intervention. As with those who had become apostate, some wondered whether it was acceptable to voice doubt, or to ask difficult questions. A number had experienced a sense of disapproval for pushing beyond 'normative' answers. Neil had felt that:

> There's an insular pattern of certain questions and answers – you have to come to a particular answer. I found my church less and less able to cope with my wrestling. I was quite difficult, people were trying to show me affection, but they didn't really get my questions or where I was coming from. Asking those questions really pushed me to the edge of the community.

Several complained that Sunday teaching was repetitive, presenting simplistic answers rather than dealing with deeper questions. One woman from a charismatic church stated:

> I know that not everything is black and white. It's difficult to blame the teaching – it is what is it – but it's not impacting my life. Because I've had an anxiety disorder from 2007 until now, I just don't believe in sudden changes. I think it takes time, and you don't need to change things quickly. I started to realize that life is a bit more complicated than just, 'Pray to love God more; pray to change your life right now.'

Theresa's long-term mental health struggles also conflicted with the 'world of certainty' of her charismatic evangelical church. She was concerned about the effects 'black and white' teaching had on the pastorally vulnerable. Similarly, Wendy's discomfort with strong pastoral control and emotive worship in her Pentecostal church grew over time: 'The emotional highs and lows of that church still take their toll now. It was so emotive, you were either literally dancing in the aisles or you were on your knees in tears. You had an "experience" every single Sunday. When [I left and] that stopped it meant, as far as I was concerned, that I wasn't connecting with anything, because church didn't rock my world anymore.'[10]

Mel was processing disappointment with God: 'When you've been so convinced that God has a plan, you imagine that the end of his plan is a happy one. I honestly thought [name] was going to be saved and then he was going to be this amazing testimony. I imagined there was going to be this huge conversion of the working class in our town. That was really hard when it didn't work out like that. It made me feel like I didn't want to be put in that position again. I'd always been passionate about evangelism and seeing people saved. After [he died] I've just backed off from that.'

Understanding that life is complex, and theology nuanced, is a normal part of Emerging Adult development. The emotional and personal problems this disenchanted cohort experienced were not unique (although for many they were profound and long term). What they were particularly concerned with were the limitations of the theological framework they were presented with. Often deep thinkers, they were living with the tension of personal difficulty and searching for a plausible, meaningful faith to live by. There were significant wrestles as to how they could continue to belong to faith communities that were not engaging with those questions in an honest or helpful way. As Parks states: 'Over and over again life will require the encounter with the unexpected. Again and again, we undergo the loss of our most cherished patterns of meaning and anchors of trust as we discover their insufficiency. Mature faith knows that the forms of faith are finite – but the promise is kept.'[11] What these Emerging Adults were hungry for were acknowledgments that their patterns of faith and spiritual anchor needed to change and help to make that happen.

Changing culture and sexual ethics

Another recurring theological tension was around sexual ethics. This is clearly a pressing issue both within wider culture and the Church in general. Millennials have been strongly socialized into a wider culture of tolerance, inclusivity and non-judgementalism rather than a world of objective or externally sanctioned morality.[12] As explored in Chapter 5, for a number, attitudes towards LGBTQi+ rights, and sexual ethics in general, were a part of their problem with church. Penny had left a church because their conservative views on homosexuality would have made her friends feel unwelcome, and Wendy didn't want her child exposed to what she perceived as prejudiced views within the congregation. Her comments typify millennial attitudes:

> It's not so much what is said from the front in terms of the pastor or preacher but some of the other things that are said or preaching done under the guise of prayer. I struggle with some of the intolerant 'Can we please pray about stopping whatever', be it abortion or gay rights or whatever. I know what I would, or wouldn't, do myself, and I believe my relationship with God influences what is right for me. But I'm not sure I have the right to dictate what that should or shouldn't be for anybody else. I want my daughter to learn that church is about loving everyone.

Olivia, now divorced and cohabiting with her boyfriend, considers that showing compassion to others, pursuing justice, and having a deep personal faith are more significant than her relational circumstances. This move towards a more permissive form of Christian faith reflects wider societal changes and a preference for personal ethics over established teaching, alongside the trend towards less conservative views among younger Christians. Olivia's views and cohabitation were rare within this sample, but a third of all the participants mentioned their concerns around church attitudes towards homosexuality.

Lifestyle conflicts and priorities

A final pattern was that other things had taken priority over their former zeal for church activity.[13] Wendy had decided to prioritize her child's sport activities over attending church. She reflected that this wasn't ideal but she didn't want her child to grow up seeing God as a kill-joy who prevented her from doing activities she loved. Her deeply held, long-established faith was sustaining her for now, and she was teaching her daughter about faith independently. Similarly, Greg and his wife were concerned to protect their children from what they saw as a toxic environment. They had found a new passion for sports, which often occupied their weekends, and were enjoying being able to visit their parents rather than serve on a Sunday. Others talked about their struggles to attend midweek evening groups as new parents or with demanding jobs and (somewhat sheepishly) admitted to preferring a Sunday-morning lie in.

Given their former commitment, it seems likely that, had they not already been struggling with theological, relational or ecclesiological issues, these young adults would not have prioritized leisure activity over church. As it was, other options were more attractive than attending a church where they struggled.

Sustaining and Developing Faith

So how is it that, when they are so disillusioned with church, these individuals have held on to and even deepened their Christian faith? Most described it as more profound than it had been in their early twenties, and the following trends emerged from their accounts:

1 Early wrestling with faith;
2 Theological changes;
3 Sources of faith community beyond the Church;
4 Perceptions on ministry and vocation;
5 A period of absence to recover.

Early wrestling with faith

Although not unique to this group, one factor was that the faith of their early twenties was not necessarily inherited. Four came to faith as teens from unchurched or nominal backgrounds. Their faith was personal and transformative, and they often described significant (positive) changes in their well-being as a result. Four more had made a distinct break away from the church tradition they had grown up with. It seems possible that having already wrestled with questions of faith at a younger age had insulated them from some of the existential dilemmas the faith-loss group experienced. Certainly, they reported having doubts, disappointments and questions, but it seemed that perhaps having already engaged with these once meant they understood them as part of Christian faith rather than a problem with it. Neil was enthusiastic about the importance of allowing young people to wrestle and question:

> For a lot of young people, in wanting to give them the best start in life, uncertainty gets closed down too quickly in church. It almost seems that it is OK to ask questions as long as you arrive at the 'right' answer. We need to allow people to carry on questioning stuff, otherwise you end up with a dual system where people publicly say the right things and that becomes separate from their private life.

Theological changes

Broader faith

Second, several explained that they had discovered theological resources that allowed them to make sense of the challenges they were experiencing. For example, two young women experienced serious health issues and found the emotionalism of their charismatic churches overwhelming; Sundays were exhausting and traumatic.[14] Both described finding a new spiritual resource within liturgical worship. The familiarity, repetition and non-emotionalism had felt safe and comforting. This, combined with academic study, meant they had found a more cerebral and theologically liberal form of faith. Both commented on how their younger self would be disapproving of the faith they now held, but it had allowed them to find a place of peace within a broader Christian tradition rather than reject it altogether.

Several others talked about accessing a wider range of theological traditions, be it through books, podcasts or other networks that nurtured their personal faith. A number referred to the influence of Richard Rohr, Brian McLaren, feminist, liberationist or Celtic spirituality. They had found a more reflective or intellectual tradition helpful in providing answers. As James Bielo noted in the United States, living within a pluralistic culture with unprecedented access to other worldviews has created the ability to explore theological alternatives and diverse spiritual resources. Several in this cohort had done just that.[15]

Again, paralleling American research, frustrations with what were perceived as restrictive or exclusive doctrines had caused individuals to explore a variety of alternatives to evangelicalism.[16] As already mentioned, Penny left the church where she came to faith partly because, wanting answers to complex questions, she felt a pull to more intellectual faith, and partly because she felt unable to invite her gay friends to attend. Although she feels her friends would be welcome at the more liberal church she attends, she can't imagine them finding much of relevance to their lives there. Neil is particularly passionate about politics and justice for the marginalized. He reads widely and is ecumenically engaged, but wanted deeper answers and greater social activism than the church he attended was willing to engage with. Having 'deconstructed' her evangelical faith, Theresa was struggling to reconstruct a meaningful way of engaging with God in the sleep-deprived haze of young motherhood. She hoped to manage that eventually.

It seems clear that a proportion of young adults, in seeking a faith that makes sense of their intellectual questions and lived experiences, move from a charismatic or evangelical faith into something broader. They are more than happy to access diverse faith resources and form a theologically eclectic patchwork of Christian practices. Why these individuals had done so when others instead rejected Christian faith altogether is not clear. However, for these Emerging Adults, broader theological forms had sustained their faith in God – if not in church.

Changing perspectives of God

Alternatively, there were also those who retained a recognizably evangelical form of faith but had somehow worked through their disappointments with God (if not the Church). For example, Greg still holds orthodox evangelical beliefs but described his theological reflections on the events that pushed him away from church: 'I link it to the fact that people are sinful. It's not God's fault people are sinful. I believe that God is all powerful and can do what he wants, but I'm more of the theology that he allows us [to] have free will and [that's why] bad stuff happens. I don't hold God responsible for what people at church did.'

Wendy, similarly, described her perspective on the failure of her marriage: 'I've never pinned it on God. God has got nothing to do with it. I'm not saying he couldn't have zapped [my ex-husband] into submission; I believe he has the power to do that, but why would I want a husband who is only with me because he has been forced to be a puppet? I don't think it ever entered my head to pin it on God. He's got, in the nicest possible way, very little to do with it.'

Another woman from a Reformed background explained: 'I hadn't lost my faith. I had never not believed in God. I don't know why I would get pregnant so many times and lose each in such horrible ways, but I think I've come to the conclusion that God is just not in control of the world like that. That it is neither his fault, nor could he have stopped it. It's probably the only way that it can make sense to me moving forward.'

There had been a process of detaching God from the source of their struggle and a move towards a more Arminian theology, or a form of open theism. This mirrors research from America where, for those who have made a theological transition towards open theism: 'The belief that suffering is random and God cannot foresee it, facilitates their ability to maintain a positive image of God, thereby avoiding the spiritual struggle concomitant with blaming God for misfortune.'[17] By their early thirties, these participants had developed an understanding that God was with them in their pain rather than responsible for it.

Several also described themselves as being less dogmatic around the intersection of science and faith. Greg was happy that all healing was God's work, whether it was overtly miraculous, through medicine, or 'the wonders of the human body'. He was sceptical about those claiming simplistic healing formulas and more interested in just making people's lives better. Wendy, similarly, wasn't bothered about apologetic questions around creation and science; a vague 'God's involved somehow' was sufficient for her. In other words, divine action could be a mystery; her faith was sufficient to withstand the tension of not fully understanding.

Sources of faith community beyond the Church

A third source of faith resilience for this group was support they had received from individuals outside their church.

Believing spouses

As mentioned in Chapter 4, for a number, that key encourager was their spouse. Although often disillusioned with church themselves, the couple had functioned as a unit to encourage each other's faith. Rick described his wife as profoundly instrumental to his faith. Even though they were both frustrated with church, she continued to inspire him as a disciple of Jesus. Theresa's husband had been her rock through her mental health struggles. His faith anchored her to church while she explored other faith-related spaces. Greg and his wife often create a 'Sunday school at home' for their children, teaching Bible stories and praying with them. Certainly, a believing spouse is no guarantee that faith will continue, and if that relationship is struggling it can make things worse (as the faith-loss group illustrate). However, a positive marriage to another believer seems to help sustain and deepen faith.

Kindred peers

Several of the participants described friendships with other similarly disillusioned individuals.

> At [X Church] which we visited for a while, we met another couple in a similar situation. He had been badly treated by another church in a different way. They were a little bit further on from us, probably by a couple of years, but they still haven't found anywhere [to settle] either. They are really good people. You find there are really good people who can't seem to settle anywhere. Some of it is not wanting to trust when you've been hurt before.

Rick had found a church that, although not ideal, contained a number of young adults with similar experiences of being 'battered by leadership roles in various denominations'. They have formed a mutually supportive community. He explained:

> It felt like we were all a bit broken and we were all there

going OK, *we have been broken but we are on the mend, but we still need to work out what on earth we are going to do with all this, and how we use it to help other people.* There's a whole load of people who are similar ages to us all going *We don't get church, but for whatever reason we are all here and trying to unpack this together at the same time.* Out of that comes a better awareness of how we do church moving forward. My real desire is to work towards that.

Unmarried individuals in this group also described the importance of kindred peers. Penny described how she prays at 6 a.m. every weekday morning with friends. That, and volunteering with a para-church group, are sources of fellowship and spiritual input that she does not receive on Sundays. Olivia had been invited to an ecumenical group by a colleague and found a faith community of women students. Where many of the faith-loss group had found themselves isolated (or intentionally isolated themselves), most of these 'disenchanted' individuals had gone looking for, or just found, like-minded Christians and formed communities beyond the walls of established Church. Repeatedly, individuals described others they occasionally, or regularly, met with to share fellowship, pray and discuss faith. It had been a vital factor in their faith continuing and deepening.

Older supporters

A number also described supportive relationships with older believers: college tutors, line managers, older clergy they had met. Oliver Robinson argues: 'The social emotion of admiration plays a crucial role through this period; an admired older person can act as an encouraging, realistic and stable ideal of positive attributes to be emulated or approached for guidance through this changeable and unstable part of the life span.'[18] That was certainly true in these cases; such mentors not only modelled faith, but exhorted them to pursue Christian service of some sort.

Penny had received vocational advice from a clergywoman she 'just happened to meet'. Rick's line manager, who he described as 'a spiritual dad', had inspired him: 'He said, "Don't worry about what the Church is doing as an institution. It's a huge organization and it has got things it has to do in order to operate. What can you do to represent the Kingdom of God rather than worrying about that? If enough people are doing that it will impact the Church on a larger scale." I found that really helpful. I still have a love/hate relationship with the institutional Church.'

Olivia's conversation with a retired canon, who couldn't use the world 'almighty' to describe God after his wife's and daughter's experiences of breast cancer, was liberating. She explained, 'It was the first time I'd heard a Christian leader be so openly honest about where he struggled with his own faith. It was just so good to hear, because that's where I was. It was so real. He was a priest and he was doing OK. I suddenly thought, *Maybe my faith can look different? Maybe it doesn't have to look the way it was always supposed to look?*'

Just as peers had made them feel less isolated and had created alternative faith communities, relationships with elders were a lifeline, creating some level of connection to the wider Church. It was evident that few of the ten in this group wanted to be isolated from Christian community; they were just fearful, sceptical or demoralized by organized church. Their faith had continued to grow and develop in part because somewhere in their journey, they had found fellowship of some sort and ongoing religious socialization.

Perceptions on ministry and vocation

A final pattern that emerged from the stories of this cohort was that the majority had found meaningful ways to express their faith beyond church. Although, for some, faith was more private, for the majority the energy they had once poured into church activity was now exerted in their professional lives, which they often described as a form of ministry. Transforming people's lives was an extremely common rationale for their chosen profession. Ed explained why he had changed from a sales career: 'I noticed a customer come in who was autistic. He was being taken advantage of. My manager said, "Sell him everything because he'll just accept it." I said, "No, I'm not doing that." I think maybe that started my commitment to disabled people and wanting to help them. It just opened my eyes to how vulnerable they are.'

Greg articulated clearly how his faith outworks professionally: 'What I love doing is helping people, and I am able to. The only downside is, I can't say, "God loves you and he made you." I am giving them the boost to move forward in their lives. Because their lives shrink down to their health, they are bound by the pain that is controlling them. Unfortunately, I can't attach God to it, but I do feel that we are massively changing people's lives. I have less time for church things, but I'm having an impact on people's lives and I'm loving having that opportunity.'

Diana likewise stated: 'I tried to do a few things in the church and some happened, some didn't, so I'm now quite relaxed about being involved in church. If I'm passionate about something, I can do it outside church. I'm working with a lot of people with complex needs; I don't want to work with people with complex needs within church as well.'

That sense of vocation resonates with the literature around young adults as altruists.[19] For most, salary was far less important than a sense that they were making a difference to people's lives. Yes, there was a need to pay the bills, but several had taken significant financial risks, or put aside professional development for a sense of calling from God. Many were deeply passionate about their local community, either in terms of meeting socio-economic needs or evangelization of the unreached, be they young, poor, marginalized, gay or vulnerable. The faith of many in this cohort was clearly in action – out in the community.

A period of absence to recover

One final observation on these ten was that for most (though not all), being outside or on the fringes of church was an intentional withdrawal to recover from conflict or disappointment. They had needed some time and space away from responsibility and organized religion. In the midst of demanding jobs, young families and emotional turmoil, particularly when they had previously been so heavily involved in church activity, some felt they needed a sabbatical. One woman explained:

> I'm tired, physically and emotionally. Part of me says I should be topping myself up more by going to church more because I know it's one of the ways that I would get that strength. But I don't have the resources with which to do that at the moment. It will get to the point where the levels of not wanting to go to church versus needing to go to church will tip and I will start to miss it. It might not be my old church. I stroll into town once a month because I can just pop in, not have to commit to anything, sit in a pew, get my fix and leave again. It is a selfish Christianity, and it isn't what I subscribe to. I think it is important to be part of a family, but I think I need to be mindful of what we need. I've done my bit for a lot of years and so I'm justifying to myself the need to be a little bit selfish for a little while and see how it goes out the other side. I'm not walking away from God. If anything, I'm walking away from church for a little while, but not for any malicious or nasty reason, just life.

Some overtly recognized that it was good for their faith to be regularly attending a church, and were heading back in that direction. Mel explained: 'I retreated. Not going [to church], though, absolutely did not help how I felt. When the new minister invited us round my husband and I said, "OK, we need to go back." So we have and they've been really supportive.' Space to process and recover from disappointment and bereavement, combined with the gentle encouragement to re-engage, had been enough for Mel, although she was still cautious.

Olivia initially found the anonymity of leaving her evangelical church and attending a Catholic one helpful. However, as she recovered from personal trauma and theological confusion, the anonymity became a problem. As she felt better, she wanted community again, something she is still looking for. Greg still wants a church where people are prioritized over programme and recognizes: 'There's never going to be a perfect church out there, and I know that, but we haven't found a church that resonates, or fits, or gets us. If we moved away it would be a fresh start and we would find it a lot easier.' Finally, Rick, despite his frustrations, considers that moving beyond church is risky. He was honest enough to say that he has stayed because he is fearful to leave, but added:

> I feel very strongly that we need to be rooted in something bigger in Christian life. I think there is more potential for us heading off on some 'interesting' path and maybe even straying into some stuff that is not healthy. For all its faults and failings, at least we know that theologically we are on orthodox ground by being rooted in institutional churches. Theological integrity and accountability and loyalty are key things.

Overwhelmingly, most of these disenchanted young adults want faith community. Their personal faith is still intact, sometimes thriving, shaped differently and sometimes a bit battered, but Millennials are profoundly aware of the value of relationship. They want authentic church where real life is shared and people are sincere about their joys, struggles, hopes and doubts. They are hungry for relationships that will contribute to living out their faith in a strongly secular culture, and are willing to serve the Kingdom of God rather than the structures of institution. Penny put it this way:

> I find church, even modern churches, pretty dull and boring, but I find God and Jesus really exciting. The two just somehow don't seem to translate to each other.

Questions for Discussion

- How far do you identify with or recognize these patterns and tensions in your own faith journey? Why have you chosen to leave/remain within a church community?

- Do you consider Millennial desire for a radical, authentic faith and altruism in faith communities to be youthful idealism and naivety, or something more significant for the Church and society? How might older generations learn from them?

- How far do you consider Emerging Adult desire (and expectation) to be involved in leadership a positive thing? How might youthful enthusiasm be valued, nurtured and developed in a constructive way?

- How might older generations model to and support Emerging Adults in processing their frustrations and doubts as life becomes complex and they have to deal with uncertainty and conflict?

- How far does your faith community model apologizing, forgiveness and reconciliation when things go wrong or mistakes are made? What effect would that have on the community if it were intentionally modelled?

- Who do you know who still has faith but is outside a faith community? How far have you really heard their story?

Notes

1 Steve Aisthorpe, *The Invisible Church: Learning from the Experiences of Churchless Christians* (Edinburgh: St Andrew Press, 2016).
2 Alan Jamieson, *A Churchless Faith: Faith Journeys beyond the Church* (London: SPCK, 2002).
3 David Kinnaman, *You Lost Me* (Grand Rapids, MI: Baker, 2011); James S. Bielo, *Emerging Evangelicals: Faith Modernity and the Desire for Authenticity* (New York: New York University Press, 2011).
4 Ibid., 30.
5 Jamieson, *A Churchless Faith*, 32.

6 James Lawrence, *Engaging Gen Y: Leading Well Across the Generations*, Grove Leadership Series, L8 (Cambridge: Grove, 2012).

7 Ibid., 81; Bielo, *Emerging Evangelicals*, 16.

8 Nick Shepherd, *Faith Generation: Retaining Young People and Growing the Church* (London: SPCK, 2015).

9 Sharon Parks, *The Critical Years: The Young Adult Search for a Faith to Live By* (San Francisco, CA: Harper & Row, 1986), 19.

10 J. K. Wellman et al. describe a phenomenon they call 'EE' – emotional energy, or a spiritual 'high', created in large, informal congregations. They do not preclude this being a numinous experience but consider it a factor in the growth of large congregations through which individuals feel inspired and empowered. '"God Is Like a Drug …" Explaining Interaction Ritual Chains in American Megachurches', *Sociological Forum*, Vol. 29.3 (2014), 652–3.

11 Parks, *The Critical Years*, 15.

12 Kinnaman, *You Lost Me*, 171.

13 Jeffrey Jensen Arnett also identifies this pattern in the USA in *Emerging Adulthood: The Winding Road from the Late Teens through the Twenties* (Oxford: Oxford University Press, 2013), 218–19.

14 Andy Frost also identifies this issue in *Losing Faith: Those Who Have Walked Away* (Milton Keynes: Authentic, 2010), 6–7.

15 Bielo, *Emerging Evangelicals*.

16 Kinnaman, *You Lost Me*, 173.

17 I. A Gutiérrez and C. L. Park, 'Emerging Adulthood, Evolving Worldviews: How Life Events Impact College Students' Developing Belief Systems', *Journal of Emerging Adulthood*, Vol. 3.2 (2015), 85–97, 92.

18 O. C. Robinson, 'Figures of Admiration in Emerging Adulthood: A Four-Country Study', *Journal of Emerging Adulthood*, Vol. 4.2 (2016), 82–91.

19 J. J. Arnett, 'The Dangers of Generational Myth Making: A Rejoinder to Twenge', *Journal of Emerging Adulthood*, Vol. 1.1 (2013), 17–20.

8

Reshaped Faith

In 20 years of ministry with Emerging Adults I have been privileged to know some genuine heroes of the Christian faith. There are young women and men I watch with pride (and sometimes awe) as they defy the statistical odds by continuing to follow Jesus through amazing highs and dreadful lows. Some of those I am most inspired by battle chronic illness or mental health problems and yet still trust God. Others have become people of great compassion and integrity, serving communities and making considerable sacrifices to do what they believe God has asked of them. Many have simply grown into devoted disciples of Jesus and are living their lives in the light of that.

The last two chapters have explored the experiences of those who have rejected their former faith entirely and those sufficiently disillusioned as to be entirely removed or peripheral to church despite their ongoing faith. This chapter will explore the experiences of those I interviewed who continue to have an active Christian faith and who were engaged with a church community at the time of interview. Unsurprisingly, they represented a spectrum of views, ranging from strongly enthusiastic through to those who were attending church out of commitment rather than great passion. One or two gave the impression that they might have tipped into the 'disillusioned' category if they'd been interviewed on a bad day but, as it was, they remained committed both to Jesus and a faith community.

Once again, each of their accounts was unique. Qualitative research does not look for formulas or try to predict outcomes, it involves closely listening to and valuing each person's journey. The aim of this chapter, then, is not to put people in boxes but rather to illustrate some of the broad trends and common patterns that emerged from just over 30 interviews. In a number of places, it will overlap with or expand on themes raised in earlier chapters to examine how these aspects of Emerging Adult faith work out in lived experience. First, it will pick up on some of the themes of Chapters 3 and 5, considering the influence of family background and a student (or equivalent) phase. Then it will reflect on how participants described their current faith in their thirties and what they believed had shaped that.

Starting Points

The influence of family

Almost all of these participants had some sort of churchgoing background: six were the children of clergy or church leaders; 14 described their parents as having a strong faith; ten had some sort of faith background and were taken to church as children (though this waned as they got older). Only two had come to faith without any form of family religiosity. Therefore, for most there was some sort of initial religious socialization and cognitive mother-structure, even if it had been nominal, intermittent or rejected at some point.

As introduced in Chapter 3, it is well documented that a sincere, active faith in parents can strongly influence their children, and siblings too can have an effect. Particularly if family relationships are warm and faith activity is seen as positive rather than coercive, Emerging Adults are more likely to internalize their family's beliefs and continue to live by those values.[1] Phil explained: 'My parents' example was a life that was wholly and completely about God and his mission. My dad has been a vicar for 27 years. He's always been passionate about the poor and seeing lives changed. I guess you can't shake that once you've got it!'

Others talked about their parents' ecumenism, encouragement to explore theology and read widely, or their consistent exposure to life-giving forms of religious activity. These patterns had created habits that, as adults, were firmly established as part of their spirituality. Many were now encouraging their own children to do the same.

Conversely, parental behaviour such as divorce or withdrawal from church had negative effects on their children's faith. Some described lengthy processes of disentangling their own beliefs from the tradition in which they had been brought up. A number had moved away from traditional, very conservative or extreme charismatic upbringings towards a different (often more moderate or contemporary) form of Christian spirituality.

Deborah was still trying to re-establish her own faith, which had been severely damaged by the semi-cultish faith community of her childhood and her father's dysfunctional behaviour. Others were critical of what they saw as hypocritical or nominal Christianity; where their parents or other churchgoers were not living out what they claimed to believe. Millennials have little truck with what they perceive as inauthenticity.[2] Danny described a cultural Catholic upbringing: 'My parents were traditional hardcore Catholics. I went to church every single Sunday as far back as I could remember. [But] I had never really experienced God in any shape or form. I didn't know if he was real. It was a fairy tale to me.' His discovery of charismatic Catholicism had been unpopular with his parents, but he described experiencing faith as inspiring for the first time.

Teenage faith experiences were equally diverse. Several remembered being bored by church. Often, they and their siblings were the only young people. By contrast, others described large youth groups, enthusiastic youth workers, summer festivals and Christian holidays. As already noted, being without peers is particularly challenging for teenagers. Developmentally their 'loci of authority' are external, meaning that they define themselves in relation to those around them.[3] Unsurprisingly, at the first opportunity, many were drawn to churches with large cohorts of peers. Having Christian friends for the first time was a life- (and faith-) giving experience and, as already described, those who discovered their own faith as teens typically did so in some sort of evangelical or charismatic context.

Research suggests that children with positive relationships and secure attachment to their parents are more likely to continue to share their beliefs.[4] As Chapter 3 described, rejecting the family's faith is a big decision and several of these participants reported that their choices were explicitly shaped by the potential consequences for family relationships. Some reported a period of 'double life': appearing compliant but having a secret second non-Christian existence. For the children of clergy, this pressure was particularly pronounced. One described spending all her early life feeling her actions must reflect positively on her parents, including following their faith. Another, after her first sexual relationship (which she kept secret) ended, explained the risks she had considered.

> I started thinking, *Actually, am I a Christian?* My parents had built their life on God and on faith. If I was going to go down the route of saying I wasn't, then that impacted on my future relationships; moving in with people and that kind of thing. It would have had a massive impact on my relationships with my parents.

This is part of a normal developmental process, the establishment of identity as independent of one's parents, but these individuals recognized the costs of breaking away from their family's faith. All of them had concluded that they *were* going to be Christians. However, for many, the next developmental phase had been crucial in consolidating that.

Early Emerging Adulthood: still a pivotal season

Despite evidence that identity and faith formation are often not fully achieved until much later than in previous generations, these accounts show that the late teens to early twenties is still a pivotal time for shaping faith. Chapter 5 began to explore some of the factors that influence the faith of those aged 17–22, but these accounts allow us to unpack that more fully. Nearly half of this cohort described this age as the period during which they decided to 'own' a Christian faith. Most had been university students, two-thirds describing participation in a Christian campus group. For many, this had been helpful: leading them to faith; providing a social network including meeting spouses; and giving opportunity to develop leadership skills. For a number, though, it had been theologically frustrating or socially isolating. Some described long-term damage to their faith, particularly in relation to assertive forms of Reformed conservative evangelicalism.

There were three particularly significant contributors to faith development at this age: peers, expanded horizons, and elders.

The importance of peers

Chapter 3 described the importance of friends during Emerging Adulthood more generally, but multiple participants told me stories of the Christian friendships they had made at university. In an American study, students reported that three-quarters of their religious experiences and discussions took place with friends.[5] These findings mirror the intensity of those relationships, with participants describing being inspired by those whose faith was more radical than their own, with whom they debated, prayed and engaged in other religious activity; learning together. A decade later, Phil still misses his 'band of brothers'. Alice and her female university friends gather regularly, from across the country, to pray, and Laura is godmother to the children of her Christian college friends. Now in their thirties, these young adults still identified how important those peers had been in helping them cement the belief system they still held. Research confirms that for Emerging Adults, healthy identity exploration also takes place within the context of secure friendships. Those who have intimate, secure peer relationships are most likely to form a strong sense of identity.[6] This in turn, helps with the formation of a coherent religious worldview. Close religious friendships are not just helpful, they are vitally important for young Active Affirmers.

As explored in Chapter 4, a quarter of participants followed the wider pattern of those in conservative religious groups by marrying at a young age. They had met their spouse as under-graduates and married them shortly after (or occasionally before) graduation.[7] These marriages were also significant in their ongoing faith, several describing the encouragement their spouse provided when their own faith was in turmoil, or they wanted to withdraw from church.

Expanded horizons

A second pattern was in the value individuals found in having their spiritual and theological horizons expanded. A gap year, or year abroad during their studies, had been significant for many (though often not easy). Opportunities to discuss beliefs that challenged what they had been brought up to understand, or to establish their own faith as distinct from their parents were mentioned repeatedly, particularly by those from strict, conservative backgrounds. For those who had done it, either at this age or later, studying academic theology had been significant, exposing them to ideas beyond their evangelical or traditional upbringing. They described finding this debate and reflection stimulating and were now typically attending congregations that encouraged rigorous theological reflection and discussion. Overall, it was widely reported that the process of exploration was important, allowing individuals to develop confidence in a personal faith, or to find a form of Christian spirituality they could engage with.

Many had also begun to explore their identity as leaders dur-ing this time. Marie had, to her surprise, become president of her Christian Union. Phil, likewise, had been involved in lead-ing evangelism and worship in his university community. Sally spent far more time on Christian activity than on her studies, and Helen volunteered as a youth worker. These roles had led into more senior roles in churches. A decade later, several reminisced about the flexibility being a student had given them to serve God, and the enthusiasm and energy they had had during this period. However, as Chapter 6 shows, there is no guarantee that those who discover leadership abilities in these formative years will continue their faith journey long term. All those who had rejected their faith had been highly involved in Christian activity at this age too. Nonetheless, the sense of purpose, self-esteem and the social capital involved in these roles did increase religious attendance and, in the case of many, a personal faith and a sense of vocation.

For financial reasons an increasing number of Emerging Adults now study at local universities, continuing to live with their parents. Others begin work, become parents or take a gap year. All these groups were represented in the sample. It became evident that for those who had remained at home, experiences of late teens and very early twenties were mixed. Some were content with the choice they had made but others, whether studying or beginning work, found themselves socially isolated. This was particularly acute for those starting work or with young children, whose lifestyle became significantly different from that of their peers. With hindsight, Clare wished that she had broadened her horizons, but her close relationships had kept her tethered to her childhood home and church. Conversely, working for a youth project had provided Felicity with new friends and wider theological exposure. It seems that it is not leaving home or attending university per se that makes the difference to faith development, but rather exposure to new ideas, experiences and a cohort of inspirational peers. Broadening horizons, social circles and theological understanding appear to be developmentally important, and churches need to pay close attention to those young adults who do not leave home if they are to receive the social and spiritual stimulation that seems so important at this life stage.

The importance of elders

Related to these opportunities were frequent accounts of support individuals had received from older members of faith communities during very early Emerging Adulthood. Marie had been mentored by a church minister who met her every week to read the Bible. Will had been intensively coached by the associate leader, who singled him out for that attention. Attending a church with a large cohort of peers (ironically) makes this sort of relationship less likely for the simple fact that any given student is one of a crowd. However, for those who experienced this sort of mentoring it had made a significant difference to the establishment, development and continuation of their identity, self-esteem and faith. They felt special, valued, and exhorted to make a difference with their lives. For some it had encouraged them into a lifestyle of radical service or ministry.

In summary

The path to their current faith position from childhood had been straightforward for few participants. Some were sufficiently disillusioned or bored by church as a child or teen that they had moved away from their family's faith, yet found their own during this early adult season. Several described reaching a point where they actively went looking for God. Nicola, a vicar's daughter, had asked the friend of a friend to take her to church. Will had rejected his parents' faith as a teen but feeling suicidal, walked into the first church he found and had a profound spiritual encounter. Suzie had intentionally 'taken a year off from being a Christian' but, after a difficult time, made a point of finding other believers at the start of university. At a point of distress, they had returned to the religion they had experienced as a child and found it to be personally meaningful.

Regardless of whether they had left home, attended university or not, these young women and men repeatedly told me how significant this period had been in laying foundations, discovering or revitalizing their Christian faith. The energy invested by churches and religious groups into Emerging Adults in this life stage is undoubtedly costly (trust me!), but this data suggests that it continues to be profoundly important.

And Now?

Ten to fifteen years later, these individuals were all Active Affirmers and part of a faith community. However, their faith can be described in more nuanced ways than this; the following is my attempt. In reality, the categories below are more of a spectrum than sharply delineated or ideal 'types'. They overlap, with some individuals situated at the intersections. As I have spoken on this material in public and academic settings, individuals have regularly approached me to tell me where they (or those they know) fit, or to express the fact that they belong to different categories on different days of the week. The aim of describing these types is not to box people in. Nor do I make any claims that these are exclusive or comprehensive. As has been repeatedly stressed, all faith journeys are unique. However, the following patterns emerged from the 30 narratives I was told. Participants could largely be described as being:

1 Disappointed but persevering;
2 Realistic pragmatists;
3 Confident and calmer;
4 Of deeper faith and greater enthusiasm;
5 Radical risk-takers.

Disappointed but Persevering

Some of those I interviewed were at a place in their lives where they were disappointed with God, or their own faith, but were persevering and hoping for better things to come. Their accounts and circumstances varied but they spoke with a note of frustration or anxiety, and some became emotional during their interview. All described struggling to fit within church. As a nurse, Deborah had spent much of her twenties working antisocial hours and relocating, often feeling disapproved of by Christians her own age. Harry described always feeling like an outsider, never fitting with the 'in-crowd', and Josh repeatedly referred to difficulties people seemed to have with some of his 'quirkier' personality traits.

All had faced significant personal battles in their twenties; combinations of family breakdown, relationship struggles, mental health problems and unemployment. Some reflected that they had made poor choices, at times with detrimental effects. Put simply, life had not turned out as they had hoped it would. Repeated professional or relational disappointments had shaped how they viewed God. Harry told me:

> You can't rely on circumstances to drop into place. You can't rely on God to tell you what you should do. You can't rely on God to tell you what career to choose, because you need to choose. It is your calling because you are doing it. Probably I should look back with more confidence now that I have managed to hold down a job for [nearly] two years. I am very wary of coincidental circumstances. I don't tend to look for them anymore. I don't tend to look for God to guide me and tell me what to do. I used to try for that and get tangled up.

Rather than a theological move towards Open Theism, this came across as resignation; he was not sure that God was particularly concerned. Nonetheless, he prayed, attended church and described how his faith helped him to manage his anxiety problems. He had friends who had rejected their faith through personal struggles, but for him that was not an option.

Deborah was conflicted about whether God was good, given all she had been through. There was a clear disconnect between what she thought she should believe and her emotions.

I know that God is a loving God, but God allowed Job to go through that. Everyone has different views, but [I think] God is a loving God overall. I don't think we understand everything he chooses for our life. At the moment, I think I'm afraid of what he is going to do next. You are meant to be God-fearing, but this is not a good fear. It is an anxiety of, *Am I going to go through something else?* I'm finding it hard to believe that God loves me. I'm trying to learn that [he] does.

At one level, their faith was profound. In the face of challenge and doubt, they were persevering, often with limited encouragement. Several spoke of the complexity of their romantic histories (or lack of any). It was also noticeable that historically, relationships with spiritual elders had been absent or strained. Where others had been supported or mentored in their twenties, several of these individuals had not benefitted from that sort of social capital or support.

So what had sustained their faith? One pattern that they all reported was of significant spiritual encounters in their early twenties. Several described these nostalgically and it seems that they created a reference point to which they returned when faced with ongoing challenges. They knew God to be real because of what they had experienced once. Josh said: '[I'm] not jacking my faith in. [Because of] things God got me through as a teenager, I know with absolute assurance and without doubt, that he is my Lord and Saviour. To walk away from that is pure stupidity. I know who I am in him. I know what I'm called to in his kingdom and I know what waits for me when I'm done here.'

Temperament clearly played a part in their determination to continue as Christians. Some used language like 'stubborn' or 'conscientious' to describe themselves. Harry was certain that the discipline of attending church was important – even if he didn't always enjoy it: 'My faith wouldn't have continued without church, but my faith certainly wouldn't have continued with church alone. The more positive aspects of my faith are probably when I am praying myself, or reading my Bible myself, but I couldn't do without church. It challenges you and makes you think about different things from what you would otherwise think about. You meet people, who challenge you. That is essential to continuing with your faith.'

Faith, then, was deeply important to these individuals, but they were living with the tension of unresolved disappointment. Without much social encouragement or support, and facing ongoing challenges, they were finding ways to persevere. They were, however, all still hopeful that things would improve. Deborah told me: 'People that I speak to in their thirties are more positive about their thirties than they are about their twenties really.'

Realistic Pragmatists

The largest group were young adults who were still strongly committed to their beliefs and serving their church community but said that they were more realistic or pragmatic about their faith. Their expectation of what a life of faith meant had changed. Over the years, it had moved from passionate zeal to something that was less intense but steady, meaningful and resilient. A number were now sceptical of what they perceived as charismatic excesses and had moved to more liturgical or theologically broader churches. However, others reflected a nostalgia for their former enthusiasm about 'Changing the world for Jesus'. Several talked about how they missed the time and energy they had had for religious activity as students. One explicitly speculated as to how feasible radical passion for evangelism was alongside a young family and professional responsibilities.

Sam described his as 'a working faith' and was typical of those who understood their working life as religious vocation. He wished churches were better at: 'valuing normal life. There is something about going away and doing mission – like that's the pinnacle of holiness! Whereas it's no more holy than doing anything else. I think it's about saying, *What is your mission field? Is it the classroom if you are a teacher? Is it your colleagues? Is it other mums in the playground?* It's not always being called to the next big thing. Actually, does God just want us to stay and do [mission] here in everyday life?'

Most of these realistic pragmatists had married in their early twenties and ascribed their spiritual development, in part at least, to their spouse. For those who were not married, the journey as a single person had been challenging. Nicola talked at length about the disappointment of being in her thirties and unmarried. She was in a place where she now understood her professional life as her service to God and was using her free time to serve the youth group. This had helped her to know a wider section of the congregation and to find support from older single women. She was determined not to follow some of her friends and leave to find a non-believing husband, but being atypical within her congregation was painful.

As explored in Chapter 4, the majority of realistic pragmatists with families described the joys and limitations it placed on their faith. Sleep deprivation, post-natal depression and distance from family were mentioned regularly. Several women talked about the challenges of motherhood; it was currently hard to engage with any meaningful form of spiritual activity. Instead, encouraging faith in their children was their priority and was personally stimulating. Some were sanguine about the season, considering that 'God understands where I'm at right now', but others described their frustration at the paucity of spiritual resources for those with small children.

Their twenties were also marked by accounts of mental health problems, professional stresses and relational difficulties. However, the support of older believers, and family (for those who were local), had influenced their ongoing faith formation. Church small groups were repeatedly described as the site for that sort of relationship and support. Whether it was providing childcare, advising them professionally, or helping them buy a house, deal with solicitors and fix the car, many described the practical and spiritual help they had received in adjusting to adult responsibility. The social capital religious groups provide is frequently recognized as beneficial for individual well-being, and these young adults had been appreciative. Most were more than happy to reciprocate support for others in the community and were usually involved in some sort of church activity within their capacity. They were largely satisfied with how their twenties had gone; life looked as they had hoped it would – although many acknowledged it had been more demanding than they had anticipated. Nonetheless, they had found social and spiritual resources from within their faith communities, which had allowed them to develop a realistic, consistent form of faith.

Confident and Calmer

Some participants described a resilient, deeper and calmer faith. They had often had a turbulent decade but having survived the ups and downs of their twenties had come to a place of certainty that God was with them. Three described long-term, traumatic, mental health problems. Struggles with singleness or volatile romantic relationships had compounded pressured work situations and they had all been unwell. Now, in their thirties, they considered themselves more rooted in God and certain of their faith. Life was calmer, and they could reflect more objectively on events and their responses to them. Counselling and good emotional support had helped them come to a place of peace and, in some cases, change of profession or relational status. Miriam explained:

I remember [there] being points where it just felt so bleak. I felt like I couldn't sense God's presence. Looking back, I could see his fingerprints all over everything, but it felt that for a long time he had just vanished. Talking to God I found excruciating [but] it was either that or talk to myself. I opted for talking to God. I think my relationship with God never disappeared. It went through rocky periods, but I think I became increasingly aware of the need to hang on to him more. I had to go deeper into him; I've seen where you can end up if you don't hang on to God and let him hang on to you.

Another reflected on the aftermath of her extramarital affair with a colleague in her mid-twenties.

We've kind of coexisted rather than what we should have been doing of having a marriage that grew deeper. We grew further apart. It's probably only in the last few years that, again, through intensive counselling we undid that and almost started again. I've never felt that God left my side. I've never felt that it was, 'You've messed up [so] I'm not going to be with you. You are going to sink or swim on your own.' I felt that God has done lots of little things over the years to rein us back in, and said, 'I'm still here and I'm still in control.'

Individuals of both genders reflected that their struggles had positively changed their faith. Gary had survived periods of loneliness and isolation, which had driven him to read popular evangelical literature and depend more deeply on God. Danny had made the decision to read the Old Testament in the face of uncertainty. In it, he had discovered a new awe for God that he felt his charismatic tradition neglected.

A common pattern was that these young adults understood God as showing himself to them through circumstantial episodes. The provision of jobs they hadn't applied for, protection and comfort within their illness (rather than dramatic healing), practical and financial help at pertinent times, were all understood as being signs of God's faithfulness. Despite their doubts, wrestling with (and sometimes swearing at) God, they believed that he had sustained them in dark times. Several emphasized that they had never doubted God's existence, even if they had had questions about where he was, or what he was doing. Interestingly, rather than significant theological shifts, most of these individuals had remained within the same faith tradition (and often congregation) throughout their twenties.

Their reflections tended to be that the change in their faith was a deeper revelation of established doctrines rather than an exploration of alternative perspectives.

It is not clear why these young adults should have retained and deepened their faith through struggle, where others abandoned it. Consistent pastoral and emotional support seemed to be a factor. It was interesting to note that the counselling they had received had typically been within a faith framework using theological resources (as opposed to the secular counselling several in the faith-loss group received). All were strongly integrated into faith communities, had geographical stability and largely came from strongly religious families. It seems likely, then, that the emotional support they received continued to reinforce a Christian worldview or cognitive mother-structure and encouraged them to see God at work in things that might otherwise have been viewed as coincidence. Ongoing Christian socialization, combined with their own temperament, appears to have strengthened rather than diminished their faith and increased its resilience through a challenging Emerging Adulthood.

Deeper Faith and Greater Enthusiasm

For others, their maturing of faith had inspired a greater enthusiasm for religious activity. Two of the African participants talked about how they were inspired by their deeper faith to return home and be a force for change. Chloe had become a passionate evangelist, and several others were pursuing a call to missions or full-time ministry. The spiritual journeys of this group were diverse. Some, having come to faith a bit later, were exploring the idea of a religious vocation for the first time. Others had been exposed to experiences that had caused them to rethink their values. Some had simply grown in confidence as they got older and had begun to believe that perhaps they might have a religious contribution to make. All of them, however, were excited by their faith, the opportunities it presented, and had an increasing sense of vocation or purpose. Whether they were undertaking religious activities spontaneously or under the supervision of their church or denomination, they were passionate about others coming to the faith that had changed their lives.

It was striking that all of them gave accounts of incidents where they believed God had intervened, protecting or dramatically helping them in some way. Aari, from West Africa, recounted:

> I was attacked. Islamist extremists train young boys [and] use them to attack people. The bus was about to leave. The person in front of me and the person behind me were struggling because [it] was too hot and they wanted fresh air. I said, 'No problem, open my window', so there was a double glass [by me]. One of [the boys] took a very large stone and threw it at the bus and it landed at my head. The first glass broke and the second one broke as well but somehow, I survived. The driver heard the noise and moved the bus and said he wasn't going to stop until he got to the next town, even if someone was dead. If I had got injured, I would have died there. It was a big lesson [in trusting God].

All the Africans gave accounts of divine protection from violence. One of them, and two of the British participants, had survived life-threatening traffic accidents. Others had suffered serious health episodes and domestic violence. Although, at the time, they had wrestled with theological questions, they now reported an increased desire to serve God. One said: 'I was a walking testimony of how good God was from [then on]. How could I doubt God? I really couldn't doubt him. When I was in hospital there was another girl who had the same injury and she died. I met her parents and went through that guilt of "Why me?" [but] I knew that God loved me and had a purpose for my life.'

For some, distressing incidents had inspired them to ask existential questions for the first time. Wayne described crying out to God from his hospital bed: 'I was on a downward spiral, thinking everything is ruined, everything is wrong and there is no chance of fixing this. There was a night I just prayed, "If there's a God, just help us out and show us. If you are real, show me that you are real. Make this better." I was begging him, I was bargaining. In an instant, I felt like someone had put their arm around me and gave me a cuddle. I just felt very comforted. I relaxed, and the sense of pain and discomfort just went. It wasn't the morphine; I just felt this real calm over me. I just fell asleep.' Although the beginning of a long journey, this episode was a significant part of his account. Wayne had experienced God as real and wanted to invest his life in explaining that to others.

Not all accounts were as dramatic, but all these participants described episodes of sensing God speaking to them, or tangibly directing them in some way. Some were charismatics who described prophetic words, or ecstatic experiences, but others were not. After her marriage ended, one young woman who had drifted away from faith, said:

When I went to church it was very comforting. [Living] on my own was terrifying. It was just this feeling [that] I wasn't really on my own; God was there and so it wasn't that scary. I went to church and enjoyed it and enjoyed praying. Praying and reading the Bible makes you feel better. I went to church and was thinking about all the extra stuff that I could do. This is going to sound really strange, but it was almost like God shouted in my ear, *Why don't you do something in the Church?* It wasn't him [actually] talking, it was my consciousness shouting in my ear. It was like a light-bulb moment and so I started looking for community work and jobs in churches.

Again, it is not clear why some individuals have this response to traumatic events and others do not. Undoubtedly, many people have bargained with God from their hospital beds or in the face of violence. Most of these participants had some sort of Christian heritage (be it parents or grandparents), which they appear to have fallen back on *in extremis*. An experience that they interpreted as divine action or answered prayer had given them a new sense of purpose, confidence or vocation. Combined with encouragement to do so (typically from their spouse or clergy), in their early thirties they were now exploring what that service might mean. Perhaps, coming to faith somewhat later in their twenties, this passion is the developmental equivalent of what others experienced as students. However, most of these individuals were not surrounded by a strongly enthusiastic peer group – if anything, the opposite. They were a minority of some sort, but still wanting to actively outwork their faith in a meaningful way. God has changed their lives and they want to share that with others.

Radical Risk-Takers

The final category from this sample is made up of those who already had a clear sense of vocation and vision for their lives, who might be described as 'radical risk-takers'. They were individuals who had spent most of their twenties pursuing an unorthodox lifestyle inspired by their faith. Several had lived without or with minimal salary, often giving up stable employment to pursue Christian activity. All of them described the challenges and demands of this lifestyle, but were deeply convinced of God's faithfulness and, at this point, committed to continuing the journey they were on.

Some had experienced a dramatic conversion or transformation in their early twenties that they attributed to God's intervention. For others, their faith development had been less dramatic. However, what they did have in common was that at some point they had all been singled out and mentored by leaders within charismatic churches. They gave accounts of being given opportunities, leadership roles, and being both supported and encouraged to take risks. This appeared to have created a sense of self-worth, confidence and willingness to make considerable sacrifices in their personal, financial and professional lives. All of them told stories of what they understood as God's ongoing intervention and provision; demonstrating what scholars call 'post-ecstatic faith growth' (which parallels post-traumatic faith growth).[8] For example, William said:

> I went three months and I didn't even get paid, but it was just incredible how God provided. I was living in this flat that I couldn't afford to live in. I couldn't afford to eat. I couldn't afford to go outside when it rained because my shoes had holes in them. That was probably my favourite year of just understanding the character and kindness of God – and his faithfulness. Friends used to come from one end of the city just to drop some lunch off for me. They bought me shoes. They bought me everything. During that year I must have cooked for myself about three times. Every other evening someone in the church was cooking for me. It was incredible. It was such a blessing.

The others had similar stories of practical and financial provision as they did what they believed God was asking of them. Accommodation, computers, holidays – things they couldn't afford on minimal income – God had given them via other Christians or seemingly random circumstances. Certainly, they had been closely integrated into faith communities, benefitting both from social capital and personal status for their radical choices, but risk-taking had worked.

Equally, they had all worked hard in demanding circumstances, often among the poor and vulnerable. They demonstrated what Lee refers to as a 'virtuous circle' – a positive feedback loop where experience of divine love gave them energy for service and sacrifice.[9] They described profoundly difficult experiences and disappointments, but also what they understood as divine direction (which at times had been very specific). All wanted to alleviate suffering and see lives transformed through conversion. They were confident that God was at work and using them. Lydia said:

I used to care more what other people thought. Now I think people can think what they want. I want to do what I think God is saying, and I'm just going to do it. I think the only disappointment in my life right now would be that I'm not married yet. [Sometimes] when I look at my brothers and my friends, and they are earning quadruple my salary, I do think, *Oh no!* But I'm not disappointed with my life. When I look back at those ten years I just think, *Wow, how many people have come to know Jesus because I decided not to be a teacher?*

Even if it was a struggle sometimes (and for all of them it had been), they described their life and faith as an adventure and spoke about the encouragement they had received in that. They could identify growth both in their faith and self-esteem. Lucy, who had struggled with self-confidence because of her background, said:

I wanted to get married and have children. I wanted to step out in faith and radically follow Jesus. I feel like I'm doing both of those. I've got a heart for evangelism and reaching the lost. Now I have more confidence in the fact that my history and my family background have all been part of God equipping me for what he will have me do. I am in a unique position where I can have an impact with people.

William commented:

God has broken things off my life that I was scared of and that I struggled with. Out of my friendship group, I am one of the only ones who is single. I think, *Why am I not [married]?* But then you think, *God has a different path for me, a different journey.* Would I forsake God for just going out and getting married? I don't want to go back to where I was. I was in a horrible, horrible place and God has transformed my life so much. I cannot turn my back on him. He wouldn't on me, so I can't do that to him.

Reflections

It is disingenuous to make universalizing statements about Emerging Adult faith development based on this sample of 30. They have different temperaments, intellects, experiences and backgrounds. The aim of describing these patterns is not to suggest that everyone who has a certain set of experiences will end up with a certain sort of faith; far from it. The task of finding a faith to live by was common to all the participants, but this chapter aimed to illustrate the diversity of ongoing faith journeys and to suggest that secure young adult faith can look widely different. Clearly, the essential step of owning a faith, as opposed to merely conforming to the one held by one's family of origin, does often happen in the teens and early twenties. However, there are also Emerging Adults who come to faith later or, without a religious background, simply go looking for meaning and find God.

It does seem to be the case, though, that young adult faith in this generation needs to be both cognitively robust and experientially significant. Intellectual assent to doctrinal truth is not sufficient (as it perhaps once was), nor are spiritual encounters or supportive community by themselves. In a sceptical and secular age, it appears that these three factors need to weave together in order to create a secure belief system. The vast majority of these 30 participants identified all three in their narratives. Having an experience, event or series of situations that they identified as divine intervention was central to their account. Psychological research shows that spiritual experiences do promote faith development by reinforcing an individual's deep mother-structure.[10] However, experiences need to be accompanied by an interpretation that affirms the person's belief in a higher power. That is, experiences need to be understood as being God, rather than merely coincidence or some other force. This is where religious community (both peers and elders) plays a significant part in faith development, by helping that process of meaning-making. Most Emerging Adults are aware that their peers (even if they are inspiring and encouraging) do not have the answers to all their questions by virtue of age. Thus, they often look to their religious elders for this sort of wisdom and support. The voices of such elders and wider faith communities are validated when they embody the Christian values they claim to hold. Faith in God, hospitality, generosity, concern for the poor, pastoral care and encouragement all convince Emerging Adults that these people – and their beliefs – can be trusted. Scepticism of religious authority can be overcome when it shows itself to be authentic, sincere and warm. It is also evident from these accounts that the narrative of 'snowflake' or consumerist millennials is often unfair. Many of these participants were profoundly loyal, not to structures or denominations, but to communities, congregations and people. Their faith and faith communities provided continuity and security during the turmoil of their twenties and they were strongly committed to them.

However, as life becomes more complex, for faith to continue to develop, Emerging Adult cognitive mother-structure needs to become increasingly complex too. This means either finding deeper ways to understand existing theological doctrines, or accessing new ideas that will facilitate that development.[11] This often looks like the spiralling process described in Chapter 5. Perspectives of God need to become more profound or sophisticated but old understandings are not simply jettisoned, instead they are modified. Likewise, understandings of the Bible or Christian doctrines have to become more nuanced. How far the support and teaching received helpfully reinforces, or constructively challenges simplistic theological understanding is important. As earlier chapters illustrated, Millennials (and even more so Generation Z) are adept at finding their own theological resources. They have almost unlimited access to information, but not always the ability to discern its implications.

Essentially, what these stories demonstrate is that individuals need to develop a faith that can make sense of difficult experiences or withstand the tension of uncertainty as naive enthusiasm comes up against the realities of adult life. As a religious minority in a secular culture, whether they have the support and opportunity to process disappointment and wrestle with doubt makes a significant difference to Active Affirmers. Throughout Emerging Adulthood, faith has to be continually reframed. It needs to be intellectually coherent, emotionally truthful and socially supportive. As Sharon Parks wrote: 'The power and vulnerability of young adulthood lies in the experience of the dissolution and re-composition of the meaning of self and world, and its challenges to faith. To become a young adult in faith is to discover the limits of one's assumptions about "how life will always be" – and to recompose a meaningful sense of self and world on the other side of that discovery.' She adds a final crucial point, which this data confirms: 'The quality of that re-composition depends on the leadership of adult culture, as mediated through both individuals and institutions.'[12]

Questions for Discussion

- Which (if any) of the five types defined above do you identify with most (disappointed but persevering, realistic pragmatists, confident and calmer, of deeper faith and greater enthusiasm, radical risk-takers)? Why is that the case?
- What do you think each might bring to a faith community and the wider Kingdom of God?
- Which do you see most frequently in your faith community (either among the young or the wider congregation)? What strikes you about that observation?
- How far do you agree that Emerging Adults are looking for faith that is 'intellectually coherent, emotionally truthful and socially supportive'?
- If this is the case, then how might Emerging Adults be holistically encouraged during periods in which they 'discover the limits of [their] assumptions about "how life will always

be"' and need to 'recompose a meaningful sense of self and world'?

- How far do you agree that 'The quality of that re-composition depends on the leadership of adult culture, as mediated through both individuals and institutions'? What is inspiring or challenging for you in that?

Notes

1 Christian Smith et al., *Soul Searching: The Religious and Spiritual Lives of American Teenagers* (Oxford: Oxford University Press, 2005), 56; Carolyn McNamara Barry, 'Religion and Spirituality during the Transition to Adulthood', *International Journal of Behavioural Development*, Vol. 34.4 (2010), 322–4; Carolyn McNamara Barry, 'Do Emerging Adults Learn What They Live? The Frequency and Importance of Childhood Family Faith Activities on Emerging Adults' Prosocial Behavior towards Family, Friends, and Strangers', *Journal of Emerging Adulthood*, Vol. 6.6 (2017), 411–21.

2 Jeffrey Jensen Arnett and David Kinnaman also identified this frustration at religious hypocrisy. See *Emerging Adulthood: The Winding Road from the Late Teens through the Twenties* (Oxford: Oxford University Press, 2004), 220; *You Lost Me* (Grand Rapids, MI: Baker Books, 2011).

3 James Fowler, *Stages of Faith: The Psychology of Human Development and the Quest for Meaning* (San Francisco, CA: Harper Collins, 1995), 112.

4 McNamara Barry, 'Religion and Spirituality during the Transition to Adulthood', 322–4.

5 A. Montgomery-Goodnough and S. J. Gallagher, 'Review of Research on Spiritual and Religious Formation in Higher Education', in S. M. Nielsen and M. S. Plakhotnik (eds), *Proceedings on the Sixth Annual College of Education Research Conference: Urban and International Education Section* (Miami, FL: International University, 2007), 60–5.

6 R. A. Young et al., 'Transition to Adulthood as a Peer Project', *Journal of Emerging Adulthood*, Vol. 30.3 (2015), 166–78.

7 Brian Willoughby and S. James, *The Marriage Paradox: Why Emerging Adults Love Marriage yet Push it Aside* (New York: Oxford University Press, 2017), 172.

8 I. A. Gutiérrez and C. L. Park, 'Emerging Adulthood, Evolving

229

Worldviews: How Life Events Impact College Students' Developing
Belief Systems', *Journal of Emerging Adulthood*, Vol. 3.2 (2015), 85–97.

9 M. Y. Lee et al., *The Heart of Religion: Spiritual Empowerment,
Benevolence, and the Experience of God's Love* (New York: Oxford
University Press, 2013).

10 McNamara Barry, 'Religion and Spirituality during the Transition
to Adulthood', 322–4.

11 Ibid.

12 S. Parks, *The Critical Years: The Young Adult Search for a Faith
to Live By* (San Francisco, CA: Harper & Row, 1986), Introduction.

Conclusion

9

What Now?

When I speak on Emerging Adult faith, people often ask me 'What do you think we should do then?' My answer to them and to you (if that is indeed your question) is that one size really does not fit all. There is no magic bullet for the re-evangelization of the UK (or if there is, I don't know what it is!). However, as a person of faith I do believe that there is a good and powerful God whose heart is for those trying to find identity, meaning and a faith to live by in the current younger generations. They have been dealt tricky cards by growing into adulthood in such a time as this. The transcriptionist who worked on this project and heard all the interviews commented 'I'm so glad I'm not young today!' Honestly, I agree with her. I can only imagine the carnage of my 25-year-old self with access to a mobile phone, social media and £30k of debt!

You will have gathered by now that I like Millennials. I really do. I have been fortunate to know hundreds of warm, kind, sincere young men and women, many of whom I now call friends despite the age gap. I also recognize that I have been privileged to live and minister in university towns and attend churches where Emerging Adults are a central part of the faith community. That may well not be the case in your context, and the Emerging Adults there may well be far more diverse and absent from your faith community. I would recommend the Church Army's report which considers ministries that are proving fruitful in reaching Emerging Adults in different contexts.[1]

The other qualication to point out is that Generation Z really do appear to be different again. Often 'Millennial' is used as a generic term that conflates the two – but they are different. Many Millennials express their concerns for those following behind them and are baffled by the values and actions of today's teens and students. I can vouch for changing attitudes and perspectives among students year by year over the past decade. Today's youth and student workers are wrestling with the challenge of supporting the faith of young people in ways that I and my peers did not have to in their position. Indeed, one could argue that retrospective research into generations is closing the gate after the horse has bolted. Someone commented to me the other day, 'Isn't it too late to be talking about Millennials now?' However, I do think there is value in understanding Millennials, in hearing their voices and in being concerned not just with the faith of the very youngest in society but of those who are now moving into positions of influence and becoming parents. What are they articulating and offering to the Church?

These concluding comments, then, are not an action plan. I hope that the questions you have reflected on at the end of each chapter have already begun to shed light on what to embrace, develop and perhaps challenge in your setting. These final findings and observations are to give voice to the participants who so generously shared their stories with us. Many of them told me that they had agreed to take part in the research because they wanted to help the Church understand the realities of Millennial life and be more effective in sharing the gospel with their generation. At the end of each interview I asked them all the same question: 'What would you like me to tell church leaders on your behalf?' These are the four sorts of answers they gave.

What Do You Want Church Leaders to Hear?

1 Get real!

Many of those who spoke with me were critical of their own generation and their own younger self. They spoke of consumerism, self-absorption, limited attention spans, compulsive screen use and social media. Emerging Adults are more than able to reflect on some of the negative aspects of the culture they have grown up in and imbibed – they are not stupid. 41 of the 47 I interviewed were also committed to their Christian faith, passionate about Jesus and wanted those beliefs to make a difference to their lives, families and communities. They believed the gospel was good news. What they wanted was help with integrating their faith with the challenges of contemporary culture and differing life stages. A number spoke about wanting spiritual wisdom and support in the areas of mental health, time management and rest. Others wanted help to counteract the pressures of online identity construction and resist the temptations of constant and immediate access to pornography. They wanted to be holistic disciples of Jesus and felt that the Church too often avoided those topics or provided little honesty or wisdom around them. Of course, they also recognized that older generations have not had to deal with some of these specific challenges in the same life stage; that the speed of cultural change meant many were at sea themselves. Nonetheless they wanted to talk about real life, about how faith informs and impacts on daily choices, patterns and rhythms. Craig considered that the most important need was to 'create a church environment where going deeper and being honest with people can happen'. What participants were frustrated with was what one called the 'I'm fine' culture of their congregation. In a world where so much is superficial and public images intentionally constructed, they wanted church to be a place of truthfulness; a place where – as one said – 'We stand against the fake-ness.'

The desire for authenticity has been identified repeatedly

throughout this book and wider literature on Emerging Adults but it was raised again and again in answering this final question. Dislike of gossip and superficiality, frustration at division from other churches and 'slickness without substance' were all mentioned. Although some had personal theological convictions that had informed their choice of church, most were unconcerned with denominational tensions. What they described was a desire for congregations to collaborate and encourage each other for the sake of their local community. Few spoke about worship style in answering this final question but those who did said 'normal church' that 'stands on the gospel' was more important to them 'than smoke machines and a concert'. A couple commented that for them there was a minimum standard when it came to music in church but that was because terrible musicality distracted them from being able to worship. Worship needed to help them connect with God in a meaningful way, but honesty about real life, advice and support in how to live out their faith with integrity was what many wanted from a faith community.

2 Talk with us

Participants also recognized the complexities of the issues they faced and believed that in some areas they were the ones with experience and wisdom to contribute. However, they were often frustrated at a lack of meaningful communication, and of presumptions being made about them. Repeatedly they said things like, 'Please don't make assumptions about us' or 'Please don't patronize us.' Amy said, 'We are not innocents. We've been exposed to so much. Please don't treat us as children!' They recognized that they were only one part of any given faith community but – as earlier chapters mentioned – this is a generation who have been raised with the expectation of contributing, and inclusivity is what many were asking for. 'Please respect us and listen to our voice' was how one put it. Participation, conversation and collaboration were what they wanted, not to be passive recipients or have church 'done' to them. Nicky pointed out that in her early thirties she carried considerable responsibility as a manager at work but, as one of the youngest members of her congregation, was often ignored or overlooked as 'knowing nothing' by virtue of her age. She smiled wryly at the incongruity of attitudes towards her professional and spiritual identities. Others had the reverse experience of having 'things dumped on me because I was the token young person', being asked to contribute too much when they were struggling to cope with the pressures of early careers or parenthood. Sally said: 'Please get to know us, don't be afraid of us! We want to be known and treated as people, not part of a programme or a name on a rota!'

This desire for conversation extended beyond involvement or being able to express ideas and perspectives. A number wanted to be able to undertake theological journeys without 'being told off' for exploring other forms of Christian spirituality. Rather than firm boundaries of denomination or doctrine often used by former generations to define their religious identity, many Millennials simply define themselves as 'Christian'. They are unaware of the historical roots or values on which different churches are based and for the most part are unconcerned with them. One described at length older members of her evangelical small group feeling it was their responsibility to correct her doctrine to make sure she 'stayed on the straight and narrow'. She and others wanted older believers to have faith in the sincerity of their explorations, to respect their questions and to 'trust God to be in that'. Greg summarized the voices of several, considering that younger generations needed help to learn to question well and discern wisely from the plethora of options available to them in a multi-cultural and globally connected culture. Central to faith, in his view, was the ability to discuss and disagree graciously; to have confidence in the gospel while being able to be respectful to those who held other views. He was one of several who noted the need for Emerging Adults to own their beliefs, not just dutifully parrot back correct doctrine. Jesus, he pointed out, did much of his teaching in parables – encouraging his listeners to wrestle with the meaning. Learning about faith needed to be more Socratic than didactic. Thus sermons (in person or podcast) should not be seen as the dissemination of authoritative answers but a starting point for learning, enhanced by mutually respectful listening and discussion. Anna summarized, 'Theological exploration and conversation doesn't have to be a threat; can't we sit down and learn together?'

Of course, there are issues with relativism, the rejection of authority, and with self as the arbiter of truth, but it seems to me that Millennial Active Affirmers are simply being honest as they try to form a religious identity in complex circumstances. The construction of unreflective 'mosaic' forms of faith can be ecclesiologically and theologically problematic. However, it is something Christians have always done: virtually all contemporary traditions have a diverse theological and cultural heritage. Faith has to become more complex as life does. Emerging adults are at a place where they are working this out and it can look messy, contradictory, doctrinally confused. It is easy for those of us who have found a place to sit theologically and a framework for our own religious identity to be impatient with the journeying of others. As I reflect, I realize it took me ten years of wrestling with the Reformed doctrine of my childhood before anyone explained Arminianism to me. I wasn't entirely convinced but I remember the relief of realizing that there was a legitimate theological alternative. (It probably took another ten years before I had language to articulate what I *was* convinced by!) Faith development is messy, frustrating, unsettling and vitally important. What participants described was wanting older generations to support and help with that process graciously, not just insist on certain answers or doctrinal positions.

Some of these participants also matched reports (from both sides of the Atlantic) of Millennial interest in ancient forms of Christianity. This also appears to be part of the desire for authenticity or rootedness – something unchanging in a culture of continual flux. Be it the writings of the Church Fathers and

Mothers, Ignatian, Celtic or liturgical forms of worship, some Millennials are finding help and stimulation in diverse forms of Christian wisdom. Like charismatic and Pentecostal forms of worship, ancient mystic expressions help them to explore the numinous – to meet God. Thus, adding ancient spiritual resources to contemporary protestant Christianity is a creative attempt to construct a religious identity that can help them face the challenges of relentless change and uncertainty. Pragmatism and flexibility are skills Millennials have needed to develop in order to navigate contemporary life and create their self-biographies; it should come as no surprise that they do the same with spiritual resources. That they want others to be part of that journeying is, to my mind, commendable. It is not a wholesale rejection of established doctrine or Christian tradition, but a desire to understand; to make sense of faith in order genuinely to own it, rather than merely comply or give nominal assent. If you are going to resist the secular narrative and be part of the 3 % with Christian faith, then you need to be sure that faith is legitimate!

3 A desire for family

As will be evident from the previous chapters, Millennials are a highly relational generation. Family breakdown, geographic mobility, uncertainty in many areas mean that church communities take on real significance for many. Related to the desire for authenticity and mutual listening and learning was the wish for secure relationships and contexts for these to take place. Craig was among those who spoke about the importance of small groups, or networks within larger congregations, and of the depth of relationships in creating a place of safety. He and others were critical of mono-generational small groups that 'hive people off into generational ghettos'. For a number the thing they wanted church leaders to know was the importance of having 'fathers and mothers in the faith'. Mark was one of many who explained the significance of the investment of older believers in the lives of those following behind them. Some used the language of 'mentoring' while others simply described it as 'walking with people'. Whether formal or informal, it was evident that for both young men and women it was not only peers that Emerging Adults wanted to do life and faith with, but elders. Certainly, many of these participants were from the North East, for whom strong loyalty to family and locality are culturally important. However, as Chapter 8 illustrated, those whose faith had thrived had found these sorts of familial relationships within faith communities.

When I speak on this research, I often raise the topic of intergenerational friendship as a core part of faith formation. Typically, Gen Xers and Baby Boomers are aghast until they reflect on their own faith journeys and the importance of those who walked with them. Millennials, however, nod enthusiastically. At one conference a couple of hundred Emerging Adults got to their feet and started clapping (the elders in the room appeared stunned!). I also point out that Emerging Adults are not after a Jedi master – an Obi Wan or Yoda whose feet they will sit at like good padawan. What they say they are hungry for are genuine older friends to walk with, both receiving and giving support. The longing described to me is for authentic, truthful communities of faith rooted in hospitality and generosity. Several described changing church during their twenties or early thirties. The big, buzzing church had been what they wanted as teens or very young Emerging Adults, but as they got older, stable family or community – deep relationships across generations – were what they were drawn to. Formerly people found these networks in villages, local communities and extended biological families. But like in so many other aspects of their lives, Millennials often need to create such support structures themselves, and when churches model this it is deeply attractive to them.

Of course, Millennials do not have a monopoly on this. Many of us, across the age ranges, cry 'I agree!' However, younger generations are intolerant of what they perceive as religious hypocrisy. There is so much spin out there, so many people projecting a carefully curated image. Emerging adults know this and are looking for sincerity; a community of people who live what they claim to believe. Certainly, with age comes understanding that everyone's life is demanding, that we are all flawed and that with the best will possible, churches are dysfunctional because people are dysfunctional. It seems to me, nevertheless, that one of the gifts of this generation to the wider Church is the challenge of sincere hospitality and cross-generational relationship.

4 Inspiration

The final recurring message participants asked me to pass on, on their behalf, was around vision for their life. One said: 'We want to commit to something bigger than ourselves.' Several articulated a desire for churches to be more, not less challenging in the message they presented. An unapologetically radical, countercultural way of living was what they advocated as attractive to their generation. Sally felt church should 'inspire people to reach for more than the world can offer'. She explained:

> that the world hasn't got it right about how to raise children, do marriage, family. The world doesn't do community. It is dysfunctional and that idea of trying to have a nice comfortable life, and aspiring to what the world tells you is the ideal – of being attractive and having a nice home, and good-looking kids, and putting nice photos of them on Facebook and having better and better material things ... I'm not saying that any of that is wrong by itself, but you have got to be 100% sold out for Jesus.

This desire for living a radical lifestyle was something Matt also articulated: 'I think people need calling to something exciting and I guess given a vision for what their life in Christ could be, not just told what to do. They need to know what their life in Christ could be like if God was put in charge of it. Not leaving them as a number in the pew, but saying 'Let's go together. I'm inviting you to this, this could be your life. Let's go on this mission together.'

Others were adamant that churches needed to look beyond themselves, to serve and be present in the local community. One de-churched individual said: 'I'd be more interested if churches met the needs of the marginal and not around the needs of white middle-class people!' Another spoke about the need for Christians to understand all aspects of their lives as service to God and as valuable because of that. They wanted church leaders to present Christian faith as something that should inspire purpose and meaning in the lives of believers. A number saw the value of a Sunday service primarily in inspiring genuine community and deep faith in order to live a counter-cultural lifestyle to bless others. Laura explained of the young adults in her traditional church:

> It is not just that we want to have modern music or change for the sake of change. I think we are looking for something more than what has become the Sunday traditional service. But we are looking for it because we want to know Jesus more, to follow him more closely, and we want to be challenged more. We want to live this life [of faith] and there has to be something more than what is currently turned out on a Sunday morning.

Felicity agreed: 'We are an odd bunch in that we're committed to faith but not in the old-school way that a different generation were. We don't necessarily want to commit to buildings and structures and tradition. We want to commit to Jesus. We get frustrated when church is about [those things]. The students I work with want to commit to something but church in the way that we know it doesn't inspire them or hold their attention enough to make them want to go for it!'

Many Millennial Christians, then, are not opposed to church – they just want it to be more honest, more hospitable, more relational, more radical, inspiring and passionate about Jesus. To my mind they carry a prophetic challenge to the British Church to be the Body of Christ in the mess that is twenty-first-century Britain.

What Causes Faith to Flourish during Emerging Adulthood?

So, to return to where we began, why is it that the faith of some Millennial Active Affirmers has flourished and for others has evaporated? In the largely secular neo-liberal culture of contemporary Britain, people of faith (regardless of religion) are often viewed as oddities at best and dangerous at worst. Younger generations are suspicious of all forms of authority and consequently developing a resilient Christian faith is demanding. To form a coherent identity as a young Christian involves choosing to defy statistical odds and cultural pressures. And yet, as we have seen, some young women and men do so, often opting for conservative forms of faith. Clearly each faith journey – be it towards orthodox Christianity (in whatever form) or away from it – is unique. I am not claiming that these final reflections are definitive or universal. However, based on nearly 50 stories (and 20 years of ministry), it seems to me that for faith to flourish among today's younger generations, four factors are pivotal (although not necessarily in this order or in equal measure).

1 *Experience*: one or more events that they understand as an encounter with God. This might take myriad forms but provides *experiential evidence of the existence and benevolence of God*. It underpins a worldview that then includes the possibility of divine activity and a sense of security that God is with them in the many uncertainties of their lives. (It also explains the current attraction of certain forms of Christianity that focus on the numinous.)

2 *An understanding of Christianity as cognitively coherent*: growing in confidence that a Christian worldview is intellectually, philosophically and historically legitimate and that they can be thoughtful, contemporary citizens while still holding to ancient beliefs. Of course, not all are intellectual or would express it in these terms, but 'It's in the Bible' or 'Christians believe this' will not wash with many. In a culture so far removed from traditional Christian values they need to understand *why* they should hold to them, or how they can understand and trust the Bible. Maturing faith, then, involves deepening understandings of doctrine, theology and the nature of Scripture, as well as developing the capacity to hold mystery and uncertainty in tension with faith.

3 A supportive, encouraging *faith community* in which to live the rollercoaster of Emerging Adulthood: this is the context in which many work out their identity and relationships, so hospitality, relationality, relevance and opportunity to grow and contribute are vital. Although peers matter, so too do elders who demonstrate how to live out authentic Christian faith and help Emerging Adults undertake the task of exploring answers to their questions.

4 A sense of *vocation or vision for their life*: Emerging Adults are in the process of establishing an adult identity and part of that is a need to answer the question, 'What am I for?' Christianity (particularly in its activist evangelical forms) can help provide answers to that question. Those whose faith was thriving in this sample often had a very strong sense of faith-based altruism shaping their choices. Whether that was focused on evangelism, raising their children to have faith, broader social transformation or the alleviation of suffering, many considered that they were following the example of Jesus, which gave them a sense of purpose and self-esteem.

Of course, personal circumstances, temperament and choices all come into this. There were individuals in the sample who did not have any of these four factors, yet they had still found a way through to a stable adult religious identity. There were those who had some of them but had left their younger faith behind. However, I do believe that for many, these are core aspects of the formation of their religious worldview and Christian faith. I also believe that this is probably true of many of us who belong to older generations. Those of us in Generation X are actually the first 'missing generation' from church (ask yourself how many in their 40s and 50s who are not in leadership are part of your congregation). However, our path to adulthood was considerably more straightforward in many ways. Perhaps the best way to test this thesis is to ask those Millennials you know what they think of it – and listen carefully to their answers!

A Personal PostScript

By way of conclusion I would like to start where I began, on a personal note – not as a researcher, but as a person of faith and Christian minister.

This research and book has been three years in the making. It has been harder than I imagined possible. My own faith and health have taken a pounding during the process. At times my heart has been broken and I have wondered if there is indeed any hope for the British Church. The work of Andy Root pulled me up short though.[2] Have we factored God out of the equation? The Church, in all its dysfunction, is the bride of Christ. We are told that Jesus loves it, loves all the generations of us. It is not over until God decides it is time, and I believe that God is stirring something among the young in our nation.

I watched the Stormzy set at Glastonbury in June 2019 (on TV, not in person – I'm not that cool) and wondered what I was seeing as thousands of (presumably non-believing) Emerging Adults sang 'Blinded by your grace' alongside a gospel choir. (Stormzy on *Songs of Praise*? These are indeed crazy times!) Similarly, the response to the sermon of Reverend

Michael Curry at the royal wedding last year was fascinating. My Millennial hairdresser regularly wants to talk about faith with me. He described attending a concert by the Kingdom Choir who were part of that same wedding service. He told me that he was overwhelmed and could not stop crying during the concert but couldn't work out why. As I was the only religious person he knew, he wanted to know what I thought about that. I told him I believed he had experienced the Holy Spirit. His response?

'I didn't know church could be like that. I'd go all the time if it was!'

More widely, student workers report a new confidence among Generation Z to invite their friends to church – and they come (some wonder if they are actually allowed to). The 2018 Christian Union Christmas services in both York and Durham Universities saw unprecedented thousands attending, young people being turned away from the Minster and Cathedral because of the sheer numbers. Those I know who minister in prisons have waiting lists of young men and women wanting to attend Bible studies or alpha courses (and they assure me not just for the biscuits!). I've heard accounts of young people watching the live streams of services for months before daring to step across the threshold of a church – because they simply had no idea what went on in that building. There is often curiosity rather than hostility to genuine faith that does what it says on the tin!

I could go on and describe young lawyers, teachers, entrepreneurs, scientists, financiers, activists, writers, musicians whose faith is profoundly informing their lifestyle and choices (I'm resisting for the sake of the word count!). The Millennial 3% may be small, but I believe them to be mighty!

I spend a good amount of my time pushing back against generalizations and stereotypes voiced about Millennials – and I hope this work will go some way to challenge those too. My desire is that it will open up conversations, inspire relationships, help different generations stand together and love each other well. The need is urgent and there is a biblical pattern to follow after all! David needed both Samuel and Jonathan. Ruth and Naomi helped each other through desperate times. Elisha was a gift to lonely Elijah, not just his disciple, and facing his own death the Apostle Paul sent for his spiritual son Timothy.

The giving, supporting, learning about how to form a Christian identity and live a life of faith is not all one way. It never has been.

Notes

1 '"Not As Difficult As You Think": Mission with Young Adults', *Church Army*, www.churcharmy.org/youngadultsresearch (accessed 06. 09.19).

2 Andrew Root, *Faith Formation in a Secular Age: Responding to the Churches' Obsession with Youthfulness* (Grand Rapids, MI: Baker Academic, 2017).

Bibliography and Further Reading

Aisthorpe, Steve, *The Invisible Church: Learning from the Experiences of Churchless Christians* (Edinburgh: Saint Andrew Press, 2016).

Arnett, Jeffrey Jensen, 'Emerging Adulthood: A Theory of Development from the Late Teens through the Twenties', *American Psychologist*, Vol. 55.5 (2000), 469–80.

——, *Emerging Adulthood: The Winding Road from the Late Teens through the Twenties* (Oxford: Oxford University Press, 2004).

——, (ed.), *Oxford Handbook of Emerging Adulthood* (Oxford: Oxford University Press, 2016).

Aune, Kristen, 'Singleness and Secularization: British Evangelical Women and Church (Dis)affiliation', in Kristen Aune, Sonya Sharma and Giselle Vincett (eds), *Women and Religion in the West: Challenging Secularization* (Aldershot: Ashgate, 2008).

Beck, Ulrich and Elizabeth Beck-Gernsheim, *Individualization: Institutionalized Individualism and its Social and Political Consequences* (London: Sage, 2002).

Bielo, James, *Emerging Evangelicals: Faith, Modernity and the Desire for Authenticity* (New York: New York University Press, 2011).

Brierley, Peter, *UK Church Statistics No. 3: 2018 Edition* (London: Brierley Consultancy, 2018).

Bullivant, Stephen, *Europe's Young Adults and Religion: Report 2018* (St Mary's University London, 2018), www.stmarys.ac.uk/research/centres/benedict-xvi/docs/2018-mar-europe-young-people-report-eng.pdf (accessed 06.09.19).

The Church Army, '"Not As Difficult As You Think": Mission with Young Adults' (2018 Report), www.churcharmy.org/youngadults research (accessed 06.09.19).

Clark, Chap and Kara Powell, *Sticky Faith: Everyday Ideas to Build Lasting Faith in Your Kids* (Grand Rapids, MI: Zondervan, 2011).

Collins-Mayo, Sylvia et al., *The Faith of Generation Y* (London: Church House Publishing, 2010).

DePaulo, Bella, *How We Live Now: Redefining Home and Family in the 21st Century* (New York: Atria, 2015).

Emery White, James, *Meet Generation Z* (Grand Rapids, MI: Baker Books, 2017).

Ford, David G., Joshua L. Mann and Peter M. Phillips, *The Bible and Digital Millennials* (London: Routledge, 2019).

Guest, Mathew et al., *Christianity and the University Experience: Understanding Student Faith* (London: Bloomsbury Academic, 2013).

Guest, Mathew and Kristen Aune, 'Students' Constructions of a Christian Future: Faith, Class and Aspiration in a University Context', *Sociological Research Online*, Vol. 22.1 (2017).

Hill, Wesley, *Spiritual Friendship: Finding Love in the Church as a Celibate Gay Christian* (Grand Rapids, MI: Brazos, 2015).

Kinnaman, David, *You Lost Me* (Grand Rapids, MI: Baker, 2011).

Lawrence, James, 'Engaging Gen Y: Leading Well Across the Generations', Grove Leadership Series, L8 (Cambridge: Grove, 2012).

McNamara Barry, Carolyn and Mona M. Abo-Zena, *Emerging Adults' Religiousness and Spirituality: Meaning-Making in an Age of Transition* (Oxford: Oxford University Press, 2014).

Osgood, D. Wayne et al., 'Six Paths to Adulthood: Fast Starters, Parents without Careers, Educated Partners, Educated singles, Working Singles, and Slow starters', in R. A. Settersten et al. (eds), *On the Frontier of Adulthood: Theory, Research and Public Policy* (Chicago, IL: University of Chicago Press, 2005).

Perrin, Ruth H., *The Bible Reading of Young Evangelicals* (Eugene, OR: Wipf & Stock, 2017).

Pew Research Center, www.pewresearch.org/fact-tank/2015/05/12/ millennials-increasingly-are-driving-growth-of-nones/ (accessed 06. 09.19).

Redfern, Catherine and Kristin Aune, *Reclaiming the F-Word* (London: ZED, 2010).

Root, Andrew, *Faith Formation in a Secular Age: Responding to the Churches' Obsession with Youthfulness* (Grand Rapids, MI: Baker Academic, 2017).

Savage, Sara et al., *Making Sense of Generation Y* (London: Church House Publishing, 2006).

Setran, David P. and Chris A. Kiesling, *Spiritual Formation in Emerging Adulthood: A Practical Theology for College and Young Adult Ministry* (Grand Rapids, MI: Baker, 2013).

Sharma, Sonya and Mathew Guest, 'Navigating Religion between University and Home: Christian Students' Experiences in English Universities', *Social and Cultural Geography*, Vol. 14.1 (2013), 59–79.

Shepherd, Nick, *Faith Generation: Retaining Young People and Growing the Church* (London: SPCK, 2016).

Smith, Christian, *Souls in Transition: The Religious and Spiritual Lives of Emerging Adults* (Oxford: Oxford University Press, 2009).

_____, *Lost in Transition: The Dark Side of Emerging Adulthood* (Oxford: Oxford University Press, 2011).

Smith, Greg (ed.), *21st Century Evangelicals* (Watford: Instant Apostle, 2015).

Voas, David, 'Religious Census 2011 – What Happened to the Christians? (Part II)', *British Religion in Numbers*, www.brin.ac.uk/religious-census-2011-what-happened-to-the-christians-part-ii/ (accessed 06.09.19).

Wilcox, Bradford W., *Soft Patriarchs, New Men: How Christianity Shapes Fathers and Husbands* (Chicago, IL: University of Chicago Press, 2004).

Willoughby, Brian J. and Spencer L. James, *The Marriage Paradox: Why Emerging Adults Love Marriage yet Push it Aside* (Oxford: Oxford University Press, 2017).

Woodhead, Linda, 'The Rise of "No Religion" in Britain: The Emergence of a New Cultural Majority', *Journal of the British Academy*, 2016 (4), 245–61.

Yarhouse, Mark A., *Listening to Sexual Minorities: A Study of Faith and Sexual Identity on Christian College Campuses* (Downers Grove, IL: InterVarsity Press, 2018).

YouthScape, *No Questions Asked: The Findings of a Qualitative Study of 16–19 year olds in Luton* (2018), http://Youthscape.co.uk (accessed 06.09.19).

Zuckerman, Phil, *Faith No More: Why People Reject Religion* (Oxford: Oxford University Press, 2012).

Index of Names and Subjects

emotion and social cost
of 163–5
isolation from church 171–2
meaning and framework
165–6
personal difficulty/trauma
170
process of faith loss 159–63
rejection of beliefs 156
shallow/deep 157
society and culture 157–8
support and 156
worldview change 167–9
see also faith
Arminianism 196, 238
Arnett, Jeffrey Jensen 5–6,
29–31
Emerging Adulthood 81–2
Astley, Jeff 125, 126
Aune, Kristin
Christian identity 38
on employment 36
gender equality 103
marriage and 82
single women in church 87,
89
authenticity, valuing 9–10,
235–6

Baby Boomers
as bosses of Millennials 14
definition of 4–5
elders and 240
faith and 125, 128
internet Biblical verse 8
Bauman, Zygmunt 26
Beck-Gernsheim, Elisabeth
99–100

Becker, Penny Edgell 65
Bell, Rob 139
Berger, Peter L. 11–14
Bethel 139
The Bible, internet memes
of 8
Bielo, James S.
on authenticity 9
the disenchanted 176–7
pluralistic culture and faith
194
Big Church Day 19
Brierley, Peter x, 17

Catalyst 19
Catholic Church xiv
family and 207
moral issues 145
retains young people xi
self-identification 10
Celtic worship 239
Centre for Church Growth
17
charismatic churches 13–14,
17
charities
Active Affirmers and 20–1
employment in 38–9
children *see* family
Christianity
authenticity of 9–10
coherence of 244
denominations 136–8
denominations and 17–18,
237
experience of violence
220–1
in a secular society 129–32

changing worldview and
168
culture and faith 129
disenchantment with
churches 191–2
faith development and
145–50
friends and 63
Millennials and 28
see also LGBTQi+
Shepherd, Nick 16, 130
sin 195
Smith, Christian 131
character of Millennials 7
Moralistic, Therapeutic
Deism 8, 128
research project xiii
social activism
in employment 38–9
Millennials and 7, 14–15,
20–1
society and culture
change of worldview 167–9
diversity and tolerance
11–14, 143–5, 194
effect on apostasy 157–8
internationals in study xiv
secularism x, 127, 129–32
tensions with theology
143–5
Soul Survivor 19, 140, 142
spiritual resources 18–20
spirituality, non-Christian
194
Spring Harvest 19, 140
Stormzy 245
Strhan, Ana 103–4
Aliens and Strangers 21

technology
adapting to 31–2
Millennial lifestyle and
10–11
theism 214
Tisdell, Elizabeth 125
tolerance
disenchantment with church
191–2
effect on faith 157–8
Millennial value 11–14
sexuality and 145–51
values of 143–5
Trump, Donald J. 129
Trussell Trust 20
Twenge, Jean 32

United Kingdom
apostasy and 158–9
culture and faith 127–9
patterns of religion in x–xii
as 'post-Christian' x
United States
apostasy in 157–8
culture and Evangelism 129
higher religious adherence
131
intern'tl preachers and
leaders 19
religious resource 138

Warren, Rick 139
Willoughby, Brian 82, 92
Woodhead, Linda xi, 130,
145
Word Alive 19
work
Emerging Adults 28, 58

faith development and
36–41
generational relations
14–15
'gig' economy 30
mothers and 101

public sector and charity 38
stages of adulthood 30
World Health Authority 32

Zuckerman, P. 157–8, 161,
167